When Life
Gives You Pears

When Life Gives You Pears

The Healing Power of Family, Faith, and Funny People

Jeannie Gaffigan

GRAND CENTRAL
PUBLISHING

New York   Boston

Grand Central Publishing
Hachette Book Group
1290 Avenue of the Americas, New York, NY 10104
grandcentralpublishing.com
twitter.com/grandcentralpub

First Edition: October 2019

Grand Central Publishing is a division of Hachette Book Group, Inc. The Grand Central Publishing name and logo is a trademark of Hachette Book Group, Inc.

The publisher is not responsible for websites (or their content) that are not owned by the publisher.

The Hachette Speakers Bureau provides a wide range of authors for speaking events. To find out more, go to www.hachettespeakersbureau.com or call (866) 376-6591.

Unless otherwise noted, photos are courtesy of the Gaffigan family.

Library of Congress Control Number: 2019944323

ISBNs: 978-1-5387-5104-6 (hardcover), 978-1-5387-5103-9 (ebook), 978-1-5387-1794-3 (B&N signed edition), 978-1-5387-1792-9 (B&N Black Friday edition), 978-1-5387-1793-6 (signed edition)

Printed in the United States of America

LSC-C

10 9 8 7 6 5 4 3 2 1

For my children: Marre, Jack, Katie, Michael, Patrick, and Bean

Foreword

by Jim Gaffigan

When I was asked to write the foreword for *When Life Gives You Pears*—which happens to be written by my wife, Jeannie, who is also the mother of my five children and my writing partner of seven comedy specials, two *New York Times* bestsellers, and one television series (*The Jim Gaffigan Show*)—I had only one question: "How much are you going to pay me?" Well, it turns out these "foreword" things pay like nothing. I know. Insane, right? So I guess my primary motivation for writing this has to be because Jeannie Gaffigan is loving, kind, talented, smart, and beautiful. I am excited for as many people as possible to read the story of this incredible woman, who writes with such humor and vulnerability about a time when she and I feared things were not going to be good. Not good at all. After having traveled down this path with my own family, I have come to realize that so many of us have gone through a loved one's life-or-death medical crisis, but those accounts of how they kept themselves sane during such a scary time are rarely shared publicly. I wish I had a book like this book prior to going on our own journey.

I've never been one for hero worship. It's always struck me as immature or naïve. Humans are, after all, *human*, and tend to disappoint. Yet there is always one exception to every rule.

If there was one person who has lived up to the hype and the grand expectations, it would be Jeannie. Of course, I'm biased, but Jeannie has consistently left me in awe. This memoir brings to life some of that Jeannie magic that has dazzled her friends, family, and any community she has interacted with since her arrival on this planet, and somehow perfectly captures the unstoppable woman I have laughed with, loved, and fought with for the last twenty years.

There have been countless moments when I've been enchanted by the life force that is Jeannie. I'm not even referring to the bravery and tenacity she displayed in the face of the pear-shaped brain tumor and the seemingly endless recovery that this book so hysterically chronicles. I'm talking about the innumerable times when I've involuntarily mumbled "Oh my God" under my breath from a sincere bewilderment at who this human is and what she can accomplish. This book brings to life some of that Jeannie magic, which has dazzled her family, friends, and any community she has interacted with since her arrival on this planet.

I met Jeannie in my early thirties. After years of failure and frustration, I had finally found a cynical confidence and was ready to pursue a life focused on my career and only my career. Yet, with Jeannie I was instantly smitten. Like most people when they first meet her, I assumed she was a decade younger than her age and clearly in need of deep breathing exercises, but I couldn't stop thinking about her. I pursued her and the more I pursued, the more I was left mumbling, "Oh my God." Here was the first time.

Jeannie and I had gone on one lunch date prior to me arriving at the St. Patrick's Youth Center on a spring afternoon. She had explained to me while sharing some overpriced eggs the day before that she was running a not-for-profit called *Shakespeare on the Playground*. I assumed she was another struggling New

York City actor teaching some kids to fill downtime between inevitable rejections. She invited me to stop by sometime so I reluctantly went to the next day's rehearsal to check it out. What I encountered stunned me. It wasn't a few kids; it was literally a hundred middle schoolers. And these weren't kids holding tap shoes and filled with theater dreams; these were street-smart kids from the nearby city projects who probably had never been inside a Broadway theater or any other one, for that matter. I looked around the room through the sea of children for any helpers and saw two weary adult volunteers from the theater world that Jeannie had caught up in the tornado that was to be my future life partner. I watched as this human cyclone choreographed and inspired the whole operation. There was no support from the school. No national organization behind her. Jeannie, the unemployed actress who did catering jobs most nights, was even paying for the kids' snacks. Most impressively, the kids were engaged, interested, and having fun. Jeannie somehow thrived and excelled in the chaos. I had never seen anything like it. Her selfless service to these children made my cynicism melt away immediately. I remember observing her orchestrate the madness of humanity and thought, *This woman can do anything. Maybe she can make me a better man. Maybe that's important. Maybe that's even more important than my career.*

Well, long story short, Jeannie did NOT make me a better man. Some things are impossible. Okay, fine. The reality is that Jeannie's influence on my life and career have been immeasurable. I guess in a way I'm like one of the middle schoolers in the St. Patrick's Youth Center that Jeannie shaped: a rebellious kid with a little bit of Jeannie-good in me. As you read this story that she so generously shares, I hope that you get to experience a little bit of that for yourself.

When Life
Gives You Pears

Introduction

Don't you hate it when you have perfected a magnificent schedule and then suddenly you get interrupted by an enormous brain tumor? That totally sucks, right?

As an overwhelmed mother of five with a touring comedian husband and a career as a writer and executive producer, I already felt that one more thing would be the wafer-thin mint that made me explode. The surreal diagnosis of a life-threatening pear-sized mass in my brain that required an urgent craniotomy with absolutely no idea of what kind of life I would be facing afterward was something that I hadn't exactly left room for in my daily itinerary. As a self-confessed control freak, I had to face the fact that I was confronted with something completely out of my control.

Ironically, "Tumorgate" turned out to be the catalyst for the radical revolution I desperately needed to reconstruct my priorities. As I am now making my journey through the recovery process, rather than asking, "Why did this earthquake destroy my house?" I find myself saying, "Awesome! I needed to get rid of a lot of that old junk anyway and wow, everyone, thanks for helping me build the new home of my dreams!"

Here I reflect on how this potentially tragic prognosis strengthened my faith in God, deepened my love for my family and friends, and renewed my hope in humanity. So, what I'm saying is that it's light reading. By the end you'll be all, "Boo-hoo! I want a brain tumor too!"

Of course, you don't have to have a brain tumor to come along on my journey. I hope my story will be valuable to everyone because life as we know it and as we have become comfortable with does not last forever. Folks who already have their priorities straight and who find love and gratitude in every little moment may be like, "Yup! This book affirms all of my beliefs, but I don't find it redundant because this girl is kinda fun-ee!" And for those people who are all like, "Why would I want to read a book about a disgusting brain tumor? It's never going to happen to me!" I would say, maybe it's not going to be a brain tumor, but it's going to be *something* because life is not in your control and the longer you live, the more things start to get crazy. Maybe it will just be a creepy cat that one day appears at your door and then follows you around for the rest of your life and then you'll be all, "Thank God I read Jeannie Gaffigan's brain tumor book because it prepared me for this. Even though I'm terribly allergic to cat dander, I will learn to love this cat. I'll just get some Zyrtec and put a scratching post in my living room because this cat is going to teach me something!"

And one more little thing: I'm not going to push the God thing down your throat. Let's just get it out of the way that my husband describes me as a "Shiite Catholic" and I am a true believer in the power and majesty of the one true God, and those of you heathens who don't get it, you're going straight to H.E. double hockey sticks. Just kidding. Through my diagnosis and recovery, I found myself relying heavily on the power of miracles. I believe that a supernatural force was carrying me through the darkest and most difficult moments of this time in my life. So if anyone has a problem believing in this sort of nonscientific metaphysical reality, let me rephrase it in an attempt to make it more palatable for you: during my diagnosis, surgery, and recovery, "The Force" was strong with me.

I wish I could say that through this journey I always saw the opportunity in the crisis, and that I faced adversity with optimism and a positive can-do attitude, but that's not what happened. I needed a lot of people to help me make pear-ade. I'd like to dedicate this book to everyone who helped lift me out of this potential undoing. Even if I didn't mention you by name, you know who you are, and I know where you live. (I don't know why I wrote that last bit; it was kind of scary.) Most of all, I would like to thank my husband, Jim Gaffigan, who let me silently yell at him while he carried me through the storm.

The Pear

"I just have one question: Am I going to die?"

I sat in the neurosurgery office at Mount Sinai Hospital, looking at a giant screen that displayed the inside of my skull. I could see a brain with what appeared to be an inverted pear-shaped glob deep in the center of it, the smaller end sinking into my neck like a cork. I thought, *I'll never eat a pear again.* I never was a huge fan of them anyway. They are either too hard and taste like nothing, or delicious but an absolute mess. Pears are sort of a metaphor for life. I guess I do like pears. Just not pear-shaped tumors.

I was strangely calm, almost numb. My husband, Jim, sat beside me and we stared slack-jawed at the screen, like it was our latest binge on Netflix; we'd just gotten to the part where they discover the thing that killed the victim was an alien that burrowed into her brain and sucked the life out of her.

* * *

The doctor's words were floating by in the air and disappearing like smoke signals from someone trapped on a desert island.

"Meningioma...," "or schwannoma...," "embolization...," "cranial nerves...," "lengthy surgery...," blah, blah, blah. It was all gibberish. I'm normally a note taker in everyday life, but I just sat there, passively waiting for my sentencing. Was I going to die? That was all I needed to know.

There are always those questions that you don't want to hear the answer to, like that incredible stress you feel when you receive the letter that might be your child's acceptance or rejection by the one school you really want them to attend. You might finger it with the trepidation of Charlie Bucket as he peels open his last chance at winning Willy Wonka's golden ticket. Or you might put the sealed letter on a makeshift altar surrounded by candles and pray that God will change the contents to suit your fancy. You might even choose not to open it because this major thing that will change your whole life is ultimately something that you really don't want to know about.

* * *

I probably *should* have felt like that, but frankly, what I experienced was the opposite. It was life or death and I needed to know right away, I guess so I could plan accordingly.

I knew the real answer to my question was "Yes." I mean, I know we all are going to die eventually. Many times throughout my life I'd come to terms with the notion that everything dies. I had lots of thoughts and opinions about death. I'd even gone through a naive period in my twenties when I thought cancer might be contagious. I'd just never faced anything as horrifying as seeing a photograph of something in my body that could kill me. And judging from the size of this alien pear lodged firmly within my command center, what I really meant was, "Am I going to die, like, real soon?" I was directing this question to someone whom I had just met moments earlier, but seeing how nice his office was, I felt like he was qualified to answer. (You don't want to enter a brain surgeon's office and discover it's a dump.)

Jim commented on the niceness of the office later. "Did you see how huge his desk was?"

I gave him my dead-eyed stare. "No, Jim, I was not looking at his *desk*," I said in a tone that really meant, "Being married to you clearly gave me this brain tumor."

But back to the moment of the answer to the whole "death" question.

The doctor looked at me carefully. I averted my eyes and looked down. I was wearing a T-shirt and sweatpants with stars on them. The starry sweats were too whimsical for the seriousness of the situation. Or the mother of five children in New York City. Or an adult. It was one of those outfits you throw on when you must leave immediately for the ER and you're showing up "as is" because in that "I might die" scenario you're not really concerned with fashion choices. I glanced down at my legs, which were crossed, but like *really* crossed, as in wrapped around each other like the string on a tetherball pole. My hands were in my lap, gripping each other for dear life. I sat up super straight, hoping my posture would make up for my outfit, and tried to act casual.

The doctor exhaled. "No. You are not going to die." The gravity of his tone implied that this was not a black-or-white answer. Did he mean "You're not going to die, *but...*" or, more specifically, "You're not going to die, but you are going to wish you had!" Regardless, in that moment, the fact that I had heard this virtual stranger—whom I was trusting to cut my skull open like a pumpkin and dig in deep to remove a 6 cm mass caught in a web of precious nerves from the middle of the most intricate part of my being—tell me I was not going to die was all I needed. I knew everything else was going to be okay.

* * *

As the doctor explained the situation to us, he simultaneously exuded calm kindness and the frank candor of a scientific genius, which is kind of like biting into a beautiful chocolate candy filled with bitter orange goo. "The tumor is expanding into your brain stem, so there's not a lot of room left in there. We are going to have to resect it right away with a craniotomy. It's going to be a very serious surgery. Probably eight to twelve hours." Serious brain surgery? Wait, is there casual brain surgery? Isn't all brain surgery rather serious and complicated? Isn't that why we non–brain surgeons refer to easy tasks as "ain't brain surgery"? I was ready to hear more about seriousness when Jim chimed in.

"Can you do it today?" The question landed with a thud. Jim was trying to help. Pitching an idea. "Hey, you know all about removing tumors, but I'm a timing guy. Sooner it's out, sooner we get back to normal." The question sounded like Jim was proposing we just swipe everything off the giant desk and throw me on it. There had to be some scalpels in one of those polished mahogany drawers. Jim is a get-it-done kind of guy. I take more time to mull things over, consider the options. Many times, I am grateful for his quick decision-making ability and I have to admit it has helped me in my life. This time, however, it *was* my life. I was still processing.

Today? I thought. *Who's picking up the kids? Doesn't Katie have tae kwon do today? Marre's at soccer, I think the boys are at Chelsea Piers ... Wait, that's Wednesday. What day is it even?*

It was Thursday. Holy Thursday. The Thursday before Easter, and it's what we Catholics remember as the day Jesus washed the disciples' feet in a gesture of service and humility. Was this supposed to be symbolic for me? Feet washing, brain surgery. I tried to make a connection. My mind was wandering. Maybe it was the pear's fault. It's hard to wax philosophical with fruit on the brain. Wax fruit. Confusion.

"No, not today." The doctor didn't sound the least bit condescending, though I knew Jim's question was a perfect opportunity for a medical professional to have a superior intellect moment. "We have to get Jeannie in here tomorrow for testing. We need to do a lot of scans of her brain to map out all the nerves that surround the tumor. Then we do a virtual surgery to figure out the best way to deal with the resection." It sounded like he was going to transform the inside of my head into an elaborate video game. I pictured a little, blurry square guy running around in there and my eleven-year-old son holding a controller, helping the doctors blast the evil zombie tumor into oblivion.

Most of these hi-tech photos would be taken in my all-day photo shoot tomorrow. Modeling ain't easy.

Tomorrow. Good Friday. The day Jesus was crucified. Obviously not comparing myself to Jesus, but I was mystified about the timing and trying to make sense of my life. This Sunday was Easter. The resurrection. In the metaphysical reality in which I exist, I should have surgery tomorrow, die at three o'clock, rise from the dead on Sunday, then take the kids to school Monday morning.

"What about the Easter baskets?" I blurted out. Now it was Jim's turn to look at me with a dead-eyed stare. "I have to make the kids' Easter baskets." I didn't have time to die right now. The doctor's assistant, a tall, beautiful blond woman who had been standing by quietly up until this point, chimed in:

"You can make the Easter baskets. I have two kids, I totally get you. Enjoy the weekend with your family. Do normal things. Don't make out your 'will,' or try to plan anything beyond the week after surgery."

I didn't understand what she was saying. The "week after surgery"? I guess I'll just call the schools and work folks and say, "Yeah, I'm going to have brain surgery, so I'll be taking about a week off."

Brain surgery? Now? I needed brain surgery like I needed a hole in the head. How did I get here?

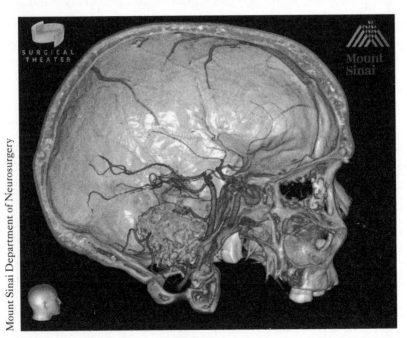

The pear.

PART I

What Happened

Chapter 1

JANUARY

After you see a picture of the inside of your brain with a pear in it, you start feeling like, well, like you have a pear in your brain. You start looking at people around you like, "Humph. Must be nice not to have a pear in your brain." But the weirdest thing was, before I saw the picture, I didn't feel it. I felt surprisingly normal. Sure, it was odd that I'd get a head rush every time I lifted something, but it must have been that I wasn't drinking enough water. Also, it was odd to feel tingling in my legs and feet after sitting at my desk for extended periods, but it was probably bad circulation. I just needed one of those standing desks that everyone raves about but soon will be overflowing in landfills when people realize that combining two sucky things like standing and work is a horrible idea. And my "allergies," wow. My constant throbbing headaches were getting worse and I was finding it harder and harder to breathe at night after I got into bed. But, as everyone kept saying, "the pollen is *really* bad this year!"

If you hadn't guessed it already, I had been compartmentalizing and explaining away the signs that I had a brain tumor. Then again, not even the most paranoid hypochondriac would imagine that these seemingly unrelated annoyances would be the symptoms of a massive brain tumor. Besides, who has time to go to the doctor when you have a bunch of little people's doctors' appointments to get to? When I was executive producing on *The Jim Gaffigan Show*, I went to work with a sprained foot and just got a cane from the props department. I didn't have time to get sick. The show of life must go on.

Perhaps the most obvious symptom I ignored was the nearly complete loss of hearing in my left ear. Over the past couple of years, I had noticed that when watching TV with Jim, I frequently asked him to repeat something a character had just said. I justified this as another example of how my "selfish" husband just had the primo position in the bed: smack between the two speakers for optimal listening enjoyment, while I, the ol' buffer, was shoved to the side in the second-class position. At crowded holiday parties or in large groups of people, I frequently found myself leaning in to hear conversations, and even then I still couldn't make out the words, so I would just smile and nod and say "Totally!" and hope to God they weren't asking me if they looked fat in their outfit.

In January 2017, on a long flight from London to New York City with my family, I was not surprised to learn that I got the bum headphones with only one side working (it figured). One of my children called me over to their seat to fix their iPad, and, after I wiped the thick layer of kid-goo (most likely

Cheetos dust and apple juice) off the screen so that it would again respond to their touch, I returned to my seat and placed the headphones over my ears. They had been twisted so that the "bad" side was now on my opposite ear. Funny thing was that the "good" side was now muffled. It took a few minutes of switching ears for me to realize that it wasn't my headphones. My left ear seemed to have stopped working. I could *kind* of hear out of it, but it was the type of sound that would register if you stuffed eight wet cotton balls in there. I don't remember being that concerned about it. I guess I chalked it up to "Well, I did stand too close to that speaker at the Chili Peppers concert in 2000; it's my fault. I guess I'll just not hear out of that ear now." I didn't even mention it to anyone. I didn't want to seem "old."

A couple of months later I was at our family practitioner's office.

The Clown Car

When I take my five kids to the doctor, it's always a big show because I bring them all at once, and there's five of them. It's like a field trip for shots. The look of confusion and empathy on the faces of the other parents sitting with one or two kids in the waiting room would entertain me for days. Is she really bringing in *five* kids? Or is she like a dog-walker for other people's kids? Five appointments equal five bills. I'm sure over the years we've financed a few doctors' summer homes.

During these visits that instantly transform any exam room into a clown car, I normally have about twenty pages of forms with me that require a physician's signature for my children

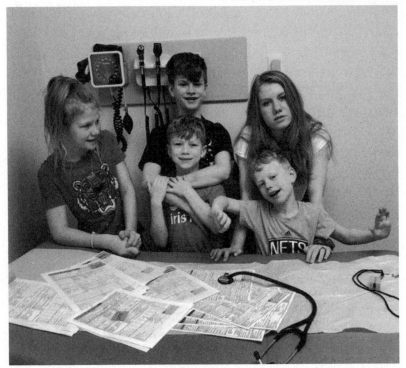

Now, if we could only fit a doctor in here...

to participate in school and camp activities. I place enormous importance on these forms and with good reason. If you miss checking off a box or leave out a birthday or a date, the form will be rejected and you will have to return to the doctor's office, which you don't want to do because that's why you almost killed yourself by bringing all the kids to the doctor at the same time. Coordinating appointments like this is a magnificent scheduling feat, and I'm not going to let some stupid incomplete form ruin my masterpiece.

*　　*　　*

During this particular episode of the circus, Patrick and Michael, my four- and five-year-olds, were climbing all over the high exam table, crinkling and ripping the paper that covered it. *Well, at least if they fall off and break a bone, there's a doctor nearby*, I thought. Jack, eleven, was dismantling a model of a body part that, unbeknownst to him, might have been a uterus (or maybe a throat; didn't get a good look). Katie, seven, was erupting in gales of laughter at the wild antics of her brothers. Marre was mortified, as any twelve-year-old girl would be. She glared at me as if to say, "Really, Mom, couldn't you just have stopped after you had me?"

I was squeezed into a corner of the exam room, shuffling through my forms while my doctor was juggling my children for weighing and measuring with the skill of a ringmaster. I was coughing, a cough that had started back during flu season, turned into seasonal allergies, and then never disappeared. I complained to her about how the last time I brought my circus into the clinic, it was for the flu shot and we all got the flu anyway and I felt like I still had it. Then Dr. Hops started explaining something to me that sounded a lot like the parent voices in the Charlie Brown cartoons. I turned my head so that my right ear was facing her and said, "Could you repeat that?"

She looked at me with concern and repeated, "I said that the flu shot really didn't work this year; but more importantly, what's wrong with your left ear?"

"I don't know, it feels like it's clogged or something. I can't really hear out of it."

"How long has *that* been happening?"

I don't know how the term "sheepish" got started because I've never known a sheep to act sheepishly. I really don't have much experience with sheep but I've seen sheep, and "sheepish" behavior as far as actual sheep are concerned is just wandering around eating grass, but I'm talking about the kind of sheepish as it applies to human behavior, meaning "embarrassedly."

I sheepishly replied, "I have no idea, but I think that ear has been bad for quite a while." You know that feeling when a doctor asks you a simple question about yourself that you don't know the answer to and you feel embarrassed and dumb? Yeah, that. I recall the time I was in very early labor with one of my children and I was feeling the tremendous pressure of the baby's head dropping lower and lower. Suddenly I had this feeling like I peed a little (sorry, guys), but it was super weird because it just sort of happened without the feeling of peeing. So I called my midwife and said, "Hey, I think my water broke!" and she was quiet for a beat and said, "What do you mean, you 'think' your water broke? Either your water broke or it didn't!"

Before you think that was a harsh reply, let me explain that this was pregnancy number four and that I'd had all my babies at home with a midwife. When you decide to go this route you are supposed to make a commitment to being aware of everything you are going through and actively participate in the process during the entire prenatal period. So, in other words, it's kind of stressful for a dum-dum like me. Although this was my fourth time in third-trimester labor, I had never experienced my water breaking early so I had no idea what it felt like, and I also was guilty of not knowing anything about it other than a sort of 1950s Hollywood version of the phrase.

"Ricky! My water broke! Call Fred and Ethel!"

"Well, I guess it feels like it broke a little." I heard my midwife sigh before she asked, "Did you feel your water break and experience a 'splash' of water?"

"No, it was more like a trickle."

"Could it be that you peed?" I hadn't peed in my pants since that time in the carpool in nursery school, and I was still traumatized by the experience.

"I didn't push down to pee."

"Jeannie, you have a nine-pound baby pushing down on your bladder. At this point you don't have to push down."

Once it was determined that my water did not break and I had in fact unknowingly peed, I was reassured, but sheepishly reassured because I became aware that I was unaware. I had the exact same feeling when Dr. Hops asked about my hearing.

She repeated, "Do you have any idea how long you haven't been able to hear out of that ear?" I looked at her the same way you would if someone asked you to perform a complex math equation in your head. "So, you just lost the hearing in one ear and you didn't think anything of it?"

I'm sure Dr. Hops was not trying to rub it in, but I felt a bit silly. I had corresponded with her many, many times since the hearing had started to go, but it was always about a kid's rash, a kid's bloodshot eye, a kid's earache, or a strange spot on a kid's foot. Notice a theme there? I rarely mentioned myself, unless it was to complain about how exhausting it was to manage my basketball team. Prior to having kids, if I had lower back pain I would go to the ER and get tested for an imagined kidney infection. Those days were over. As any mother or other busy person can tell you, there is little time for superfluous doctor visits.

She looked at me, concerned, and indicated my left ear. "Can you hear anything at all on that side?"

"What?" I joked.

Dr. Hops looked in my ear with that ear-looker thing. "I

don't see any swelling. I'm going to write you a referral to a specialist." Great. Another appointment. She must have seen that expression on my face that said, "Maybe I'll find some time next year to call this guy," because she looked me in the eye and said, "Promise me you'll follow up on this." I'd like to think if she hadn't been so firm, the course of my life, or the lack thereof, would have been dramatically different.

At this point the younger children, taking advantage of being unsupervised, were going completely bonkers, running amok in the tiny exam room, germing up all the stethoscopes and various instruments, blowing into rubber exam gloves, and possibly breaking the model uterus. I hugged my precious school forms to my chest lest they become additional props for the clown show, looked her right back in the eye, and agreed to follow up.

The first ear, nose, and throat (ENT) specialist I called about a week later was not available to take new patients. Who knew ENT doctors were in such demand? I always figured they were combo doctors because there weren't enough patients to cover those specialties individually: "There's enough people who need an eye doctor, but the ears, nose, and throat? We'll just make that one position." It's as though they're trying to cut overhead. Or it's random, like how alcohol, tobacco, and fire-arms are also oddly thrown together.

It took me three phone calls and about twenty minutes of hold time to figure out that this ENT doctor was not taking new patients. I fired off a quick email to Dr. Hops, letting her know that I had indeed fulfilled my part of the bargain by fol-lowing up, but unfortunately, I was unable to be seen. I was kind of hoping that she'd respond with, "Well, you tried. See you next time your kids need some forms filled out." Instead, she emailed back quickly with the name of a different ENT specialist to call.

"I want you to see Dr. David Godin. He's good. Call him." I know, the fact that I get quick email responses from a doctor seems more unrealistic than my surviving a brain tumor with flying colors, but I'm telling you the truth. Having a personal correspondence with a doctor has become a thing of the past, so Dr. Hops is an anomaly in the medical community—she responds immediately. I chalk it up to her being Canadian. She has a small-town, hang-a-shingle-out style of doctoring that is a welcome oasis in the desert of New York City. I have so much love and appreciation for Dr. Hops.

Normally, to contact a doctor you must deal with the "front of the house," which is analogous to being caught in a house of mirrors with no lights on. To be fair, I am sure it's a tough job to have to deal with whiny, angry sick people all day. Even getting a simple message to a doctor is like getting a bottle of water past airline security. For anyone who has dealt with a crabby medical receptionist, you know what I am talking about. I dreaded calling this new doctor so much I forgot about my ear. I literally forgot the reason I was going to the doctor. I was only on a mission to make an appointment to please Dr. Hops. She deserved it.

Chapter 2

FEBRUARY

A Bedazzled Hearing Aid

I called Dr. Godin's office fully expecting to get the runaround, but, surprisingly, they got me in right away. I arrived at the spacious office waiting room and filled out the paperwork. I'm not sure why the way they process medical forms hasn't changed since the era of Bob Cratchit. We live in an age where a robot can vacuum our floors, but we still get a clipboard and a pen to fill out forms in the doctor's office? I have a theory that the paperwork at doctors' offices is total busywork to distract you from the fact that after rushing to get to your appointment on time, you are forced to wait forty-five minutes before you can see the doctor. There are like ten pages of redundant questions and fill-in-the-blanks on a clipboard, including name and medical history, even though they literally have your name in the system from when you made the appointment and the referring physician already sent your medical history. They call your name to hand you a paper that asks for your name. Do a lot of people change their names and/or birth dates since the last time they were in a doctor's office?

If all these forms are eventually being entered into a computer, why are you filling them out again? Can't they just email the forms from the referring doctor's office? Are you waiting so long in doctors' offices so they can retype the same information over and over again?

Then you sign that you have acknowledged your rights as a patient, but you never read the rights because you are too exhausted from filling out the ten pages of forms. The best is the page where you release the rights to share your data with other doctors. You sign the page, but they never share the data, or else we would not be filling out ten pages of forms! And you're not done yet! Next, they have you copy down the tiny numbers on your insurance card even though they are going to make a copy of it. You know those stacks of magazines on the side tables in doctors' offices? No one is ever reading them because they are too busy filling out forms. Maybe the publishers of the magazines should solve the form problem—it would be in their best interest.

Finally, my name is called. I say, "Hold on, I only have three more pages of questions to answer."

"That's okay," they say. "You don't have to fill the rest out." I knew it! Busywork. Theory proved.

Before I see the doctor, I go into a tiny booth with a technician to take a hearing test. It's like a recording booth where I put on giant headphones. The technician's on the other side of a window with some contraption that plays sounds while she measures my response. The purpose of the test is to see if I can hear a variety of different tones at different frequencies. When I hear a tone, I raise my hand. First, the "good ear." I hear the variety of tones, and I raise my hand after each one. Easy. Now, the "bad" ear. Here's where I discover that I'm determined to beat the test, even if I can't hear the tones. Something in me wants to "pass," even though I should be focused on getting my hearing problem diagnosed.

I hear nothing. Or do I? Was that a tone or just ringing in my ears? I raise my hand. After that, there is a pause, where a tone should probably be. I might have heard something. I tentatively raise my hand. Was there no tone? Are they trying to trick me? Did I just raise my hand after no tone and now look stupid? Like I'm cheating? But wait, in the other ear, there was always a tone. Do I need a hearing aid? That might be the end game here. Maybe I'll just get a hearing aid. I mean, hearing aids are so small and discreet now, no one would ever really see it. It would be kind of cool. I could turn it up and hear people whispering from across a room (hushed): "Is Jeannie Gaffigan wearing a hearing aid?" "I HEARD THAT!" Or else I could get a huge hearing aid and wear it proudly. Maybe it would look like the Bluetooth earbud my dad always wears, with the strap around the ear. He loves that thing. I think it makes him feel like he is in the Secret Service or something. I could get a hot pink one, or bedazzle one with rhinestone stickers, and my seven-year-old would then steal it and wear it to school. Maybe I would start a trend: "What do you mean, you *don't* have a hearing aid? All the cool kids have them!" I continued to raise my hand at the phantom tones until the technician said, "Okay, you are all done. I'm going to take you to the exam room where the doctor will see you."

The good thing about going to an ENT specialist is that you don't have to take off your clothes and put on the paper gown. There is rarely anything to take off that covers the ears, nose, and throat. Even if you have on a hat and a ski mask, if you take them off, you don't need to put on a paper hat or ski mask that is all open in the back. At this point I realize that the taking off of the clothes and changing into the paper robe is a welcome distraction from the fact that you are now waiting in a different room.

Mental note for future set design: Just change the poster of the specific "inside of the body" chart on the wall, and the model of the body part on the counter, for different doctor's office sets. That would save a ton of money for the scenic department.

Did the doctor forget about me? Have I been in this appointment all day? I have a job. What the hell are they pulling here? Should I look through the drawers? Are they watching me in here? Do doctors use a patient cam? Anyway, I have things to do. Finally, enter a man in his twenties. I'm impressed that the doctor is so young, until I realize that it's the doctor's assistant, Kurt, who apologizes for keeping me waiting. "That's fine," I lie. "At least you're here now."

He then looks at the computer and asks my name and my birthday. *Okay*, I think. *I get it. They obviously should make sure they have the right person. It's a safety issue so they don't remove my gallbladder when I am just here for a bedazzled hearing aid.* But then he proceeds to ask me a series of questions that I *already filled out on the ten pages of forms!* I try to be calm as I answer: "Yes, that is correct, as I previously stated on the ten pages of forms I filled out in the waiting room!" He obviously thinks I'm just another crazy impatient patient. Or some weirdo who would use a term like "impatient patient."

"Okay," he says. "The doctor is seeing someone else now, and he will be in shortly." I've heard that one before. He exits and I go to my phone to catch up on emails. I don't know what anyone did in a waiting room before smartphones. I guess they embraced their human emotions. Even the times when I am wearing the paper robe, I go straight to my pile of clothes on the chair and dig out my phone. What if I miss something? I view the ability to catch up on emails all day the same way I view laundry. Don't let it or them pile up.

I grew up submerged in the opposite philosophy. I was the eldest of nine children. No, that's not a typo. Nine children. There was a total of eleven people in one house. When I was really young, like elementary school, we would have a dreadful ritual once a week known as "Laundry Day," where we would head down to the laundry room and confront a literal *mountain* of dirty clothes that would be daunting even to the Sherpas of Nepal. The mountain was at the foot of "the chute," a large vent that ran along the inside of the walls down three stories of our house. And it was not always laundry that went down there. Our laundry chute, aside from providing hours of entertainment for a group of unsupervised, rambunctious children ("let's throw water balloons down the chute!"), also served as a sort of pneumatic tube delivery system for those of us who were too lazy to carry items down three flights of stairs. So the laundry sorting process was also a kind of mining expedition to locate nonlaundry items such as pens, homework, toys, and the occasional dirty diaper, all of which, if accidentally scooped up and put in the washer, could add hours onto the already brutal laundry sweatshop.

The next eight hours would be spent sorting, mining, washing, sorting again, and folding. There were no organized shifts, but the four oldest of us would work as a team, normally to "earn things" like free time in the neighborhood, which would be individually promised to us by Mom. Occasionally someone would do the "slip-away," and then we'd all start complaining loudly until our mom would track them down. The "putting away" phase was sometimes reserved for another eight-hour day. Even with the two-day process, there was an entire basket or two of socks to sort.

There were seemingly hundreds of mismatched socks that almost looked identical, but never really lined up with one another. They would be the same size, but one would be a tube and the other shaped like a foot. Or they would be the same type, but one would be huge and the other tiny. Or they would be identical, but one was bright white and the other dingy gray. The Rubik's cube was easier to solve. I was so traumatized by "Laundry Day" that I vowed when I had my own household (and I had no idea at the time that there would be seven of us) I would do small loads all day and never have anything close to a mountain, or even a tiny hill. I kept that vow—I run my dang machine all day. Don't tell Al Gore. I transferred this same concept to my email behavior. Deal with it throughout the day. Never have a mountain of email.

I took the opportunity to catch up on those emails while waiting to be seen by the ENT doctor. It only took me fifteen minutes. I didn't even "keep as new" the long and complicated ones. I dealt with them. I was done. Still no doctor. I started to feel like I didn't even care about not being able to hear in my left ear. As a matter of fact, I was angry at myself for wasting half the day on this stupid doctor's appointment. I was angry at everyone. Except Dr. Hops. I just couldn't bring myself to be mad at her. I lay back on the exam table and sighed loudly. I closed my eyes and tried to meditate. "Breathe in, breathe out. Breathe in, breathe out." I must have dozed off because I remember being startled awake by the doctor knocking on the door before he entered in a cascade of apologies. Someone had had an emergency. Now I felt guilty. I wiped the trickle of drool off my cheek and smiled my best "no problem" smile.

The doctor went over the results of my hearing test. "Your hearing is within the normal range in both ears," he said.

"But it's not!" I exclaimed. "I can barely hear out of my left ear!" So not only did I waste my whole day, but now they're telling me I don't even qualify for a hearing aid?

"The hearing in your left ear is *slightly* less than the hearing in your right, but it's within the normal range."

After a pause, I blurted out, "I cheated on the hearing test!"

He seemed perplexed. "I don't understand…"

I continued my confession. "I raised my hand when I heard nothing, but I kind of heard something, like a tone. But it sounded like it was more in my head. Like more of a ringing. But I guess I shouldn't have raised my hand." He looked at me like I didn't need an ENT, I needed a PsyD. He explained that they were also measuring other things like vibrations and such that I really couldn't "cheat" on.

He gave me an assignment. Use Flonase three times a day and start a listening enhancement program online, which is like a workout for lazy ears. *Okay, I'll just add that into my free time.*

I'm a rule follower. When I got home, I pushed aside the huge pile of work on my desk and immediately googled the online sign-up for the auditory exercises. I committed myself to completing one exercise a day. It was $99 to sign up, but probably less than a hearing aid.

The exercises instructed me to "listen to the male voice" and then played the sounds of a ton of people speaking in a crowded room and then I zeroed in on the male voice. *This is misogynistic,* I thought. Then, after a minute, the next screen asked me to write or gave me choices to guess what the male voice said. I was pretty good at the exercises, but there was no way to really block my good ear. Still, I religiously followed doctor's orders: selective hearing exercises and snorting Flonase like an '80s coke fiend for a month. The left-side hearing didn't return, but at least I got a new addiction out of it. Always looking for that kick of the first hit.

Chapter 3

MARCH

The MRI That Wasn't

When it came time for my next appointment with Dr. Godin, I felt like I had accomplished something. I had gone with the whole family to Asia for Jim's tour over spring break and I'd packed the Flonase. I had totally completed the online auditory exercise program. (In English, of course.) The problem was, the hearing in my left ear had not changed one bit. This time I was honest during the hearing test. I was basically deaf in my left ear. The doctor came into the room promptly after the test. I happily reported that I'd completed the entire listening program he had prescribed and did he know of a good Flonase rehab program?

He looked at the results of the latest hearing test, looked inside my ear again, and sat in silence for a beat. After an awkward pause, he explained to me that my hearing functions appeared to be normal, and that sometimes there is something in the inner ear that he cannot see through the otoscope (the medical name for the ear-looker thing). In very rare instances, there may be something small blocking the internal auditory canal. But that's very rare, like ten in one million. The only way to see if there was anything in there was through an MRI scan. Sure, I said. Why not? Another appointment to schedule. Hope they can get me in soon. I guess I'll start playing phone tag with another medical office for the next three weeks. He explained that I didn't have to make an appointment. He would just write me a prescription, and then I would show up at a radiology center, check in, and wait. Sounded simple. I would just go early in the morning when no one else was there. Appointments at 9 a.m. are my absolute preference.

Jiminy Cricket

My mornings go something like this:

6:00 a.m.   Wake up to iPhone alarm, hit Snooze.

6:10 a.m.   Wake up to iPhone alarm, hit Snooze.

6:20 a.m.   Wake up to iPhone alarm, tempted to hit "Snooze."

6:25 a.m.   Babysitter enters and tells me to stop hitting Snooze.

6:30 a.m.   Drink coffee and stare.

6:40 a.m.   Panic that five kids need to eat breakfast, brush teeth, do hair, get in uniforms, find their shoes and backpacks (I have helpers, don't worry).

7:00 a.m.   Get picked up by Sixto car pool. My kids are the whole car pool.

7:30 a.m.   Drop off Marre at her middle school on East Ninety-Seventh Street.

7:37 a.m.	Drop off Katie at her school on East Eighty-Second Street.
7:40 a.m.	Cross Central Park on Seventy-Ninth Street down the West Side Highway to Chelsea.
7:55 a.m.	Get dropped off with the three boys, take Jack and Michael into school.
8:10 a.m.	Take Patrick down the street to the second-floor Early Learning Center. Play with blocks while we wait for his teacher to open the doors, then do "Kissing Hands." We kiss each other's palms and put the kiss in our pockets to save for later if we are having a bad day.
8:30 a.m.	Totally done with drop-offs. Now I am sans kids until 3:30 p.m.

The sprint has begun to get anything at all accomplished in the next seven hours.

*   *   *

Since we made the brutal decision to end *The Jim Gaffigan Show* at the end of season 2 for the sake of not missing our kids grow up, we moved our production company to our home office. I made a commitment to spend more time with my children, which is no better exemplified than by my willingness to commit the 2.5 hours before school to this epic and expensive journey around Manhattan every weekday morning. Even though I'm not at my best in the wee hours, I feel like, in a way, the kids are. Maybe not the crabby eleven-year-old and twelve-year-old, but the little ones are filled with gems ("Mom, am I allergic to baths?").

I can get to an appointment by 9 a.m. This is simply the best option for me. I can drop off the kids, make it across town to the dentist's office, get my teeth cleaned, get home and be at my desk at 10 a.m. and have a full day of productivity *and* clean teeth.

The worst option is a 10 a.m. appointment. Then there is not enough time to get back home and leave again. I have to stay out and find something to do for an hour, and I can't even run errands to pick up a bag of stuff because:

1. I'll have to carry the bag of stuff I picked up along with me to the appointment, which inevitably means that I will leave the bag of whatever at the appointment and then spend the rest of my day chasing it down; and

2. nothing in Manhattan opens until 10 or 11 a.m., so I couldn't pick up the bag of stuff even if I wanted to, because there is no stuff to be bought until 11 a.m.

I imagine that shops in New York used to open at 9 a.m. but then they changed the time because of the shabby customers. Maybe a few moms came in after drop-off in yoga pants with dried toothpaste in the corners of their mouths, and they were like, "We need a classier clientele. You know, the ones who sleep until ten, go to SoulCycle, then hit the showers and salons for a makeover and a blow-out before we open the doors at noon for these decent New Yorkers." The only things open are the pharmacies. I went into CVS one morning to get something I needed before a 10 a.m. appointment. I spent way too long in there and then left with a bag of stuff I didn't need, forgetting the thing I went in for, and then ultimately left the bag of other stuff in a cab. I'm not good at killing time. Jim and I are always involved in writing and producing a comedy show or making a film, and a 10 a.m. random appointment upends the whole day. The next day, I go to the radiology center with my "script" (what we insiders call prescriptions), take the elevator to the lower, lower level (for some reason radiology centers are always on the lower, lower level. Trust me, I am now an expert), and go to the front desk where I exchange my script and insurance card for, you guessed it, a clipboard with a stack of forms.

I look around the room and notice that almost everyone in Manhattan also decided that 9 a.m. was the perfect time to come to the radiology center on the lower, lower level. They each have a clipboard of forms. Since I was a pro at filling out forms at this point, I resolved that I was going to fill out my stack quicker than everyone who had arrived before me. It became an imagined competition. The room transformed into an SAT test center, with all of us lip-biting students determined to finish better and faster than the next. That's when I hit a question that stumped me:

Are you pregnant or is there a possibility you could be pregnant? Y/N

No fair. There is a total sexist disadvantage to the females filling out the forms. All the guys can skip that question. Plus, for me it involves math. Because of my and Jim's "let go and let God" or, as Jim calls it, the "no goalie" approach to birth control, there is *always* a possibility I could be pregnant. I had to think. I mean, we weren't *trying*, but we weren't not trying. Also, Jim is out of town a lot, so I really didn't know. I checked the calendar and I was smack-dab in the middle area where it was too early to take a test. Instead of just "*Y/N*," there needed to be an "*Other*" section. Or a "*Maybe.*" Even a small essay section would suffice. I could ace this thing. I just needed options. I glanced around the room for a nurse or other medical person. Nothing. I looked up at the front-of-house reception desk and there was an old man yelling at the women behind the desk. I moved up behind him, knowing my unsure-pregnancy question would be a welcome reprieve from this guy.

"I have been here for THREE HOURS!" barked the man. It was only 9:23 a.m. I wondered what time they opened or if the guy was exaggerating. Did he sleep outside last night like he was getting the next iPhone? "I have rights!" he continued. Apparently, he'd had enough time to read the Patient's Bill of Rights at the bottom of the stack of forms. I guess he *had* been there for a while. This was a true New York moment. People just go off here. I grew up in a midsize city, but if you heard more than one siren outside, everyone would come out on their front porches to see what was going on. In New York City, fifteen firetrucks could be blasting down the street and you just turn up the volume for your earbuds. The old guy kept yelling and began to bang his fists on the counter. The unfazed receptionists continued what they were doing (probably entering redundant data from forms) and didn't even look up at him. "I was here before the last person you called!" His complaining was falling on deaf ears. Or, in my case, deaf ear.

"Sir, there are many different tests that go on here. Patients get called as their specific testing room becomes available."

"This is RIDICULOUS!" he barked. I thought of how awful it must be (a) to be really old; (b) to be getting a scan for I'm sure nothing good; and (c) to be old, getting a scan for something not good, and waiting for what he perceived as three hours to be scanned for something not good.

I peeped around him. "Hi," I said to the stern front-of-house person whom I hoped would be happy to see me.

"Can I help you?" she asked, without looking up and in the same tone with which she'd answered the man I felt sorry for one second ago.

"Yes, um, on these forms here, it asks if I could be pregnant, and I don't think I am at all, but it's possible, like, not probable, but there is a small, tiny possibility, like, really remote, like, if I was pregnant it would be like, five minutes pregnant. I mean not five minutes, that would be TMI, but like, it would be really, really early. Like, if I did a test now, it would say 'negative' even though it might be 'positive,' you know? I mean, I could be in the early stages...but I could also just say 'No' on the form because I'm not pregnant, to the best of my knowledge, but I could be. You know?" The old man looked at me and rolled his eyes. Now I was the raving lunatic. Maybe I *was* babbling a tad. The receptionist still didn't look up.

"We can't answer any medical questions. Please direct all questions concerning your test to the radiologist." *Right*, I thought and sat back down. I looked up at the TV that had no volume. *The Chew* was on. *I'm starving*, I thought. I left the question blank and continued to fill out the rest of the form.

Eventually a woman in pink scrubs came out and called my name:

"Janine?"

I didn't even look around to see if there was coincidentally someone named Janine there. When most people read the name "Jeannie" I guess it just looks like "Janine." I once had a summer job where I was called Janine for two months because I didn't want to correct the person. Wait, do Janines get called Jeannie? Maybe if I changed my name to Janine, then people would call me Jeannie. Anyway, the woman in the pink scrubs guided me to the back where there was a row of curtained booths.

"Take off your clothes and all of your jewelry and put it in this bag. Someone will come get you when it's time for the MRI." She hurried off. Whatever happened to romance? I realized I'd missed my chance to talk to her.

Now probably wouldn't be the best time to ask the pregnancy question, I thought. As I struggled to take off my small earrings and necklace, I was mad at myself. *Why did I wear jewelry to an MRI?* To be fair, I didn't purposely put it on to attend the MRI like it was the social event of the season. I just never take it off because

I'm afraid I'll lose it. I realized I didn't know what MRI stood for or what it actually was. I just always thought of it as a glorified x-ray that measures how truly claustrophobic you really are.

However, with all the form questions about having metal implants in one's body, such as "aneurysm clips" or "bullet or shrapnel wounds," I could guess that the "M" stood for "magnet," and if you wore jewelry in the tube, it would be ripped right off. I put the tiny hoop earrings and the Miraculous Medal I never remove (so I won't lose them) into my shoe (so I won't lose them). I put on the paper gown and sat shivering in the little curtained booth waiting for the technician. Thankfully, they like to turn up the AC in the areas where you wear the least clothing.

A not-so-short time later, a pleasant-looking man in his forties, with glasses and more hair on his face than his head, approached the booth with the curtain that stopped about six inches shy of actually covering the door. "Hi, I'm ready," I said, letting him know he could open the curtain because I was decent. He was carrying a clipboard with my forms on it.

"Hi, Ms. (reads) *Nawth Griffin?*"

"Yes, that's me. Kind of. It's actually pronounced 'Noth,' like rhymes with 'both,' *Gaffigan*."

"Do you have any metal in or on your body?" Again with the not reading the forms.

"No, I'm good." I realized now that this was my chance to explain why I had left that one question blank. Not that anyone noticed. After all, we have already concluded that no one reads these forms. I would have rather asked a woman, but this guy would do. "I do have one question. On those forms, it also asked if I am pregnant. Although I don't think I am pregnant, there is a slim, slim chance I might be, although it would be way too early to know." I impressed myself with my ability to consolidate the communication about this after my undeniable similarity to the lunatic in the waiting room. "It's still okay that I get the MRI, right?" I waited for him to tell me it was fine in his haste to get to the next patient.

"I wouldn't," he said easily.

"What?" I was shocked. I had already taken my jewelry off, for God's sake. I was in the gown and everything. I don't know why these plastic and paper ponchos are called gowns. When I think *gown*, it's evening wear. If calling this thing a gown was an attempt to glamorize the poncho experience, it wasn't working.

He continued without hesitation: "Even if there is a small chance you could be pregnant, we really don't know if the test could have an adverse effect on the baby."

"But there is no baby! I mean, I was just being *cautious*."

"Better to be cautious. A lot of things can go wrong at the early stages of pregnancy. I'm sure if you *are* pregnant, and something goes wrong, you'd hate to think you had something to do with it because you went ahead and got the MRI."

Wow, who was this guy, Jiminy Cricket? Now, after all that, I couldn't get an MRI today. Frustration and anger bubbled, followed seconds later by an overwhelming feeling of guilt. How selfish of me. I was totally ignoring the health and well-being of the baby that may not exist, for an MRI that I didn't even need. So I left with no MRI, grumbling that I hoped Dr. Hops would be happy that her little "assignment" for me had turned into an epic saga.

In a few days it became clear that I was certainly not pregnant. When I called the radiology center, I learned that they had held on to my script, and my forms, so all I had to do was show up, change the date, sign something, and I would be good to go for the MRI. Just knowing it would be that easy to get another MRI, I put it off for another week. It was almost Easter, and I was busy.

Chapter 4

APRIL

The Margarita Guy: *Houston, We Have a Problem*

The following week, on a day when I had my sacred 9 a.m. hour free, I headed back to Union Square to the lower, lower level. Just another thing on my to-do list. I had one of my usual splitting headaches, which meant doing anything at all seemed like a tedious chore. There weren't a lot of people waiting, so I waltzed into the barely curtained booth with no issues. I'd left my earrings and metal medal home like a pro. That too-small-curtained booth was not so bad without the wait. I effortlessly put on my gown like I was getting a massage at a fancy spa, and I was quickly called into the MRI room.

If you've ever had the privilege of entering a walk-in freezer at the back of a restaurant, then you have a rough idea of the temperature inside an MRI room. The technicians were wearing fleeces with the logo of the radiology place like they were

Arctic scientists. The room was gray, and in the center, there was a large white tube that looked like a cross between a futuristic escape pod and an open-air coffin.

"Hey!" Jiminy Cricket walked in.

"Oh, hi!" I said. After our encounter about the fake baby, I felt like we were close friends. He introduced himself as the technician who would be conducting the scan. It became immediately clear he did not remember me, or his important role in my life's ethical milestone concerning the choice between getting my MRI over with, or the health and well-being of my imaginary baby. Still, he was bursting with energy, sunny and cheerful.

"I hope you're not claustrophobic!" He laughed.

"Not really," I said. "How long is this going to take?"

"It's about an hour, if you hold still. You must stay completely motionless so we can get the clearest images. If you move, it might be longer." Suddenly I doubted my ability to hold still. "I'm going to put an IV tube in your arm, because in the second part of the scan, we will be injecting a contrast dye into your bloodstream to allow us to see certain parts of your body more clearly, particularly the blood vessels."

"Why not?" I replied. I knew all about the dye. Several questions on the forms were dedicated to it. I was to get an MRI scan "with and without contrast." I was intrigued by the expression "with and without" because it seemed so beautifully paradoxical. I had only heard the phrase in relation to the scan and couldn't really apply it to anything else tangible. "Would you like some coffee, with and without cream?" I could easily apply it to more abstract concepts: "Would you like some marriage, with and without conflict?"

The technician applied the tourniquet and began to insert

the IV catheter. The familiar smell of rubbing alcohol filled the air. I stared at the contraption stuck in my arm with morbid fascination. "You can leave this in after the scan if you want to inject a margarita later." He winked.

I was impressed by his demeanor and understood it was part of his job to make the scanee feel relaxed before inserting them into the escape-pod coffin. I wondered how many others had heard his margarita bit, knowing I wasn't the first.

"I noticed on the forms that they asked, 'Have you ever had an allergic reaction to contrast dye?' How would I know if I was allergic to the dye if I have never had it before?" He'd probably dealt with this question a million times. I'm sure in the past it had occurred to a few people that getting a foreign substance that has been known to cause allergic reactions injected into their bloodstream right before they are slid into a claustrophobic, soundproof coffin, where they are not allowed to move, was cause for a modicum of concern.

"Reactions are extremely rare, and you don't have any kidney problems," he said. "And don't worry, I will be communicating with you over a speaker the whole time, letting you know how long each picture will take. The first one will be about twenty-five minutes. You'll be hearing loud noises so we're going to give you some earplugs."

"I have five kids, so I know from loud noises!" I thought it was a good move to slip in that I had five kids, because they would probably be more careful with me than a less important person who had, say, four kids. The jovial technician whom I now no longer thought of as Jiminy Cricket and currently referred to as "the Margarita Guy," was pleasant and reassuring.

"Don't worry, you will be out of here soon."

It was clear that I was one of the easier scans. Although

there are no "routine MRIs," I was a healthy, youngish person, and this was a "rule-out" MRI due to left-ear hearing loss, that's it. Ruling out that something inside my body was causing hearing loss. Meaning, nothing was. After the margarita comment, it was clear that I was one of the more "fun" patients, so I decided to have fun. I lay on the plank.

"Do you want a warm blanket?" he asked.

"Yes, and can you read me *Goodnight Moon?*"

He chuckled as he handed me a rubber ball attached to a cord. "If you need to get our attention, just squeeze this."

The Margarita Guy moved toward the exit to station himself behind the protective glass that shields the technicians from the poison magnetic rays that were about to happen.

"If I need to get your attention, can't I just start screaming?" I called out.

"No need," he replied. "We wouldn't be able to hear you anyway." Wait, what? Shouldn't we test if the ball thing works? The machine started up with a whir and the plank slid me into the tube.

Inside, I was alone with myself. A rare occasion for a mother of five. I felt disconnected from my body. The voice of Margarita Guy shifted to a speaker. I felt like I had been launched into space, and the voice was Houston.

"Okay, this first test will be about twenty-five minutes long. Try not to move." I realized that I'd forgotten which hand the emergency squeeze ball was in, but I was afraid to slightly clench my hand to remind myself for fear I would break the no-moving rule. *How am I going to do this for twenty-five minutes?* Then I heard something like a hammer methodically banging on the outside of the tube. That can't be good, right? Had it malfunctioned? Was I trapped inside and they were trying to crack me out? Had I left some jewelry on like metal in the microwave?

The rhythmic hammer bangs turned into full-fledged jackhammer pounding. This time it was not orderly at all; there was no rhyme or reason to the banging. It was so loud the whole tube should have been shaking, but it wasn't. This was obviously part of the test. If they were trying to break me out, that tube would have already cracked like an egg dropped on the kitchen floor. Have you ever been at a circus and you saw a clown with one of those huge horns with the rubber ball on it and just for fun they put it right next to your ear and honked it? Well, neither had I, but now I knew what it sounded like. But not a short goofy honk. Imagine that sound, but sustained for somewhere between five seconds and twenty-five minutes. The irony was that the loud honk was in my good ear. The little rubber earplug they'd put in was somehow acting like an amplifier. The horn was periodically interrupted by what is best described as a shotgun firing into my ear, but without the reprieve of instant death. I had a feeling that my "good ear" was no longer going to be very good. I finally understood the animated graphics in the 1960s Batman series: *Pow!* *Blam!* *Ka-POW!* I now saw flashing before my eyes. Then, more incessant banging that morphed into jackhammering. It was great for my headache.

I tried not to breathe. If I moved, even a little, I would have to do this again. I needed no other motivation to keep perfectly still. Suddenly I got an itch on my eyebrow that felt like a mosquito was trolling around looking for a lunch place. I realized that I normally took for granted the simple gesture of the scratch. Do people in comas who can't move or talk get itches and experience this unbearable sensation? Let it pass;

let it pass. Say some Hail Marys. Wait, I can't remember the words, even though I've known them since I was five. Twenty-five minutes turned into twenty-five hours.

Finally, I heard from Houston: "Okay, great job. This next scan will be about ten minutes." Ten minutes. Easy peasy lemon squeezy. I could do this standing on my head, or even lying on my back, unable to move in a freezing coffin. I became one with the test. I chose to accept it. Embrace it. The banging, horns, and shotgun blasts became like white noise to me. This wasn't so bad. Much easier than trying to get five kids to brush their teeth. In fact, I may invest in a banging isolation chamber for my own house just to get some peace, if not quiet, every now and again. I think I might have even dozed off.

"Okay, good job, now we are going to inject the dye." I startled awake. I felt a rush through my blood, first cold, then warm, and tasted a sharp chemical flavor in my mouth that was kind of like drinking a shot of rubbing alcohol. It wasn't a warm feeling as in a "warm and fuzzy" feeling, but it didn't hurt or anything. It felt as if I had released my bladder in the tube and the liquid had spread out and enveloped me in a blanket. Pleasant and unpleasant at the same time. With and without pleasant.

The rest of the scan moved along without incident. I stayed perfectly still, encouraged by Margarita Guy periodically telling me I was doing a "good job." I didn't squeeze the help button even once.

And then it was over and the auto-slider ejected me slowly from my noisy chamber of peace. The on-time dismissal meant they did not have to redo any of the pictures. Another of life's experiences tried and over with. I'll never have to do that again. As I sat up on the plank, I thought about which of the witty remarks I had been thinking up for the past hour and a half to use on Margarita Guy. He entered the room.

"I'll take that margarita now!" I said. That's what we improvisers call a "yes, *and*." But he didn't "yes, *and*" me back. In fact, he didn't even crack a half smile.

"You can go get dressed and wait in the reception area." He avoided looking me in the eyes as he spoke. What happened to "good job!"? He was complimenting me over the microphone through the whole test, and now that I had survived *and* held perfectly still, he was just going to blow me off? I thought we had something. Before, he was my improv partner; he was my conscience.

"Can I just go then?" I was eager to put this whole experience behind me. I mean, I was glad I'd had the test—knowledge is power—but I wanted to get out of there as soon as I could.

"You should wait in the reception area. Your doctor will call you." Our eyes met briefly before he turned abruptly and exited the room. A creepy chill went down my spine. Despite his best attempts at a medical poker face, Jiminy Margarita had looked at me with horror. Like he was looking at a corpse.

I walked back to the reception area and sat down to try to figure out what had just happened. Why the sudden change in demeanor? I had to be imagining it. I'd walked into this appointment to tick something off my to-do list, but now I was overcome with a sense of dread and foreboding. I stood and walked over to reception.

"Hi, my name is Jeannie *Noth* Gaffigan. I was just told to wait for my doctor to call me here? His office is uptown, and I was just supposed to make a follow-up appointment with him two weeks after the scan."

The icy receptionist looked up this time. "He must have ordered a rapid response. We sent him the report, and we are waiting for him to call."

"Okay, thanks," I replied dutifully and sat back down. I checked my phone. Nothing but spam emails. I couldn't focus. "A rapid response." No, that's not true. He just sent me in for a "rule-out." I remembered this vividly. Get the MRI scan to rule out anything wrong with my inner ear, then make a follow-up visit in two weeks. Nope. Nothing about a rapid response. I called Jim.

"What's up?" he asked curtly when he answered the phone. He was clearly in the middle of something. This is the primary way we communicate: answering each other's calls in a hurry and sounding annoyed when we are in the middle of something.

"Jim, I just had an MRI scan." I recalled that this appointment was so minimal to me, just another thing I had to do to interrupt my busy day, that I hadn't told him I was getting an MRI. I hadn't even told him about the first attempt to get an MRI. It was just another thing I had to do.

"Are you okay?" Jim sounded concerned.

"I don't know. I think so. I went in because I had hearing loss in my left ear, but now everyone here is acting strange and they won't let me leave."

"Do you want me to come there?" he asked. Amazing Jim. I knew he was busy, but he would drop everything for me.

"No! I want to go home!" I didn't want to sound whiny, so I decided to get mad. "I'm leaving! I'll be home in a minute." I hung up and marched over to the reception desk. "Excuse me. Can I see the order from my doctor where it says, 'rapid response'?" The receptionist seemed to be surprised by this question.

"Pardon me?" she asked.

"You just told me that my doctor wanted a 'rapid response,' but he told me nothing of the sort. He just sent me in for a rule-out MRI. So, if he indeed told you I was supposed to get an MRI scan at this radiology center, that has no doctors' offices connected to it, and that I was supposed to sit here all day while we waited for him to call you so you could give him a 'rapid response,' I'd like to see where he wrote that." I craned my neck as though I were trying to see her top secret computer screen. I had turned into the old man. Clearly I was not going to let her blow me off.

"Hold on." She picked up the phone. "Have a seat just for a moment." I stood there for a beat to be sure she was not just faking a call to get rid of me, and then I slowly backed into a chair, not taking my eyes off her. I wasn't playing. Then, the original woman in the pink scrubs appeared from the back. Smiling and totally pleasant. "Hi, Ms. Gaffigan?"

I stood up. "Yes, here!"

"You can go home. Your doctor is in surgery now. He will call you when he's done." I was confused. I no longer sensed any weirdness about the attitude of the staff, but my doctor will call me? That was not part of the plan. As I mentioned before, I was pretty positive he'd said, "After you get the MRI, make an appointment in two weeks." Maybe at this lower, lower level place, deep in the basement bowels of the building, they always assumed the doctor would call after the MRI, just as a courtesy that anything unusual had been ruled out. That had to be it. Yet, something was nagging at me about this whole situation. I left and walked home from Union Square. I needed some air.

Chapter 5

LIMBO: An uncertain period of awaiting
a decision or resolution; an intermediate
state or condition

About fifteen minutes after leaving the radiology center, I walked into our home office, where Jim was in the middle of an interview for a documentary we were producing. Sky, our right-hand man, was filming him. Sky is a guy. His name, when it appears in an email, often causes people to assume he is female. He finds this error a constant source of amusement, and he is never offended by it—it's just his "Janine." Because I have a million kids and have been exposed to every uncommon name under the sun (and sky), I happen to know that the female version of the name "Sky" is actually spelled "Skye," but many people do not, and whenever Sky and I were on an email together to a business associate that we had never met face-to-face, it was not uncommon to have the sender begin the email with something like, "Hey Ladies!" at which Sky and I would react with amusement, and have a fun debate over whether or not to ever tell the person that Sky was actually not a lady. Also entertaining was when we occasionally did correct the sender, informing him or her that Sky was indeed a member of the male persuasion. The reaction was always the same: Way too much overapologizing and admitting humiliation. As if they had accidentally assumed a woman who had put on a few pounds was pregnant.

"Oh my God, I am *sooooooo* sorry! I am such an idiot. Whoa. My total bad! I should not have assumed that. Open mouth, insert foot. Please forgive my stupidity and ignorance." Since it really was never a big deal, many times we just chose to let Sky remain a lady to keep things less awkward. He doesn't care. He's twenty-four years old going on wise old man.

We didn't actually "meet" Sky; rather, we stumbled upon him. Very early in season 1 of *The Jim Gaffigan Show*, our writer's assistant had to leave abruptly while we were in the middle of shooting and it could have been a disaster. The head of the production company we were working with was quick to help. While he was gathering candidates for us to interview, he gave us the name and number of one of his best office PAs to assist us in the meantime. When I got his number, it was Sky. I recalled that I had heard our former assistant speak his name before ("I'll just send Sky to pick that up"), but I had never met him. When I was entering his number into my phone, I noticed it was a 414 area code. The same as I had growing up in Milwaukee. So I sent him a text:

> **Hi it's Jeannie Gaffigan, Executive Producer. Thanks for helping us out! Are you from Milwaukee?**

Yes!

> **Where in Milwaukee?**

The East Side.

> **Where on the East Side?**

Newberry Boulevard

> **Lake Park fireworks?**

Every 4th of July!

This person, whom I had randomly met by chance in New York City, grew up a few blocks away from me in Milwaukee, Wisconsin, and we shared many identical childhood experiences. We knew tons of the same people, and as it turned out, our fathers were both film historians and his grandmother and my father worked together for years at a Milwaukee newspaper. His childhood best friends lived in the house next door to my parents.

He started working for us immediately as a temporary replacement. That's when we discovered that he was already thoroughly familiar with our work. Within a day we realized that he had been acting as an assistant to our former assistant. He knew everything about what we were doing—from the scripts, to the promos, to our coffee orders. He worked as hard as we did and he actually cared as much as we did, which was rare and unique. Sky stepped right into the role of being an essential part of every aspect of our very intense creative process. Even after the show ended, we brought him into all of our other projects, and our kids started to view him as one of the Gaffigan clan.

So when I came in that day, distraught from the MRI confusion, and Jim and Sky were working on the documentary, I had no problem interrupting them to say I was concerned. I was with family.

"You guys, I think something is wrong with me."

I was admitting this to myself at the same time. Now that I was in a safe place, I was no longer channeling my fear into anger about waiting around at the clinic. I was terrified.

"What happened?"

I told them all about Margarita Guy and the sudden change in his demeanor. I told them about the suspicious "your doctor will call you" scenario.

"I'm sure it's fine." Jim did not seem too concerned. In retrospect, he was probably very concerned but he couldn't show it. In our relationship, as in most good relationships, if one of us is freaking out about something, the other one's automatic role is to remain calm. It's a natural reflex that transforms couples into "good cop/hysterical cop." If you are at a restaurant and the service is horrendous, one of you will be furious, and the other will be all, "Honey, calm down; maybe she's having a bad day." In other situations, the reactions will be reversed. It's a couple survival instinct. If you know couples who both lose it at the same time, you probably aren't friends with them anymore. Jim and I have been through so much together, including a lot of medical scares while I was pregnant. Some of these scares turned out to be nothing, and some were indeed worst-case scenarios, and we survived them all. Jim's stoic confidence had its familiar calming effect on me. I felt better.

I put it out of my head and jumped into working on the

documentary with them. We were in the middle of creating a "making of" film about the difficulties of writing a comedy special while our lives were so busy. Very meta concept, to write a film about being busy while we were actually too busy to write a film, but very standard practice for Jim and Jeannie. We wanted to finish it by September. It was April. We had plenty of time. Or so we thought. Less than an hour into work, the phone rang, and I saw it was Dr. Godin. Needless to say, after that call, the documentary never got made.

"Hi, Jeannie, it's Dr. Godin. How are you?"

"I don't know. Actually, I have been waiting for your phone call for *you* to tell *me* how I am. Did they find something wrong with my ear?"

"Well, I'm looking at your report now, and it appears that you have a large mass growing in your brain." He sounded so casual.

"Okay," I said. Jim and Sky were staring at me, not hearing the other side of the conversation.

He continued. "A lot of the time, these things are benign growths. To tell you the truth, my own mother has several of them, called *meningiomas*, and they just kind of watch them. That's what it might be."

"Okay," I said again. I looked at Jim and Sky. They must have seen the panic in my eyes because they looked really scared.

"This sort of thing is out of my area of expertise. I'm going to give you the names of two really great neurosurgeons. I mean, normally I would refer you to a neurologist, but in this case the neurologist would just refer you to a neurosurgeon anyway." I picked up a pen to start writing this down. My hand was shaking uncontrollably.

I tried to match the calmness in the doctor's voice. "Okay, um, so, there is some mass in my brain? And you want me to make appointments with neurosurgeons?" I repeated this for the benefit of Jim, who was obviously wondering what the hell was going on.

"Yes. This is what I want you to do. Go back to the radiology center and get the scans. Normally they are like $15 or $20 a copy. Then make an appointment with either one of those doctors. Both are really great." I tried to steady my hand to write down the names of the surgeons. Jim and Sky were frozen in their spots.

"Okay," I said. That word seemed to be pretty much my side of this conversation. "Um, so what do you think the neurosurgeon is going to do?"

"Well, as I said, this is really not my area, so I can't give you any real medical advice. But I would imagine they would try to resect at least part of it."

"What does *resect* mean?"

"Remove."

"But…it's in my brain, right?"

Dr. Godin cleared his throat. "Look, I am not sure what they are going to do; as I mentioned, it's not my area, but don't worry. Just get the scan and make the appointments. These doctors will know what to do."

"Okay." My new favorite word.

"And let me know after you make the appointments. I want you to follow up with me."

"I will." I hung up and sprang into action.

"I have to go back to the place and get my scans."

Jim grabbed his jacket. "I'm coming with you." We hurried down the block silently, lost in our thoughts but holding hands tightly, and got in a cab. We were at Union Square in five minutes. We went together to the lower, lower level and

I approached the desk with confidence and determination, emboldened by Jim's presence. Team Gaffigan.

"Hi, I need the scans from the MRI I got today." Jim stood behind me with his arms folded over his chest, staring down the receptionist like my bodyguard.

"They're $25 a disc."

"I'll take three copies. No, four." Money was no object in this situation. I don't know why I thought I needed all those copies of my scan, but it made me feel better to have them. It was like how everyone in New York City bought all the water in the stores after the planes hit the World Trade Center, even though there was no shortage of water. The four scans gave me a false sense of control. Who knew? Maybe the fourth one would save my life. We sat in silence as we waited about thirty minutes for the scans. What do you even say to each other in this scenario? "So. How is your day going?" After we greedily collected the four discs, we immediately went back to our office to see what all the fuss was about. The problem was, we'd forgotten our computers didn't have disc drives in them. Damn those technological advancements.

"Wait! We have an external disc drive!" I started opening drawers and file boxes. In my office and my home, I have this super OCD way of labeling everything. Everywhere you look in my house, there is a sign, note, or label designating where things belong. Even if I am not there, it looks like I'm bossing everyone around. In reality, the signs and notes are for me so I don't forget where things are, which is just what happened in the case of the external hard drive. I knew I'd put it in a logical place, but since it was the only one, it did not have its own label. Would I have put it with storage hard drives? No. What other things were like things that you plug into your computer?

I was lost. Suddenly all my labeled organization meant nothing as we frantically searched for the technology that would allow us to view the scan. Where the hell was that drive? Finally, I found it in the top drawer of a side table where we also stored the extra Wite-Out. No logic.

I plugged it in and inserted the disc. Jim and I stared at the computer screen, nervously waiting for it to load. When it finally showed up, we clicked open the file, and, instead of an image, we saw a string of numbers. "We can't open this on our computers! We need a hospital computer." Okay, that's fine, we could just call the neurosurgeons to make the appointment. Maybe they would let us swing by and look at the scan. I dialed the first number and got the receptionist. I was frantic but remained calm and fake-dignified. "Hi. I'm a patient of Dr. Godin, and he recommended I call the doctor because an MRI I had today detected a large mass in my brain and he wants me to meet with the neurosurgeon." I paused briefly for the concerned and sympathetic reaction in this urgent situation. "Are you a new patient?" came the disinterested response. I was taken aback.

"Of course I'm a new patient. I just told you my MRI showed a mass in my brain and my referring doctor told me to call your office!"

"Do you have the MRI *report?*"

"No, I have the scan. Do you want that?"

"We will need to see the report first before we see the scan. And I need the report if you want to make an appointment as a new patient." How many people are making fake appointments with brain surgeons with no report? Why would I make this up?

I called my ENT doctor and got his assistant, Kurt. "Hi, the neurosurgeon the doctor recommended needs the report from the MRI in order to make the appointment. Can you please send him the report? It's urgent." Kurt agreed to ask the doctor to send the report and told me the neurosurgeon should have it in an hour. An hour later, to the second, I called back. They had the report. Still not concerned. The job application for medical receptionists must have the requirement: "has worked as a maximum-security prison guard." I put the call on speakerphone so Jim could be more involved.

"The doctor can see you at 2 p.m. on May 16." That was over a month away.

"Do you have anything earlier?"

"No, you can call back on Tuesday of next week to see if we have had any cancellations, but the doctor is all booked up. Especially for new patients."

Okay. "Do you want me to drop off the scan?" I was hoping Jim and I could just get a look at it on their fancy computer. See what all the fuss was about.

"Just bring the scan with you to the appointment." I hung up. Jim looked as frustrated as I felt.

"Call the other guy," he said. I googled the other neurosurgeon's number. The receptionist answered. It was the same office. Both of these guys were in the same office.

"I . . . I just called and made an appointment with Dr. (blank). My ENT also recommended that I call Dr. (other blank). Does he have any appointments before May 16?" He had one on May 8. I took it. They already had the report. I'd just bought eight days.

"Would you like to cancel the appointment with Dr. (blank)?" I looked at Jim. He shook his head.

"No," I said. "I'll keep them both." The receptionist acted

annoyed, but for the first time in my life, I didn't care or apologize. "Well, that was horrible," I said to Jim.

There wasn't much else to do at that point except wait until May 8, and bring in the scan. I was in limbo. Jim and I agreed we should not call my parents, or anyone really, to tell them what was going on. We certainly were not going to scare the kids. "The good news is that it must not be that big of a deal if they aren't rushing you in," said Jim. That was true. If they were really worried, I'm sure they would have had me come in immediately, right? So, I decided to let go and put it in "God's hands." Oh yeah. God. I had totally forgotten about him. He was the perfect person to turn to in a time like this.

I tried talking to him. "Hi, God. I'm pretty concerned about this thing in my brain. Obviously, you are going to take care of everything, right? I know I got really busy and forgot about you, but just so you know, I am relying on you to fix this situation." I felt like maybe just my talking to him wasn't enough, since I still had this horrible feeling about sitting on this "not knowing" feeling for three weeks. Who did I know who was buddies with God? It dawned on me. It was time to bring in the big guns. I called Marita.

Marita Haggerty is my mom's first cousin. She is what is called a "spiritual warrior." She runs this ministry at her church on Long Island that is for cancer patients who have lost all hope. Her group has healing Masses and prayer sessions for people who are facing the unimaginable and in many cases has had miraculous healings, or so she says. It was time for me to believe it. Marita was something special.

When I first moved from Milwaukee to New York City, I didn't have any family here that I knew of, which was kind of strange since both of my parents were originally from New

York City. My mom grew up in Flushing, Queens, and my father in Manhattan. The roads of their lives intersected when they met at Marquette University in Milwaukee. They settled there and had nine kids. That's a lot of roots to put down in a new town and a great excuse as to why they lost touch with cousins on the East Coast.

After I graduated from Marquette myself, I did a brief internship at the Milwaukee Repertory Theater, where it dawned on me that New York City was the place I actually wanted to live. Once I got there, it wasn't easy. After struggling for several months with no money, trying to lock down an apartment and a job, my second cousin Anne, Marita's daughter, looked me up. She was about fifteen years older than me and had a super-prestigious job at Condé Nast. I hadn't known her at all growing up, but she heard I'd moved to the city and took me under her wing. We instantly got along. Her mother Marita's parents had passed away when Marita was still a girl, and Marita and her younger brother Bill had to move in with my grandfather and grandmother, who were at the time young parents raising five very young children of their own. So, essentially, Marita and Bill grew up as older siblings to my mother. Geography had separated everyone for years, but now that I was back in New York it was like no time had passed at all. When I met Anne, we were immediately family. We were related by nature and nurture. She called me "cousin Jeannie" so I called her "cousin Annie." It was a cute, warm title that started as a joke and then just stuck.

Soon Anne invited me out to her childhood house on Long Island for the weekend. The second I met her mother, Marita, I could tell she and my own mother were like sisters. She sat me down at the kitchen counter, gave me some food, and leaned in, peering over her glasses and looking me right in the eye. "How are you *really* doing, dear?" she said. It was as if my own mother were sitting in front of me because that was exactly what she would have said. Even the sound of her voice and her mannerisms with the glasses were virtually identical. This should have totally freaked me out, but instead it moved me to tears and I threw my arms around her in a giant hug. I had left home, and I missed my mom, but God had brought me here to this new family with their wraparound-porch farmhouse on Long Island. Anne's siblings, Beth, Greg, and Laura, adopted "cousin Jeannie." They were a terrifically fun bunch. Every time I had a weekend off or I felt homesick, I was invited to the Haggertys'.

As I got closer to my distant cousins, I became drawn to Marita's incredible connection with God. At the many celebrations, dinners, weddings, funerals, and parties I attended at their farmhouse, I noticed Marita would often slip away to her room with a serene smile on her face and pray the Rosary. I imagined her up there in her bedroom, listening to the hooting and hollering below, and spending quiet time alone with God. Growing up I had witnessed my own mother slipping away to pray, and it always struck me as weird and annoying. As a rebellious teen, I literally would tell my mom she was crazy and I would hide her little prayer books when my friends came over. As an adult, witnessing Marita doing the same thing, I found myself admiring her. Maybe I was just older and more mature, but seeing this replica of my own mother doing her thing with God made me better understand my childhood and filled me with a newfound love for my mom. I felt shame and joy at the same time, a feeling that perhaps other cultural Catholics reading this book may totally relate to, and that some of you will probably just think is odd and pitiful, but it's a feeling. I call it "shoy." What really struck me about Marita's rich, spiritual life was that in spite of all the hardships, sickness, and tragedy that inevitably come with life and having a big family, she always kept her faith and kept praying. She kept holding her family together, loving people and God. I didn't understand how she did it, but she did. Now, in my moment of confusion and despair, I knew I had to call her.

I dialed her number and got an answering machine. I forgot people still had those, I thought maybe they were all in museums at this point. Since Marita is in her eighties, it made perfect sense that she had an actual answering machine. While I was listening to the creepy robotic male voice of the factory-recorded outgoing message, I remembered that with answering machines, all the privacy that comes with modern voice mail is lost. You press Play on an answering machine and everyone in the room can hear the message. She might be having some fancy neighbors over for tea, and in the middle of biting into a jelly donut, they'd hear my voice saying, "mass in my brain." I was not actually sure what my message would say anyway. I couldn't just hang up, because I remembered the scene from *Sixteen Candles* where the hunky guy hangs up on the grandparents and they think he's a pervert. *BEEEP.* "Uh, hi, Marita, it's cousin Jeannie. Um, I'm wondering if you could call me about something when you have a chance. Bye!"

I sat staring at my phone. I felt unsatisfied. Would the message get to her? Should I have said it was urgent? I didn't want to upset anyone. That's why I wasn't calling my parents. I mean, my mom is a prayer warrior too, but asking her to pray for me because I might have brain cancer is kind of like asking an ob/gyn to deliver their spouse's baby. Was Marita even in town? I knew I could ask her oldest daughter, Beth. I felt really close to Beth because we had a connection as eldest female children of big families. We had also been joined at the vein as blood sisters when we were in the hospital together while Anne was so sick with cancer. Beth was in the hospital all the time, long after Anne lost her speech. She was the one who made sure there was always someone with Anne and managed everyone's comings and goings. I remember each time I walked into Mount Sinai to see Anne in her hospital bed, Beth would be there, circles under her eyes, but always with a smile and a hug. "Cousin Jeannie! I'm so glad you are here." Even though we'd grown up half a country apart, I understood her intimately. Her role in the family was the caregiver, and no one was taking care of her. We bonded. I didn't want to worry her by telling her what was up with me, but I knew she would know where Marita was. I shot her an email.

To: Beth Haggerty Steers

Subject: Marita?

Hi Beth, it's cousin Jeannie! How are you? I just tried to call Marita and got her machine. Do you happen to know where she is or when she will be back?

Thanks!
Jeannie

Beth replied immediately, another way we eldest children are alike.

To: Jeannie Gaffigan

Subject: Re: Marita?

Cousin Jeannie! How are you? Mom should be at home. Sometimes that phone doesn't ring, it's always giving them problems. Is everything OK?

Love,
Cousin Beth

To: Beth Haggerty Steers

Subject: Re: Marita?

Hey! Thanks, I will try her again. I was just calling her because she's a prayer warrior and I have some concerns about a medical thing that I'm dealing with. Hopefully it's no big deal.

Love,
Cousin Jeannie

Then my phone rang. "Cousin Jeannie, what's going on?" I guess Beth wasn't going to let my cryptic message stand for itself.

"Well," I said. I told her about the mass in my brain and how I couldn't get anyone to tell me what to do or what was going on.

"Jeannie, you have to go to Mount Sinai. They are the best."

"I think these neurosurgeons that I'm seeing are near NYU."

"I'm sure they are good, too, but Mount Sinai is tops." She then went on to describe her family's special relationship with Mount Sinai. Of course, there was Anne's long stay there during and at the end of her illness. Beth also had treatments at Mount Sinai herself and was back on the tennis court. Marita recently had lung surgery at Mount Sinai and loved all the doctors. "Mom knows absolutely *everyone* at Mount Sinai. She has *connections.* She's like the mayor there." I told her how I was very frustrated because I had to wait so long to even get in to see a doctor, and I was hesitant to call new doctors. "You need an inside push," said Beth. "Marita will help you. Hey, I just remembered, my friend had something with her brain too. An aneurysm. What was her doctor's name? Bederson. That's it. He was terrific. *Tops.* You know, I have this strong feeling that you should go to Dr. Bederson." What was an aneurysm? All these names and hospitals were just making me stressed.

"I really just want to call Marita because I know she has a direct line to heaven."

Beth agreed. "Mom has a huge network. Her prayer group will all be praying for you. I'm going to drive over to her house and tell her to call you." I thanked her profusely because I needed all the prayers I could get to release me from this limbo. Now that the spiritual battle was under way, I needed some science warriors as well. I remembered that my childhood friend John was a neurologist. He lived in Milwaukee, on Newberry Boulevard. A stone's throw from Sky's family.

John and I had been friends since grade school. In high school, he went to prom with my joined-at-the-hip BFF, Shana. I knew they wanted to go to prom together, but they were each too shy to bring it up to the other. Shy was one thing that I was not. Prom was coming fast, and someone had to make a move. I decided that person would be me. I remember the scene like it was yesterday. I was sixteen, and I was driving a red Toyota Corolla home from something on a weekend night. I had just dropped off the person in the passenger seat, leaving John and Shana in the back. They were each staring out their individual windows. I pulled over and turned toward the backseat to face them.

"Hey, Shana, are you going to prom?"

> **SHANA:** I don't know.
>
> **JEANNIE:** John, are you going to prom?
>
> **JOHN:** I don't currently have any plans.
>
> **JEANNIE:** Hey, I've got an idea! Why don't the two of you go together?

And so, I asked them to prom. With each other. Now they are married with two kids. Yes, I take complete credit for their getting married. And partial credit for the kids. John ended up becoming a neurologist, which turned out to be very convenient for me—this wasn't the first time I had been the beneficiary of his career choice.

In 2007, my sister walked into my dad's office in Milwaukee to find him lying facedown on the floor and not responding. I was in New York, and I got a call that my dad was in the ER. No one knew what happened, but it appeared he'd had a stroke. I spent an hour on the phone, pacing around the apartment and trying to get information from members of my family. There was no cell service in the ER, so my siblings would have to go all the way outside to give me updates on the situation. They also had to translate medical gibberish. Even though I had no idea what was going on, it became clear that the people in the ER had no idea what was going on either. Jim was able to book us on a flight at 6 a.m. the next day. I was losing it. I had to wait eight hours to even get on a plane to see my father. Anything could happen. I asked Jim to help me pack. I saw him put his good navy suit in the suitcase.

"What the *hell* do you think you're doing?"

Jim stopped packing and looked at me with an unusually grave expression. "Jeannie, I lost both my parents and you always have to be prepared for the worst." I stared blankly at him for a moment before the reality of what he was implying sank in.

"You think my dad is going to die and you are packing a suit to wear to his funeral? Have you no faith? What kind of a *monster* are you?" Jim took the suit out of the bag and moved to hang it back in the closet. I was overwhelmed with emotion. "What the hell do you think you are doing? You don't have the common decency to wear a suit to my father's funeral? What kind of a *monster* are you?" Did I mention that Jim couldn't win in this scenario?

I called Shana. Even though we lived half a country apart, that high school best-friend bond still held strong. She and I had been pregnant with our second children at the exact same time and often, through texts and emails, we would complain to each other about our workaholic husbands. John was at the hospital constantly and Jim was on the road constantly and we were home juggling the babies. This was a position neither of us thought we would be in: two strong women with vision and purpose in our own careers, home in a sea of dirty diapers and spit-up while our husbands were out pursuing their dreams. Shana understood me more than any person I'd met in my married life because if you knew me in high school, you would have voted me "Least Likely to Marry a Comedian

Who Sucked All the Air Out of My Spotlight and Have Five Kids with Him." She knew the frustration and helped me find meaning, joy, and humor in domestic chaos. That's what BFFs do. When my dad was in the ER at Columbia Hospital in Milwaukee and I was helpless in New York, the first person I called was Shana.

"Hi, Shana! My dad is in the ER at Columbia and it appears that he may have had a stroke. I am not getting a lot of information from the ER doctors, so I was wondering if I could call John to see if he could find out what is going on." At the time, John worked at Froedtert Hospital in Wauwatosa, Wisconsin, round the clock. It was unlikely I would be able to reach him, but I suspected his wife could. We wives have that kind of power.

"Oh my God! Actually, I'm with John right now. It's his one night off and we are having dinner at my parents' house. Let me put him on with you." I was astounded. Shana's parents' house was two blocks away from the ER where my dad lay unconscious. I spoke to John briefly, and he arrived at the ER within five minutes. He knew just what to do and was already acquainted with the neurology team at Columbia. John got my dad into the ICU and on the right medicine so he woke up without suffering any brain damage. To this day my father is John's patient, and John is my family's hero. Since then, I had tried not to reach out to John for anything except friendship and avoided asking him for medical advice. I compare people asking their doctor friends for medical advice to people at parties finding out Jim is a comedian and asking him to tell a joke.

This time, however, since I had a mass in my brain and John was a neurologist, I felt like it was okay to bother him.

I texted him:

I realized that although I knew a report existed, I didn't have it. It was the secret property of the doctors. I knew the radiology center had sent it to Dr. Godin, who called me to give me the not-so-great news. I also knew that Dr. Godin had sent it to the elusive neurosurgery office, who needed it to make the appointment. It seemed that everyone had this report but me, and I was the only one who really cared about it. I called Dr. Godin's assistant, Kurt, who informed me that the report would become available on the radiology center website portal. I gave John the login information. We waited several hours for the report to show up. Eventually I called the center. I found out that it could take forty-eight hours for reports to be posted for patient viewing. This seemed incredibly asinine, since the doctor had read the report to me hours earlier.

Why would people in an office who did not have my potentially urgent medical condition have access to information that I didn't? I called the doctor's office. Kurt answered.

"Hi, Kurt. I assume you guys have my report since you read it, correct?"

"Yes, we do."

"Can you email it to me?"

"It will be available soon for you to view on the portal."

"But I need it now. Can't you just send me my own report?" There was a beat of silence while he placed me on a brief hold, I assumed to consult with the doctor. Maybe it was because I was now on a first-name basis with Kurt, and sometimes humanity trumps bureaucracy, but for whatever reason, they broke protocol and sent me the report almost immediately. I forwarded it to John. He called me seconds later.

"It reads like you have a 6 cm mass on your posterior fossa, but it doesn't make a lot of sense because the circumference of your brain stem in that area is about 3 cm. I would need to see the scan to make sense of this."

I explained to him that I had the scan, several copies, in fact. Jim would run to FedEx and overnight a copy to him. When Jim got back, the kids were getting home from school and I had nothing for dinner, so I ordered pizzas. It was a spontaneous choice made from necessity, yet it was the absolutely perfect one. The joyful excitement caused by those three easy words, "Who wants pizza?" was a welcome distraction, so they didn't notice that Jim and I were both secretly gripped with anxiety. We sat around the dinner table as we ate our pizza, and conducted our regular "best and worst things that happened to you today" interviews. Jack's "worst thing" was, as usual, "this dorky interview," a joke that never gets old. God, I love these kids. Everything they did around the table seemed ten times sweeter and funnier that night.

The laughter was interrupted by someone buzzing the door. It was one of our babysitters. With the unexpected whirlwind that turned our world upside down that day, Jim and I had totally forgotten that we were supposed to go out that evening. Jim was concerned about me and asked, "Do you want me to cancel us going to that film premiere?" He had recently been cast as a lead (that's right, a lead—not a taxi driver or a funny friend) in a film. That night, we were invited to attend a premiere, with the director of Jim's film, for another movie she'd produced.

"We can't just cancel," I said. There was no new information that was going to become available to us before tomorrow, so we went on with our regularly scheduled lives. Not that there was anything regularly scheduled in our lives, but we'd had this "date night" on the books for months. The kids would be in bed soon. Why stay home? We had God *and* science working on this. We were in limbo, so we might as well go out and have a rare fun date. Acting like nothing was wrong helped deal with my fear of the unknown. And it was an unknown. Maybe there was really nothing to fear. Besides, my friend Trish the makeup artist was on her way over to help me get ready, and I needed a blow-out while I still had my hair. We agreed not to say a word about the scan.

These Shoes Ain't Made for Walkin'

Getting my hair and makeup done by Trish is always a fun break from the stresses of reality. We talk and gossip like old friends, because we are. Old friends. Not *old* old, but like longtime old. Note: Never call female friends "old." Trish was the head of the makeup department on *The Jim Gaffigan Show*, and we have been through many a rough shoot and late night together. I was rarely in her chair, but I saw her transform people at 6 a.m. from looking like they could play the zombies on *The Walking Dead* to cover girls. She never caused any drama or stabbed anyone in the back, a rarity on a film set or in a hair and makeup trailer. "I'm Switzerland," she would always say.

I have loved Trish since the first day I interviewed her for the department head job years ago. She brought her dog and a suitcase to the interview. She didn't need the job; she was working on another series that was wrapping up its season, but she was curious about our show based on a big Catholic family living in the middle of New York City. Something about it felt familiar to her. Something about her felt familiar to me, as if I'd grown up with her. I bet you're sensing a theme here—me responding to people I feel like I grew up with. I remember saying to her that Jim was either going to love her or be like, "Get this crazy lady with the dog away from me."

She said, "Jim sounds exactly like my brother." Ever since the show ended, Trish has been my go-to for all things beauty. Every special we shoot, I force her to travel to us and do Jim's beard. She's the only one who can take it on. "I can do beards!" she says.

But that day, as she was doing my hair and makeup in my office before the premiere, I tried to act normal, chatting about old stories, laughing about the stresses and complaints of everyday life, but my heart wasn't in it. I was distracted, deep in thought. She stopped curling my lashes for a beat and stared at me. "What's wrong?" she asked.

"Nothing, why?" I lied.

"Something's wrong," she said. "I get it if you don't want to talk about it, but just know I'm here." I debated saying something. I didn't even know what was wrong, so where would I begin? What if the mass turned out to be a smudge on the MRI screen or something? Then I would feel really stupid.

"I'm just tired," I said. It was the truth. I had been getting more and more tired over the past couple of years, but instead of resting, I just doubled my caffeine intake. It wasn't normal "kids are exhausting" fatigue, but more like the feeling of being drained in pregnancy, and we'd already established that I was not pregnant. Most evenings, when everyone was settled I would just collapse. In fact, this was going to be the first night Jim and I had gone out together in months for something that was not work or an obligation. I'd been missing all the "moms' night out" events at the schools because I was so zapped by day's end. I cherished my "mom's nights in." Having five school-age kids is some kind of wonderful, but there is always something crazy going on. Many people with large families choose to homeschool their children because it is way more practical than dealing with multiple schedules and pickups. "It's easier," they say. I would never be able to homeschool. How do I know this? Because at night when everyone is home and has different assignments to work on, I get a little taste of what it would be like, and it is overwhelming and physically and emotionally draining. It's like "Home Night School." We hop from kid to kid, like other people go to bars, to answer questions, break up arguments, check math we don't understand, listen to sometimes excruciating piano practice, and wipe spaghetti sauce off schoolwork sheets. Lately, I prefer the insanity of homework time to "free play," though. I have renamed this activity "fight to the death to keep them off screens." The obsession my kids have with getting on an iPad makes me pine for the days of picking hundreds of tiny Lego pieces out of the couch cushions.

Still, I prefer to be fighting the good fight at home. I love being with the kids even in chaos. My role as the family boss and problem solver becomes most apparent when I leave. Whenever I go out to an event at night, I can time my sigh of relaxed relief with an inevitable text from the babysitter or Jim that someone threw up, hit a sibling, said a curse word, or, even better, the water is off in the building or some other disaster only I can deal with. That night, however, we were going out, and no text or call from the babysitter could be about anything worse than what might be growing in my brain.

As Trish finished her transformative artistry on me, I ran into the bedroom to get my heels on. I have a shelf in my closet of great heels that I've accumulated for occasions over the years but that I've used less and less. They're like a historical exhibit of my past social life. I probably had to dust them off, it had been so long since I'd worn them. I came back in the room, and Trish had her arms folded across her chest and was looking at me, concerned. Sky was typing away silently. "You can talk to me, Jeannie." I looked at Sky, clicking away on the keyboard. Had he said something?

"All right," I said. "This may be nothing, but an MRI revealed that I have something growing in my brain and I haven't even had my follow-up appointment yet." Trish gave me a big hug.

"Jeannie, you are one fierce lady. Whatever it is, I know you are going to crush it with both hands."

I needed to hear that. I *was fierce*. I was strong. I was the girl who'd rescued a friend's diamond bracelet out of a public toilet! I was going to get through this, come hell or high water. I am a fighter, and I was ready to kick some brain mass ass.

"The only people who know about this are you, Jim, Sky, and the doctors."

"My lips are sealed," she said. "And, by the way, I just asked Sky what was wrong with you and he straight-up lied right to my face, so you sure as hell don't have to worry about him saying something!" Sky just gave a sheepish shrug. That's right. Sheepish.

Jim and I left for the premiere in silence. As we walked down the steps of my apartment building to the street, I stumbled in the heels, grabbing the banister with both hands. It had been awhile since I'd walked down stairs in high heels. Jim broke the ice by joking about my shoes: "I just don't get the heel thing. You literally can barely walk in them."

"They are not made for walking," I quipped back. "They are made for standing next to you and looking hot, so, you're welcome!" I stepped down another stair and grasped on for dear life.

Jim looked at my feet and shook his head. "Those are ridiculous!"

I'd gotten them for a superchic '70s party three years ago and I had great memories of wearing them; we'd made a great team. They were like an old gal pal. I defended the shoes: "These are spectacular!"

"So are stilts at the circus," Jim reminded me.

Film premieres are odd events, really. There are no separate fancy theaters for premieres. They are held in regular movie theaters with moderate inclines and sticky cup holders. Jim pointed out that the one we went to that night was actually the same theater where we'd taken our kids to see *Cloudy with a Chance of Meatballs*. The only difference between going to a movie theater and going to a movie theater for a premiere is that, for the premiere, you are overdressed. Definitely too overdressed to sit in a chair and watch a movie.

We sat with Danielle, a close friend of mine who was the production manager on *The Jim Gaffigan Show*. When I saw her, I felt compelled to tell her what was going on, but I decided against it. I was not going to let this scary secret I was carrying around ruin anyone's night. Except Trish's, and Sky's, and John's . . . but that was it!

I barely remember watching the film. I sat silent in the darkness, unable to focus on anything but the insidious mass in my brain. Was Jim thinking about it too? I tried to read him with psychic energy while pressing my knee against his. He reached over and took my hand. My mind was swirling. Every so often the audience would laugh, so I would force a guffaw even though I had no idea what I was laughing at. I didn't want to be rude. We both sat looking ahead at the screen until the film ended. When I stood up to exit, I felt my legs give out. I could barely stand up. *This is peculiar*, I thought. I said to Jim, "You guys go ahead. I'll meet you in the lobby. I have to check my messages." The screening room was on an extra-steep slope even for the normal slant of a theater. To get to the exit, I had to hug the wall and slowly put one foot in front of the other like I was totally inebriated.

I'm sure that's what the rush of exiting audience members thought as they pushed past me, eager to get to the after-party. "Wow, that girl got wasted *before* the film. Sad." I let people by. I felt stupid and out of shape. I wondered silently to myself why suddenly I couldn't walk in heels. Balance was never a

problem. Could it be I was getting old? Connecting the dizzi-
ness to my recent diagnosis never even crossed my thoughts.
If it did, my vain fear of aging drowned out the efforts of my
logical mind.

*I have to go out more, or at least wear heels around the house
during homework mania*, I thought. I checked myself for past
judgments of the "hot moms" who wore heels to drop-off.
They had more practice. I bet they weren't leaning on walls at
movie premieres.

When I found Jim in the lobby I was relieved to finally stand
on flat ground, but I still felt dizzy. I found a column to lean
against. Jim and Danielle noticed my unsteadiness.

"Are you all right?" they asked.

"It's these heels!" I showed them off. Jim was right. I was a
clown on stilts, only clumsier.

Getting to the postpremiere party in New York City is
always an adventure. Sure, all the actors and film folk have cars
waiting, but everyone else is on their own. Essentially it turns
into a hundred people Ubering, Lyfting, or cabbing from the
same destination. It has the chaos and charm of the American
evacuation from Saigon at the end of the Vietnam War.

Jim suggested that our group walk to the corner and try
to get a cab. In 20/20 hindsight, it seems obvious that there
was another reason for my inability to balance that night, but
like everything else, I explained it away as something minimal. In this case, impractical footwear. I stumbled along with
the group, cursing myself for wearing "ridiculous shoes" and
glancing around for an empty wheelchair. "Walking to the corner" turned into walking three blocks looking for a taxi. Feign-
ing a public display of my love for Jim, I leaned on him like
a drunken prom date. My relief from getting in the taxi soon

turned to horror when I saw that the after-party was being held in a private room on the roof of a club up three flights of stairs. Jim looked at me, staring up in disbelief. "Do you want to just go home?" he asked. That was very generous of him, because I knew the purpose of this outing was for him to get to know the director of his upcoming film.

"No, I'm good," I replied. "I want you to have a good time. Is that three flights?"

The rest of the night, I was obsessed with finding a place to sit. I wanted one place to park myself and not have to move. Ironically, the medical issue was totally "out of my head" as the heel issue dominated my every thought. Once I sat down at the after-party, I found myself scheming about how I could just stay in that same spot for the entire night. I wondered if the people in the club would notice. I could just pretend I was a statue, like *The Thinker*, but in high heels and sitting on a lounge couch, until a guy sweeping up in the morning kicked me out.

When it was finally time to go, I just took off the heels and walked down the stairs, blending in with the drunken crowd. Though totally sober, I was so off balance in those heels that it was safer for me to walk barefoot through the streets of midtown Manhattan. Who cared if I might step on a dirty needle? Anything was better than those heels. If I'd had a kingdom, I would have given it all for a pair of ratty house slippers!

Chapter 6

THURSDAY

The Bat Signal

The next morning, I took the kids to school as usual (in my comfy Converse). Inside, I was incredibly anxious to hear from Dr. John, who would be getting the scans today, but I was determined to stay positive. In the car, the girls were reading their books like literary angels and the boys were fighting like rabid monkeys. Michael alleged that Patrick put a booger on him, an accusation that Patrick vehemently denied, and Jack started screaming that they were both disgusting. The girls were now whining, "Shut up!" which is equivalent to a curse word in my household. I didn't have my normal instinct to yell at them to pipe down and threaten to make them all walk to school. I just wanted to grab them, boogers and all, in one big, endless embrace. It wasn't easy for me to say good-bye to them at school drop-offs that day, but at the same time I wanted to rush back home to Jim. I'd let him sleep, his favorite activity, because I knew he was emotionally drained, holding it together for me. Now it was wake-up time. I didn't want to be alone when I got any news, good or bad. John would surely call at some point this morning, but it was an hour earlier in his time zone, so it would have been only 7:45 a.m. in Milwaukee.

I checked my messages when I got back to my office and was surprised to see Marita's name on my iPhone voice-mail list several times from the night before. A wave of guilt washed over me. After I had called her the day before with an urgent prayer request, I'd ended up going out on the town and stumbling around Manhattan in high heels like a common dock whore. Jim walked into the office half asleep with a cup of coffee in his hand.

"Well, call her now!" Jim might be really private about his spirituality, but he knew the direct line to heaven was what this situation called for, and my family had the contact number.

Early on when Jim and I were dating, I mentioned to him that my mom was praying for a good outcome to a big audition he'd recently gone on. Jim responded with a polite but confused look on his face: "Gee, thanks." I know he was thinking, *Uh, can we keep your mom's voodoo out of my career?* Of course, after he got the callback, he casually mumbled, "Uh, Jeannie, could you have your mom, you know (cough), pray for my callback?"

I dialed Marita. She picked up. "Marita. It's Jeannie!"

"Oh, Jeannie, Jeannie, Jeannie!" She had this way of exuding pure comfort. "Don't you worry, Jeannie! The Lord has you in the palm of his hand and you are going to be just fine. I have the entire Eastern Seaboard praying for you. My friend has a radio show and she is spreading the word for a special intervention for you." This was like the Catholic equivalent of putting out the Bat Signal.

Marita was no stranger to medical crises. She'd had a number of run-ins with the grim reaper, yet she'd survived them all. She was so well-versed in various diseases that she even had a favorite hospital: "Jeannie, Mount Sinai is the best!" What was with this family and Mount Sinai? Mount Sinai was somewhere on the Upper East Side past One Hundredth Street; it might as well have been on the other side of the planet. At that point I didn't care about the best hospital; I wanted the closest hospital where they would tell me what was wrong with my brain and I could move on.

Since I gave birth to all my children at home, I knew very little about New York hospitals. I was confused by the notion that there would be a dramatic difference in quality between institutions where sick people went. A hospital was a hospital, and I didn't like being in any of them.

She continued, "And, Jeannie, I called my friend at Mount Sinai. I know everyone there..." Marita really *was* like the mayor of Mount Sinai. I pictured her walking down the halls, shaking hands with everyone and kissing babies in the labor and delivery ward. "...Now she's in pulmonology, but she knows a lot of great people in neurology..." She then went on to list about five names of doctors she wanted me to call. Jim was furiously writing them down as I repeated them out loud. "They have the top neurology department in the city. People come from all over the world. Mention my friend's name and I'm sure they will get you in!" I wasn't trying to make a restaurant reservation. My heart sank at the prospect of calling more doctors. Especially ones with world-class waiting lists.

"Marita, thank you so much, but Mount Sinai Hospital is

really far away, and I already have appointments on the books with a couple of other great surgeons at a hospital near NYU, which is much closer to where we live…" I tried to be gentle. She was in her eighties.

"Jeannie! You have to go to Mount Sinai; they are *tops*. They took care of me, they took care of Beth, they were so good to Annie…" She meant well, but this advice was giving me anxiety. I didn't want to have to think about getting "the tops" neurosurgeon. Thinking that way made this too real, and some small part of me was hoping it would end up being nothing and we could quickly go back to life as usual. Marita may well have been giving me the best medical guidance yet, but because of my state of mind, I couldn't hear it. I am a compartmentalizer. I was calling her for one thing (prayer), and I was calling John for another (science). I didn't need another referral, another receptionist, another appointment. I needed a prayer warrior. "Marita, thank you so much for all of this. I have not told my mom and dad about anything yet because I really don't know how bad it is, but my friend who is a neurologist is going to call me today and give me some advice on how to go about dealing with this. As soon as I find out any more information, I am going to call you. I just need prayer right now."

"Jeannie, we are going to keep praying and praying and praying." I hung up feeling uplifted. I pictured this prayer chain happening on old-fashioned telephones, like "The Telephone Hour" in *Bye Bye Birdie*, but instead of teens spreading gossip, the prayer warriors were spreading Hail Marys. There was this whole faith community out there that didn't know me at all, but they were for sure storming heaven. I could feel it.

My own experience with faith is complicated. I am too rebellious, hardheaded, and scattered to have ever been "religious."

Rules and regulations scare me and make me run for the hills. I grew up Catholic, so that's what I was. I went to public school. My family attended church every Sunday because that's what Catholics did, and my mom made us, so we went. It was ingrained in me as a regular part of life. As a child, I never felt "damaged" or "shamed" by my Catholicism; it was just a normal part of my identity.

At home, my father was a secular intellectual, always writing a story for the paper, reading a thick novel, or lecturing us about how Reaganomics was going to be the end of civilization. My dad rarely spoke about God, although oddly enough he was known to play a mean rendition of "He's Got the Whole World in His Hands" on the banjo at the occasional Newman Center family program on the University of Wisconsin–Milwaukee campus. I guess being in a Catholic ministry center surrounded by a secular university made it more his thing. My mother, on the other hand, was constantly praying. She kept an enormous statue of the Virgin Mary in the living room, surrounded by much smaller family photos. If she wasn't dancing around the house to praise music, she was telling us, "The Lord is working!" or "Offer it up!" If we had our feelings hurt by a kid at school, she would say, "Let no weapon formed against you prosper!" or some other oddly poetic tidbit of biblical wisdom. Sure, I was painfully embarrassed of her because absolutely no one else's mother acted anything like she did, let alone had an altar in their living room, but growing up with her as my mom, something happened to me, no matter how much I tried to run away from it or hide it. God was a real character in our house. He lived there. He was always with us and always protecting us. Even though I never went to Mass when I was away at college, I remember being alone and having pretty extensive dialogues with God about exams, boys, and money problems. If I was doing something I shouldn't, I'd have the thought, *Hey, God, don't tell my mom I'm here.* I was more worried about her judgment than His. God was my therapist and my consigliere. I was always aware He was there. Even if I found a good parking spot, I'd be like, "Thanks, dude." I had become a unique blend of my crazy spiritual mom and my pragmatic lefty dad. A semisecular spiritualist. In my current situation, Dad would have called John, and Mom would have called Marita. I called them both.

As I got older and life started to get a whole lot rougher, my relationship with God matured as I did. When I moved to New York, I started going to Mass regularly again. I was far away from family, and a church smelled like home. I realized that after all those years away from it, I felt a deep connection to the rituals. Being inside a Catholic church anchored me and kept me from getting lost in the thousands of shiny object distractions in Manhattan. No one was making me go to Mass anymore; I wanted to go. When I got married and had kids, things got way harder. Jim was on the road. I was jealous. I had miscarriages that brought with them emotional pain like I'd never experienced. God became less of a buddy and more of a mystic all-knowing presence that was there to remind me, "This is all part of my plan, even though it seems to suck righteously." And I did believe in miracles. I'd witnessed unexplainable medical healings in people close to my family that were attributed to prayer. I'd been the recipient of my own significant miracle, which I'll tell you about when we know each other better. So, when Marita told me her friends were praying for me and that whatever was wrong in my brain was going to be all right, I believed it 100 percent. After speaking to her, I felt like there were angels around me. I may have been in limbo, but I had a team of celestial beings breaking me out.

The Man with the Plan

My phone rang. It was John. It was only 8 a.m. where he was. I looked at Jim and announced, "It's John! He's probably calling to say he got the FedEx!" I picked up. "Hey, John!" Apparently, he'd received the scan at 7 a.m. and drove to his hospital first thing to look at it. He was not one to mince words.

"Jeannie, I'm looking at your scan here. It's not good." He texted me a screen shot: the inside of my brain with an absolutely enormous tumor in it.

"Oh my God!" I said. I put him on speaker and showed the phone to Jim. The blood drained out of his face. John continued. "Do you see that area to the left of the tumor?" It was the first time I'd heard the word *tumor* used. Until now, it had been a "mass," which seemed less real. He was telling me to look at the area around it, but all I could see was that giant bulb. "…That's where your brain stem should be, and it is almost completely compressed to the side." I looked at the black-and-white image in disbelief. This horrific view into my own skull revealed there was a huge blockage in the part of my brain that connects the nerve signals for the motor and sensory systems to the rest of my body. This couldn't be good.

In Jim's comedy, he characterizes himself as lazy. He is anything but. Jim is always in motion. Sure, some of that motion might involve climbing in bed for a nap or sticking food in his mouth, but he's continually moving forward to the next task. This man, ever consumed with his next project, was suddenly a statue next to me. Not defeated, just frozen.

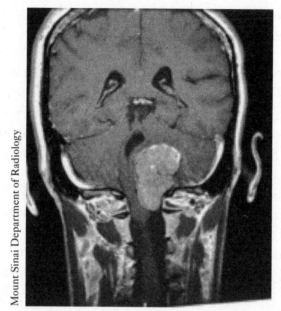

Mount Sinai Department of Radiology

Tick, tick, tick…

I explained to John that the two neurosurgeons I was referred to said to bring the scan to my first appointment in May. "May?" John replied with uncharacteristic panic in his voice. "This can't wait three weeks. You need to get into the OR right away."

"But I need a doctor to go to the OR!" I was practically shouting. "And their first available appointment is not until May 8!"

John was steady, firm, and decisive. "If you were here, I would send you to neurosurgery right now. You need a plan. You need a plan today." I had no plan. Even calling a doctor and getting past the gatekeepers seemed beyond my capabilities.

"John, give me a plan!"

He didn't even pause. "Okay. Find the hospital with the best neurosurgery department in the city, go to the ER at that hospital with your scan. Tell them you have headaches and feel like you're passing out." It wouldn't be a lie. I did have chronic headaches (that I had explained away), and I certainly felt now as if I were about to pass out from fear. I pictured myself walking into a dirty New York City ER and having some sleep-deprived intern cut open my skull with a rusty butter knife.

"I can't go to the ER with a *brain tumor*!"

John was focused and direct. "Go to the ER at the best neurosurgery hospital in New York with that scan. They will get you to the top guy."

Tops. I thought of Marita. I knew where we had to go. "Jim, get your coat. We're going to the emergency room at Mount Sinai."

The Parting of the Red Sea

Jim and I were speeding up FDR Drive in a taxi. Jim was texting people to make sure the school pickups were covered. We had a plan. At least the first part of a plan. Go to the ER with the scan. See the top guy. Then, wing it. I imagined us walking cold into the ER, and it made me shudder. I had to call my doctor in New York. We needed an inside push. I'd forgotten Marita's friend's name. Could I just tell them I knew Marita Haggerty, the mayor of Mount Sinai?

Then it suddenly occurred to me that my own Dr. Hops was somehow affiliated with Mount Sinai because I'd seen the logo on the computer screen in her office. In all the chaos, I'd never followed up to tell her what was going on. It dawned on me that if she hadn't forced me to get my ear checked out...I shuddered to think of it. She could be my inside push. I called her office. They informed me she was on vacation and couldn't be reached, and would I like to leave a message for the doctor on call? "No!" I hung up and called Dr. Godin. I got Kurt. "Kurt, it's Jeannie Gaffigan. I'm going to have to cancel those May appointments with the other neurosurgeons; that's too long to wait. I'm on my way to the ER at Mount Sinai." Kurt was stunned.

"What? Don't go to the ER. Just wait twenty minutes, and Dr. Godin will call you." I wasn't having it. Poor Kurt.

"Too late. I'm almost there. My friend John, who *loves me* and is a *neurologist*, told me to go to the ER. And I'm going. Bye!" I looked at Jim. "Gotta stick to the plan."

We passed the old-fashioned Pepsi-Cola sign across the East River in Queens. It reminded me of Mimi, my mom's grandmother. I never met her, but every time my mom comes to New York City and we are on the FDR, she brings up being in Mimi's Tudor City apartment as a child and looking out at that sign beyond the water. My mom's memory was now my memory. I wondered if I was going to be able to have memories anymore. What would that be like? Not to have memories? My kids might not have a mom who gifted them her memories. My phone rang again, jolting me out of the spiral.

It was Dr. Godin. "Jeannie, I had no idea that you couldn't get into those doctors until May. You should have called me." Dr. Godin was really concerned. I think he thought my suddenly going to the ER was an impulsive, ill-informed decision.

"I'm almost to the ER at Mount Sinai," I said abruptly. My manners went out the cab window as I was in full fight mode and flight mode at the same time. Truth is, it never even crossed my mind to call him back to get in earlier.

"You don't have to go to the ER. I know people at Mount Sinai too. I just referred you to the other hospital because it was close to you. I'm sure I can get you an appointment at Mount Sinai with one of my colleagues by tomorrow, or Monday."

"I appreciate that, but right now, I'm going to the ER. My best friend John told me to!" I realized that I was actually looking forward to going to the ER. I had a plan. In this whirlwind of confusion and stress, for a moment I felt like I was not falling. The appointments that may or may not happen did not seem serious enough for my taste. I may not be a doctor, but I know the *E* in *ER* stands for "emergency," and I felt like I had an Emergency with a capital *E* on my hands.

"Look, I am going to call my colleague at Mount Sinai and tell her that you need to see her as soon as possible. I'll call you right back." I remembered he had not actually seen the scan, just the mysterious report.

"Great," I said. "I'll take your call in the ER." I thought of my kids misbehaving in the car that morning. Was I being a baby?

My kids. They were all in school like it was any other day. Completely unaware that their lives were about to be upended. What was going to happen to me? To all of us?

Dr. Godin, who now was heavily involved in my saga, called right back: "Okay, I spoke to my colleague, a neurosurgeon. She's actually in Florida right now." I pictured her getting interrupted on the golf course by the call. "She can see you on Monday." I probably didn't have until Monday. John had told me a story about referring one of his patients to neurosurgery; they took a "wait and see" approach, and the guy had a stroke over the weekend. I marveled as I recalled the cold, clinical responses I had received when I tried to make those initial appointments with the neurosurgeons. What was going on there? Maybe there are a ton of folks making casual checkup appointments in neurosurgery departments. I just accepted it. When I heard "May," I was like, "Okay, guess I'll find out in May." With the knowledge I had now, surely just accepting that appointment wait time could have cost my kids a mother.

Dr. Godin continued, "She also said she was going to advise someone in the neurosurgery department to call you today. I gave her your number. I hope you don't mind." I didn't mind at all. Dr. Godin was on the team. I thanked him profusely and continued my race up the FDR to the ER. Jim was staring out the window. I wondered what was going through his head. It was probably as scary as what was growing in mine.

An unknown number popped up on my phone. I was getting so many calls in the cab, I could see the driver in the rearview mirror piecing together the drama of the drive. He began the ride not realizing it was a life-and-death journey, but by this point I saw only empathy in his eyes. He clearly understood the gravity of the situation by now. "Hello?" I answered the phone. I hoped it wasn't a school nurse notifying us about a lice outbreak or a kid with a broken limb.

"Hi, is this Jeannie?" Yes. Not Janine. Good sign. "This is Leslie Schlachter from the neurosurgery department at Mount Sinai. One of our neurosurgeons called from Florida and said you might have a problem that is in need of immediate attention?"

"Yes, I do," I said casually, as if this complicated chain of events wasn't unusual. "I've actually been expecting your call."

"Great. Where do you live?"

"I live downtown, but right now I'm about a block away from the Mount Sinai ER."

"Really?" said Leslie. "That's great; c'mon up to Eight West. Dr. Bederson just happens to be here because his surgery just got delayed." Bederson? The one Beth told me to see. The "tops."

I turned to Jim. "We are not going to the ER! We are skipping that part of the plan and going straight up to the top guy! His name is Bederson."

Jim was googling like mad on his phone. "Jeannie, Dr. Bederson is the *chairman of neurosurgery* at Mount Sinai!" You could almost hear the Hallelujah Chorus. The Bat Signal was working.

"This is God!" I exclaimed. The cabdriver looked back with a smile to indicate his relief that he might be participating in a happy ending. I imagine after he dropped us off, he probably pulled over to the nearest church and converted to Catholicism. "The plan" was unfolding. Maybe the world was spinning our way. We jumped out of the cab and took the elevator up to Eight West: Neurosurgery.

There were two receptionists waiting at the door of Dr. Bederson's office like greeters at Buckingham Palace. "Come in, sit down," one said. "Do you have your scan?"

"I have four!" I said, showing off the multiple copies I had obtained for my soon-to-be-canceled preliminary consultations.

"We just need one." She took my scan and disappeared deep in the office. I handed the other woman my insurance card. "Thanks," she said. At that moment a tall, blond woman in a lab coat appeared.

Her height was overshadowed by her beauty and her beauty was overshadowed by her warmth. "Hi, I'm Leslie!" She was wearing a funky necklace. It was a sunburst and some other shape. She smiled. "Dr. Bederson is ready to see you." I was astonished that there was no wait.

"Don't I have to fill out a stack of forms?"

"No, that's not necessary now, c'mon in. Dr. Bederson has surgery in forty-five minutes. He normally never sees patients on Thursdays. I guess you got lucky."

Jim and I looked at each other. We knew that luck had nothing to do with it, unless luck parted the Red Sea for Moses. We walked right into the office of the top neurosurgeon in New York City. No appointment, no wait, no forms. And there, in front of that big polished mahogany desk, stood Dr. Joshua Bederson, chairman of the Department of Neurology at Mount Sinai Hospital. The man who would save my life.

Leslie C. Schlachter, PA, and Joshua Bederson, MD

Chapter 7

THE ELEPHANT ON THE CLOTHESLINE

"What surprises me," said Dr. Bederson after he had laid out the Good Friday scan plan, "is how you are walking around with this tumor. Do you have headaches?"

"Terrible ones," I said. "But I do have five kids."

"She's been complaining about headaches for months," Jim offered.

I shrugged. "I thought it was allergies."

"Do you have breathing problems?"

"When I lie down in bed at night I have a coughing fit," I admitted.

"She gasps for air in her sleep," Jim confessed.

"I do?" I looked at him angrily. "I didn't know that!"

"You told me you had allergies," Jim replied.

Dr. Bederson nodded. "That's from the pressure on your brain stem when you lie down. Your cranial nerves are severely compromised. What about your balance?" Oh my God, the heels. It was like the *Seinfeld* episode, but mine would be called "It's Not Shoes, It's Me," and feature me stealing a wheelchair from a helpless grandma because of a wardrobe malfunction. Also, those dizzy spells and head rushes when I stood up. I recalled a curriculum night when I had to hang back in the classroom while the rest of the parents exited to the auditorium because I had the spins for no reason at all. I was mortified that I had been neglecting these things, and now my husband and kids were going to suffer for it. Of course, over the past few years it had crossed my mind more than once that it was not normal to get head rushes all the time, but who goes to the doctor for a head rush? I thought I would put it off until I was older. Only old people got sick. To me, admitting I was not feeling great was like complaining about being old. I guess I felt like I could force myself to stay young if I didn't complain about my health.

Dr. Bederson gave me some tests that I can only describe as the same tests you would get if you got pulled over by the cops because you weren't driving your car straight.

"Hold out your arms to both sides, then one at a time try to touch your fingers to your nose." I tried and I missed my nose by a mile. "Can you stand on one foot?" That would be easy. I used to do yoga every day. When I had one kid. How long ago was that? I lifted one foot behind me. I almost toppled over. Dr. Bederson moved his finger in front of my eyes. "Can you follow my finger?" I felt like I could, perfectly, but he noticed a major delay with one eye.

"Are you going to give me a DUI?"

"How's your spatial perception?" I thought for a minute. I'd walked into doorframes more than once. I thought I was just clumsy. I was baffled by my lack of self-knowledge. How could I have not noticed any of this? And wait a minute, why had a giant tumor grown in my brain anyway? Was it from my iPhone? I felt like Jim and I were ignoring the eight-hundred-pound gorilla in the room. I had to ask: "Is it cancer?"

"I don't think it's cancer."

"Why?"

"Cancer cells grow really rapidly, and if this tumor grew rapidly, we wouldn't be having this conversation right now."

"When will we know if it's cancer or not?"

"After the surgery, we will send the tissue to the lab to get the pathology. It will be about two to three weeks after the surgery. We won't know until we get the lab results, but judging from the characteristics of this tumor, I would say that there is an 80 percent chance that it's not cancer." I chose not to focus on the other 20 percent, but truth be told, what I really wanted to hear, what anyone would really want to hear, was that it was 100 percent not cancer.

"How long have I had this?"

He explained that judging from the size, and in conjunction with how functional I was, it was likely the tumor had been insidiously growing for years, and that my nerves had found ways around it, suppressing any serious symptoms that would have caused immediate alarm. Leslie explained it this way: It's like if you put an elephant on a clothesline, the clothesline will obviously break. But if you slowly, over time, keep pinning small items onto the clothesline, eventually it will stretch lower and lower to the ground, until, ultimately, you can put an elephant on it and it won't break. For those of you who can't follow the large animal metaphors, the clothesline was my brain, the elephant was the tumor, and the eight-hundred-pound gorilla had a 20 percent chance of being cancer.

An eight-year-old's medical diagram of the brain adapting to a tumor.

"Can you get it out?" I asked. Dr. Bederson took a deep breath.

"One of the things I am very concerned about," he began as Jim and I leaned to the edge of our seats, noticing the shift in his tone, "is that your facial nerve is running right through the center of the tumor. There's risk that one side of your face will become paralyzed."

"I don't care!" I blurted out. At this point I could be a head in a jar as long as I could raise my kids. I'd just be that mom with the paralyzed face. What did I care—I already had a husband.

Leslie would handle scheduling the full day of scanning that would begin early the next morning. A word about Leslie and PAs (physician assistants): Being a surgeon is obviously no small task. You want the brain surgeon focusing all of his attention on the surgery. Leslie dealt with everything else. It was a relief knowing someone was handling all the hospital logistics who was knowledgeable about every aspect of what was going on and able to field the never-ending questions from people like me and Jim, who were obviously not brain surgeons. Dr. Bederson was the star out on the stage. Leslie was coordinating the whole production. Leslie was the Jeannie Gaffigan to Dr. Bederson's Jim Gaffigan. With the team of Leslie and Dr. Bederson, we had hit the jackpot. Leslie is one of the most incredible people I have ever met. She is like six feet tall and drop-dead gorgeous. A former basketball champion in the NCAA college league at GWU and overseas on the Israeli Olympic team, she has a brilliant mind, is the master of Dr. Bederson's schedule, and still keeps a million other balls in the air, all while being nonstop charming and genuine.

She explained that the MRI scans, the CT scans, the angiograms, and the ultrasounds would be integrated to render the brain's anatomy in a virtual reality 3-D scenario. This new type of augmented reality surgery, blending digital images with physical structures, was the most advanced way of removing tumors in a procedure where even the slightest miscalculation could cause irreparable damage. This "CaptiView" system overlaid data and 3-D models to the eyepiece of a surgical microscope and combined rare technologies that were being used individually by only a "handful of experts." The first doctor to use CaptiView in neurosurgery? As luck would have it, Dr. Joshua Bederson. The pioneer. Guess we barged into the right office.

Chapter 8

GOOD FRIDAY

VIP MRI

The next day, Good Friday, our schools were closed. I covered my bases with the kids by farming them out on playdates, not telling them or any of the other parents why our plans had changed. They didn't need to know what was going on yet because we barely did. I generally look forward to these days off and spending quality family time (slipping away from time to time to deal with the huge stack of production work on my desk), but this day I couldn't get them out to their friends' houses fast enough.

Good Friday is a pretty significant holy day, and since I wouldn't be making it to Mass, it was important to me that I was "spiritually covered" before I went in for my day of scanning. Luckily, I had the nuns. Many years earlier I'd gotten involved with the unique Sisters of Life order. Unique in that they are all really young (as nuns go). I think the average age is like under forty. I'd met them in the hospital during a difficult situation with one of my pregnancies and they were there for me in a real time of need. I never stopped reaching out to them when I needed some support. I would call their convent and rattle off a list of requests, normally involving scary worries about kids, babies, or pregnancy. Never underestimate the power of calling nuns. They really should charge an hourly fee. Try as we may, we non-religious-order people cannot even come close to the spiritual lives that religious-order people live. Their day is literally built around prayer time, including quiet chapel time that allows one to go into a deep state of communication with God.

Technically Catholics are supposed to be doing this type of God consultation once a week at Sunday Mass, but for me that time is normally spent taking kids to the bathroom (that ol' childhood trick), picking up crayons off the floor, or making a shopping list in my mind. The more I learn about my Catholic faith, the more I realize what a bad Catholic I am. In times of deep spiritual need or crisis, I have resolved to stick to a prayer schedule, and almost every time I have failed miserably. That's where the nuns come in. "Can you please pray for me and Jim and the kids on Good Friday? I won't be able to make the three o'clock service because I gotta get scanned for a 3-D rendering of my brain for a craniotomy on Monday."

"I think God will understand," said the nuns. God probably understood better than all the people whose emails were going to sit unread, whose phone calls would go unanswered, and whose appointments had been canceled, but for the first time I could remember, I couldn't have been less concerned about my to-do list.

Jim went with me to radiology on the lower, lower level at Mount Sinai. This time it really felt like going to a spa. At the last place, the robes were sort of shabby, and all random colors and patterns. I remember that during the fateful MRI with Margarita Guy, I was wearing a faded olive green with a brown floral print, and the time before, when Jiminy Cricket was concerned about my fake baby, it was a washed-out pale blue with a black paisley pattern. The robes at Mount Sinai all seemed brand-new and they were supercute. The solid Cyrene gown was to be put on first with the back open. Then over that, you wore a soft seersucker robe with pockets and a real belt. It was like a little outfit that you could easily show up in at a post–Memorial Day garden party in the Hamptons after your MRI.

I was escorted into a spacious booth where the curtain totally covered the opening, and then some. I was also given a nifty tote bag for my clothes, as well as a little Tupperware container for my jewelry. There were even socks with teeny pads on the bottom. As I prepped for the full day of CT scans and MRIs of my head and neck, I felt comforted for the first time since this crazy diagnosis. I knew I had a colossal brain tumor that had an 80 percent chance of *not* being cancer (still ignoring that 20 percent), but I felt like I was finally doing something about it. I had a plan. I was not in limbo anymore. I was in really great spirits under the circumstances and I felt strangely peaceful. It was the not-knowing part that caused me anxiety.

In the room, they gave me a heated blanket and headphones that played music during the incessant banging of the scan. I mean, I still heard all the horns and jackhammering, but I felt like they were at least putting forth an effort to make it more tolerable. There was also a little skylight inside the tube, directly over my eyes, so it definitely felt less claustrophobic. I wondered if the resort-like scanning was unique to that hospital, or if it was simply because I had something life-threatening, so now I was in the VIP room: Very Important Patient.

Regardless of why, I felt waves of gratitude: To Dr. Hops, for insisting I get my ear checked. To Beth, for telling me she had a feeling I was going to see Dr. Bederson. For the text exchange with John, in which he told me he needed to see the scan. To Marita for the Bat Signal. For Dr. Godin calling his friend in Florida. For walking with Jim into Eight West at Mount Sinai and seeing the doctor who was the most qualified in the world to deal with the specific type and location of my brain tumor. None of it was an accident—God was with me. Not some scary guy with a long white beard who punished bad people and helped only good people, but a real force that guided me to this point of peace because I asked him for help. If you just decided to stop reading because I got too Jesus-y, check out this photo I took of Jim in the waiting room when I was finished with all my scans:

When I saw Jim in this state I had my first good laugh in three days.

Chapter 9

EASTER WEEKEND

HOLY SATURDAY

The next day I was obsessed with making Easter baskets. If my kids are reading this book, let me make it clear that I was *prepping* the Easter baskets so that the (real) Easter bunny would know which of my kids wanted what color and which items. I mean, the Easter bunny has a lot of kids to visit, and I wanted to help him or her understand that the five-year-old has different needs than the twelve-year-old. I was just *prepping*. Now that we've got that out of the way, I'll go on. There was one point when Jim came into the office where I was doing this important (prepping) work: "Don't you think you should be spending time with your children instead of doing this?"

"This is spending time *for* my children!" I replied way too defensively.

"All right, all right," he said while exiting. But I knew he was right. I realized that the Easter basket making had some kind of a

complex symbolic meaning. They weren't just part of the autopi-
lot, ticking off the to-do list that had helped me carry off the last
ten years. Maybe the Easter baskets were a way for me to procras-
tinate on telling my kids the truth and I just wanted to act normal and give them pretty things and candy to mask the harsh
reality of life. Maybe I felt that I could make baskets for my kids
better than anyone in the whole world, and I was showing my
love through service to them. Maybe I was afraid that it would
be the last time I would be the one responsible for this highly
anticipated annual tradition and I wanted to give it my all. Whatever those Easter baskets meant, I wanted to be making them
more than I wanted to tell my children what was about to happen. Maybe telling them would make it too real for me, and then
I would finally feel the fear I was not feeling. Finally, the baskets
were complete and beautiful and it was time to act. I checked my
inner task list: call parents, tell kids, call Nora. I decided to call
my dear friend Nora first. This would be my warm-up call.

I first met Nora Fitzpatrick in October 2003. Jim and I had
gotten married earlier that year in July at St. Patrick's Old Cathedral in lower Manhattan, on the same block where we both lived
and met. Yes, I moved all the way to New York City to marry the
boy next door. Later I found out that during our wedding there
was an international retreat going on at St. Patrick's and they
had run out of food for all the missionaries. Nora was a volunteer at the missionary retreat and was trying to figure out how
to feed fifty people on a Saturday night at midnight when at the
same moment, a wedding reception (ours) at the Puck Building
around the corner let out and a team of girls in gowns and boys in
tuxes (my siblings) showed up at the church with pans and pans
of high-end wedding food. Nora laughs later when she recounts
this as our first introduction. The French missionary priests were

especially excited about the champagne grapes and the pâté. Our parish priest at the time, Father Thomas, officiated at our wedding and was of course the guest of honor at the reception. When he saw all the leftover food we had at the end of the night, he pointed out that there was a huge retreat going on at the church, and isn't that the way the world should always work.

In October of that same year, I found myself volunteering at another food-centric event at St. Patrick's, "A Taste of NoLIta" (which stands for "North of Little Italy"). Neighborhood restaurants donated a batch of their specialty dishes to the church, and the public could buy a $20 ticket and sample all the local fare. It was a pretty great fund-raising idea as well as a community builder. Though I was nearing the end of my first trimester of pregnancy with my first child (yes, Marre was a "honeymoon baby"), I signed up to volunteer. Collecting dirty plates and garbage was not the best activity for someone battling the nausea of early pregnancy, but this parish was dying on the vine, and getting married and expecting a child awoke in me a newfound desire for a community in which to put down roots.

The enchanting little church with the redbrick wall around it was the center of our neighborhood and made New York City feel so personal, almost provincial. The parish's heyday was long past. The Italians of the neighborhood had long ago moved to Long Island and beyond, and were replaced by Dominican immigrants who were getting priced out by models, artists, and, I guess, Jim and me. I felt a responsibility to the beleaguered, once thriving parish of Italian grandmas and Dominican die-hards that was now the center of the most secular community in Manhattan.

As I hauled a huge rubber bus tub full of slop to the back, I noticed another woman, who stood out because she was below the age of eighty, doing the same activity with an energy that mirrored mine. She was tall and gorgeous with jet-black hair and pale white skin. Most significantly, she was about eight months pregnant, which seemed to make her even more powerful and beautiful. As we emptied the slop into the garbage and slid the sticky sauce-covered plates into the sink, I noticed our husbands holding court with the priest as the last of the patrons were leaving. I felt the situation definitely called for one of my signature sarcastic remarks: "Let the pregnant women carry the garbage. What's a little more weight?"

"It's good exercise for them," she quipped back. "It prevents varicose veins." And a lifelong friendship was born. Practical, funny, and empathetic, that was Nora.

It feels strange to characterize Nora and Trey as simply friends. They are most certainly friends, but also so much more. Do couples have the equivalent of a soulmate couple? Like-minded childbearing fools who walk beside you down the thrilling and treacherous path of parenting? After Nora gave birth to Joseph that December, I had Marre in May. After she had Nellie in August, Jack was born the following November. The simultaneous pregnancies continued until we each had five children. This was not a coordinated effort, much to the disappointment of the little old ladies at our church.

Every time they would notice Nora with a bump, they would encircle me after Mass like a small pack of wolves. "You better catch up! Nora is winning!" We would insist it was not a competition, but what fun was that? We realized we were really spicing things up for the daily Mass crowd. They were gleefully intrigued by each new development and at the same time a little disgusted: "Again? What, don't you have a TV?" The ten children gave our families star status in the parish, the congregation of which at the time comprised us, the aforementioned little old ladies, and some neighborhood regulars who were the same regulars of the corner tavern in the evenings. When there were other families with small children (or a child) at Mass, they sat far away from our group of rowdy hooligans.

There was an infamy to our celebrity, as Nora and I were often found gossiping in the church vestibule during Masses with a couple of babies and a lot of Legos. We were the bad Catholic girls turned bad Catholic moms. I remember Father Thomas confronting us about it one time. "You shouldn't take them to the back when they cry. They should get used to sitting in the church." I was so impressed with us for getting our five kids to Mass on Sundays that I secretly felt we deserved some kind of all-access pass.

"Father, they are *one*-year-olds! They are not quite getting the concept of transubstantiation at this point."

Father was not having it. "You see that little boy, Cooper? He is three years old and he sits quietly in the front pew." Father Thomas was right. Cooper did sit quietly in the front pew. Cooper also sat quietly at the park where we all took our kids after Mass. Kids from smaller families had a different disposition. In other words, they behaved.

Nora and I had been through many of the ups and downs of raising a big family in the city together, and we were bonded like sisters. We traditionally spent Halloween, Mother's Day, Fourth of July, and innumerable weekends together. Doing anything with ten young children in Manhattan feels like a field trip, and the Gaffigans and the Fitzpatricks did it with regularity. We would literally overtake city sidewalks and parks. We found amusement in the horrified reactions of New Yorkers who encountered our combined brood. It must have felt like an invasion of children.

* * *

This Easter we had planned a similar brunch following the egg hunt that the Fitzpatricks spearheaded each year after Mass at St. Patrick's. Finding seating for fourteen-plus at the bougie NoLIta restaurants was always an adventure, but through trial and error, we cracked this dilemma and always had an adventure finding a back room or a downstairs area that would accommodate our herd of children and where we adults could have a fabulous salmon benedict and mimosa while the kids barely touched their $30 French toast because it was served with a dollop of gross-looking ricotta on it. Nora always brought a big bag of thematic kiddie crafts, and the trendy café would be transformed into our idealized entrepreneurial venture where a "family-friendly" experience did not have to mean bad food.

We had one of these plans for the next day, and I thought it would be best if I let Nora know about the craniotomy prior to the mimosa. Nora's reaction to my phone call confirmed the love I felt for this woman.

"Just wanted to give you a heads-up that I have a large brain

Imagine looking up and seeing this crew entering your brunch spot.

tumor and I have to go into Mount Sinai Monday for an urgent craniotomy." I knew her well enough that I could hear her heart bursting with compassion while her voice remained measured and calm.

"Everything's going to be fine. Don't worry about us." She went on, "We totally can cancel the brunch."

"No!" I replied. I wanted everything to be normal. "I want to have the best Mass, egg hunt, crazy take-over-SoHo brunch and let the kids trash their fancy Easter clothes at 'Dirty Park' " (our pet name for our local NoLIta playground where a trip down the slide would result in blackened pants). Nothing sad, nothing scary, just fun and love. Like we do it.

"Okay," she replied. We would stick to the plan.

"I have to call my mom and dad," I said. "They don't know yet."

"Okay, do that. Bye." She hung up. Nora is not one for long good-byes. Practical and empathetic, that was Nora.

Telling My Parents

Saturday went by like any other typical weekend day in the Gaffigan house, except Dad was home. Jim was usually performing on weekend nights, but this was a special family holiday and he had committed to be home months ago. Fortunate and unfortunate at the same time. With and without fortune. It was the night before Easter so the kids were riled up. After a normal, chaotic dinner, we got the kids ready for bed, but they were wide awake. I pulled Jim aside.

"Jim, can you put on an Easter movie in our room for the kids so I can call Dom and Weezie to tell them about the surgery?"

My matter-of-fact demeanor was all he needed to reply

nonchalantly, "Do they have a kid's version of *The Passion of the Christ* or something?"

I ignored Jim's borderline sacrilege. "I think it's called *Hop*, and it's not great." If I survived this, I decided, I had to do something about kids' movies. I sat down on the couch in my living room and dialed Dom and Weezie. I started referring to my mom and dad as Dom and Weezie a few years ago because that's what Jim called them, as he is vehemently opposed to spouses calling their in-laws "Mom and Dad." Jim's parents both unfortunately passed away before I met him, and like most comedians, he covers the pain with dark humor. For instance, if I say, "What should we do for Dad's birthday?" he says, "My dad's dead. Thanks for bringing it up." So, I call them Dom and Weezie. I still, of course, call them Mom and Dad to their faces.

I distinctly remember calling them from my darkened living room. It seemed more appropriate than doing it from the home office where I usually make private phone calls. This wasn't a business call. It was a human call. The most human kind of call. A private, somber grown-up call. I guess I initially left the lights off as a deterrent from a kid walking in. But in retrospect I realize that it was the mood lighting I needed. A dramatic kind of a setting for me. The right ambience. I'd been putting off this call, and now it was time. As a parent, all I do is worry about something happening to one of my kids, and now I had to tell my own parents that something was happening to their kid. I took a page from Nora's playbook for the tone of the call: serious, but under control. You may be wondering why it took so long for me to call my mom and dad about something so life-threatening. I had enough experience under my belt to know that I shouldn't call my mom and dad about something in the middle of chaos.

"Mom, Dad, I just found out I have a mass in my brain and I

have no idea what to do!" would have been the call to them two days ago. The reaction would have been my dad consulting Dr. Google for "mass in the brain," and my mom calling her ob/gyn for advice before telling me I wasn't taking enough fish oil. Her father was an ob/gyn, so in her mind those doctors were the leaders of the medical community. She would call her ob/gyn even if she had a head cold. I realize this sounds like an exaggeration, but, as much as I love my parents, I understand how they process bad news. I called their landline. I know, I know. No one calls the landline anymore. But this seemed like a landline kind of call because I wouldn't have to choose between calling Mom's or Dad's phone. I was calling them both.

"Hi, Danielle, can I talk to Dad?" Danielle is my sister who lives at home. She was born with a rare chromosomal disorder, Williams syndrome, that is characterized by moderate intellectual disability, distinct facial features, and cardiovascular problems. For those reasons, she will probably always live with my parents. Williams syndrome kids are the friendliest, nicest people and often, like Danielle, have advanced musical abilities. Danielle is the fifth child, smack in the middle of the nine, and she is the soul and anchor of our family. She is love incarnate, and I just couldn't tell her about the surgery yet. One step at a time. "Dad, hi. Can you get Mom on the other extension? I need to speak to you guys about something serious." Being one of nine siblings, I very well could have been the sixth or seventh call they got that day that opened with the same statement.

I heard my dad calling, "Louise!" The way they rallied together in situations like this was impressive and made up for all the needless bickering that occurs after forty-eight years of marriage. (Or fourteen years in Jim's and my case.)

When I was sure they were both on the phone, and out of the

earshot of Danielle, I asked them if they were sitting down. I know that's kind of a cliché way to open a call, but I meant it. I'd never really said that to someone before, but I didn't want to be the reason either of them fainted and hit their head. I'd never hear the end of it from my eight siblings. "You told Mom and Dad you were having brain surgery without telling them to sit down and they fainted and hit their heads! How selfish of you!" I suppose I also said it to keep them focused so I wouldn't have to repeat myself. I led with the right statement: "I am not going to die."

"Glad to hear it." This from my father, the die-hard pragmatist. His dry response indicated he was over the drama and wanted me to get to the point.

"Okay, um...I have a brain tumor, and on Monday I'm having brain surgery to remove it." (Pause)

"What kind of a tumor is it?" said Dom/Dad. I could hear his fingers clicking on the keyboard, Dr. Google at the ready.

"They think it might be a meningioma, but there's no way of telling until they get a sample of the tissue."

"Did you get a second opinion?" asked Weezie. My mom loved second opinions. I wondered if she was texting her gynecologist.

"Meningioma are benign," my dad/Dr. Google informed me.

"It still needs to come out, Dad, regardless of if it's benign or not. It's very large and it's pressing against my brain stem. I've been consulting with John Broderick, and he thinks I have the right plan. I also found my surgeon through Marita and Beth Haggerty."

"Oh, then that's fine. Do whatever John says," said Dom.

"Marita knows all the best doctors," said Weezie.

My dropping these names was all my parents needed to feel satisfied that I had done everything I could. As my mom would say, now it was in the hands of God, and as my dad would think, it was in the hands of the secular universe. However rocky the road ahead, they would walk it with me, each in their own way. "We are coming to New York for as long as you need us."

"Thank you, but Jim will let everyone know how it goes. I don't want anyone to panic or put themselves out." No big deal. It's just brain surgery.

My mom and dad were obviously curious as to how I found out that I had a tumor and how this was all happening so fast. I went on to tell them about the hearing loss and all the delightful "coincidences" that had brought me to this place. I made it a happy, positive story because in reality, it was.

Once I knew that Dom, the lifelong journalist, would handle the family press release, and Mom would get on the local *Bye Bye Birdie* Hail Mary chain, I was ready to move on to the next step in my plan: telling the kids.

Dom and Weezie

Telling the Kids

Anyone who has had to have a serious talk with kids, or who remembers their parents calling them in to "talk to them alone" when they were a kid, knows that feeling of dread before the actual conversation. As the one giving the news, you know you can't just blurt it out, or bring it up right before school or bed. You have to give a warning that something needs to be said in private. You know from experience that you have initiated the dread feeling, and that makes you all the more anxious as you dread the reaction. Basically, there's a whole lot of dreading going on. A talk like this is done with a level of formality, where you must sit facing each other, free from all other distractions. It's not really appropriate to be fixing a car engine or stacking boxes like you're being interviewed at your job by detectives on *Law & Order.*

Jim brought in the two oldest, who at the time were eleven and twelve. There were a few fears and concerns I'd had about this talk. One, that the kids would think, before we said anything, that we were going to tell them we were getting a divorce, not that there was any real reason for them to think that, but they could. Sure, Jim and I sometimes fight in front of the kids about idiotic stuff, but so many of their friends' parents have suddenly announced they were divorcing, and it kind of comes out of the blue and surprises us all. Of course, that's not what we were going say, but the way Jim and I decided to tell them—"Jack and Marre, come in here, please; your mom and I need to talk to you"—I knew that even for a moment they might look at each other and think, *Oh no, divorce!* When they eventually came in, I didn't want to lead with "We are not getting divorced!" Because what if they weren't thinking that at all and now I'd put the thought in their minds?

The second fear I had was, what if they asked me, "What will happen if you die?" I really couldn't give them an answer there, because Jim and I had not even entertained that as an option. We had decided that we would get the two oldest together and tell them the truth, the whole truth, and nothing but the truth, so help us God. Tell them that we loved them and that we were hoping for the best. The pickle with this honesty approach was that if they asked "Are you going to die?" and we said "No way!" and then I did die, would they spend the rest of their lives thinking we'd lied to them? Jim and I realized we had never, ever had one of those "come in here please, your mom and I need to talk to you" talks with our kids before, and we knew nothing about how to deal with their reactions. What we did have going for us was that we didn't really hide much from our kids, and we had been relatively honest about bad things happening in the world and other adult stuff. Therefore, we knew our kids were strong. Well, strong about some things. If we told them that iPads were being outlawed, well, that reaction, especially Jack's, might have been something that we would need a child psychiatrist on standby for. The other concern I had was that they might not care. They might be like, "Cool, it will be nice to have you off our backs for a while."

We sat down facing them and took their hands. I hesitated for a moment, unsure of how to begin. Jim jumped in: "Your mom is very sick and needs to go to the hospital for surgery." My oldest, Marre, was silent. She is very introspective and thoughtful in her reactions to everything. She was processing, but I couldn't read her. Being the oldest myself, I could relate to feeling like it was my role to be the most responsible and mature one, and I hoped she was not thinking that this problem was being dumped on her like she was supposed to fix it.

Jack blurted out, "Is it cancer?"

"It doesn't look like cancer. If it is cancer, we will cross that bridge when we come to it, but for now it's a brain tumor that has grown very large and it has to come out." Jack's and Marre's eyes looked like that spinning thing on a computer when it's working really hard to search for something.

"Did you get it from a cell phone?" Jack seemed certain. All those empty threats we had given him about overuse of screens must have brought him to this conclusion.

I debated momentarily about answering, "Yes. Cell phones, iPads, and walking too close to the Xbox definitely caused this tumor."

"No," interrupted Jim, who saw my hesitation and probably knew I was thinking about turning this personal crisis into a sham teachable moment. "We don't know what caused it, but Mom has to go into the hospital Monday so they can try to take it out and she might be gone for a while. As in, not at home." Marre's eyes dropped to the floor. I imagined her thoughts: *Good-bye, childhood.*

Jack was fascinated. "Are they going to pull it out your nose or cut your head open?"

"Cut my head open," I tossed back. I met his gross-out challenge. I'll see your "pull it out your nose" and raise you a "cut your head open." Jack stared wide-eyed at the wall.

"Are you going to tell Katie, Michael, and Patrick?" Marre asked. I saw the haunted look in my oldest child that I read as "I'm too young to take over this circus."

"Yes," said Jim. "But we are just going to tell them tomorrow night that Mom has to have an operation and will be in the hospital for a while. They don't need to know the details."

"Can you keep it?" Jack asked. Maybe he thought leaving the hospital was like leaving prison. "Here you go, your wallet, keys, tumor…" I pictured the tumor in a jar on the mantel. The ultimate trophy. I wanted to explain to him that it would likely have to be removed bit by tiny bit because of all the vital nerves entangled in it, but that might freak him out. The thought of it was freaking me out. I kissed them good night and left, by myself, to go to the Easter Vigil Mass. Hardest conversation I'd ever had with my kids, check. Jim, the designated babysitter, was going to have to field the residual questions. Now that the cat was out of the bag, I knew I had to give up having Jim at my side for every moment of my personal trauma so he could be there for the children. I would need a different support system for myself. One that could give me undivided attention. It was time to bargain with God.

The Vigil Mass

I had not been to an Easter Vigil Mass by myself for years. In fact, probably not since before I had kids. It takes place the night before Easter, and it's the extended remix version of the Easter Sunday Mass. It goes a little late for small children, so for the past twelve years I'd been putting kids to bed at that time so I could, you know, help the Easter bunny hide the eggs and candy. Then, in the morning, we'd all normally go to the shorter, more upbeat version of the Mass, the one of fancy-hat fame.

The Vigil is very theatrical, beginning in a darkened church by candlelight. Tonight, it was more than just a show for me. I was going "backstage" to receive the sacrament called the Anointing of the Sick after Mass, and the whole night was me getting ready for this beautiful and terrifying blessing. I had already called Monsignor Sakano, the pastor of our church, to arrange my anointing. I couldn't help but think of it as preparation for my own personal crucifixion. Not to diminish the actual crucifixion, which did not involve any anesthesia, but it would be the closest I had come to anything like this in my life. The real point of getting this kind of blessing was accepting that I might die, and that I had an expectation that death would not be the end. I had to believe that to have peace with this surgery. There is nothing more deep or profound than that kind of feeling. Having faith because I simply had to. No atheists in foxholes.

After the Mass I found Deacon Paul, an extraordinary soul and talent, who was going to perform the anointing with Monsignor. I'd known him for years. He'd officiated at Katie's baptism and called all the children up to the altar and delivered the homily like it was a fun segment on *Sesame Street*. No Muppets but clapping and singing. The whole ceremony was totally unlike the more formal service at our previous St. Patrick's baptisms. St. Patrick's Old Cathedral had its fifteen minutes of fame as the church in the *Godfather* baptism scene. Our other baptisms there were similar to the movie, but instead of the baptismal vows being intercut with mafia massacres, think me and Nora in the back with screaming kids.

Deacon Paul is a three-time cancer survivor and believes in miracles, so I was thrilled to have him as part of the anointing experience. The resident expert. He was like the Dr. Bederson of the sacrament. After the Vigil, I pushed down my fear and boldly walked back to the sacristy, guns blazing, and announced, "Hi, Deacon Paul! I'm ready for you and Monsignor to anoint me!" After pointing out that his multitalented son Eric had refinished the gleaming antique credenza that was the centerpiece of the room, Deacon Paul sat me down in a chair and got ready for my anointing, which I equated with "last rites." His showing off the credenza made this moment so personable and less terrifying for me. I'll never forget the credenza. Focusing on these small details grounded me in reality and stopped my mind from wandering off to all the "what-ifs." I readied myself for whatever Deacon Paul was going to do or say to make me feel at peace with this journey I was about to take.

Appearing like an angel at his side was Helen, Deacon Paul's devoted and marvelous wife (meeting her stopped him from becoming a priest, so you know she's got it!). She placed her hands on my head, not as part of the ritual, but as if reading my mind that I was looking for a strong and supportive mother figure in that moment.

The blessing began. I couldn't ever repeat the words that were spoken, but that tight circle around me offered a glimpse of the power of good that surrounded me in my life. I closed my eyes and felt the oil dripping on my forehead. A week before, if someone would have told me that I would be in this bizarre setting, next to a refinished credenza backstage at a church happily having oil poured on my head as if getting ready for the rapture, I would have asked if they were high. The absurdity of the situation was obvious, yet I felt part of something larger, much larger. The blessing of the new fire, the water, the oil, Helen the Saint, and the holy men in robes elevated me to another place.

What had happened the previous day at Mount Sinai with all the scanning of my body was happening now for my spirit. I was aware of the nonphysical part of me in a way I'd never been before. I was alive for now, and I needed supernatural help. I knew there was a presence larger than the physical world. I knew there was a God, and he would take care of me and my family. I felt covered from all angles. I believed with all my heart and soul that I was in the right place at the right time for all of this to happen now, and the fear and doubt that were so intertwined in the deepest part of me were released. It was kind of like getting a pedicure before going into labor, but way better.

EASTER SUNDAY

I woke up on Easter morning with total confidence. Normally it is a time of extreme chaos in my home. There's the Gaffigan house egg hunt, where Jim and I essentially set ourselves up for failure by letting the kids find—then trying to stop them from eating—baskets full of chocolate bunnies, Peeps, and handfuls of jelly beans just before Mass. My children don't really grasp the idea of "saving some for later." They take after their father. Then there is the wrestling match of getting everyone into cute outfits and to Mass in some proximity of being on time. It usually explodes into me yelling, Jim cursing, and the kids all having a contest to see who can cry the loudest. If you were to walk into our home during this time, you would think you'd stepped onto the set of *The Exorcist*. Getting them to church on Easter morning, the most joyful holy day of the Christian calendar, has basically the same effect as a ritualistic invocation of Satan.

But not this morning—I was floating through life and everything was easy. It may have been a result of my soul cleansing from the night before, or just a heightened appreciation for every moment spent with my amazing kids, but the energy was jubilant and enthusiastic. The kids were overjoyed at finding their personalized baskets, and the cute outfits went off without a hitch.

I chose not to pack any after-Mass play clothes, because for the first time in my life, I didn't care if they trashed their Sunday best. In the past, I'd brought two sets of clothes on Easter Sunday and changed my kids in tiny bathrooms of restaurants so they would not ruin their white-and-pastel ensembles. Last year at the end of the Easter adventure, I discovered I had lost one of a pair of brand-new good shoes, an expensive white hat, and a navy wool blazer that could have been handed down to two more boys. I imagined the staff at the restaurant finding them and thinking, *Whose kid is walking out of our restaurant with one shoe?* The collateral damage from the Easter quick-change was costly and maddening, but I used to do it just so I could enjoy seeing them play rather than biting my nails about the white dress getting stained at Dirty Park. This year, however, I was looking forward to watching the good clothes get wrecked. It was as if I'd just remembered that people are more important than things.

We got to Mass on time and everyone was well-behaved in anticipation of the big parish egg hunt in the courtyard. In the church, there were fresh flowers everywhere, and I felt like I was in heaven. This was heaven for me: flowers and Jim and my children and love and meaning.

* * *

After Mass and the egg hunt, we walked with the Fitzpatricks down to Grand Street and all of our kids held hands and skipped. Even that journey to the restaurant was glorious. The Gaffigans' and Fitzpatricks' Easter Parade. Jim, not usually one for small talk, commented on the amazing weather. It was breezy and sunny, not a cloud in the sky, unlike a few years ago when it had snowed on Easter. "At least it will be nice when they inevitably kick us out of this restaurant."

When we arrived, we were escorted downstairs to a semiprivate area that was already set up for our huge party. There was another large table down there that appeared to be a bizarre bridal shower brunch (one of the ladies was wearing an ironic white veil), much to the amusement of Katie and Gigi, our two families' seven-year-olds. "Mommy, is that lady getting married to all those other ladies?" What do you expect? They're

New York kids. The food was fantastic, and Trey ordered a bottle of champagne. One little sip wouldn't hurt me. We toasted the success of the operation and the mood was euphoric. The older kids who didn't want to do the arts and crafts projects that Nora pulled out of her giant handbag were allowed to go into the "lounge" area with money and order "mocktails" from the bar.

Jim, Trey, Nora, and I were reminiscing and laughing about our many adventures with all the kids together when another priest friend we knew from days past, whom I had not seen in years, walked in. Father Jonathan had been a major figure in our lives, heaven-sent, after Jim and I went through the darkest three years of our marriage from around 2006 to 2009. Jim's touring theater career had exploded unexpectedly, and neither of us was prepared for this major change. At the same time, I was at home, overwhelmed with the treacheries of young motherhood: I'd had two pregnancies that didn't end well, while at the same time nursing a baby and chasing after a rambunctious toddler. Then I was pregnant again—in my eighth month—and I found myself riddled with anxiety. Jim was gone all the time, physically and mentally. I wanted to talk to him about all my angst, but he was consumed fully with work. I had always been at his side and now I felt like an afterthought. I was at the end of my rope and having drastic thoughts when Father Jonathan was assigned to take on some responsibilities at our parish. He was young, and from a familiar world, as he was a frequent TV and radio commentator and had been the dramaturg on feature films. He'd counseled us out of the dark ages and witnessed our marital renaissance.

Since Father Jonathan had been reassigned to a parish in the Bronx, getting together with him was a rarity. Now he was walking into the NoLIta brunch spot on the most significant day of my life. I was stunned at this incredible coincidence until I found out that Jim had sent him an email regarding what was going on with me, and he had loosely invited him to meet us after Mass. It was a long shot because inviting a priest on Easter is like inviting a retail executive on Christmas Eve, but he showed up. It was exactly the right time in the party to have our guest of honor appear. Who doesn't want a priest to show up to the Easter meal?

We squeezed him in between us, poured him a glass of champagne (after the Vigil and morning Masses at his parish he was off duty), and apologized for eating all the food. We tried to get a waiter to come over and take his order. He looked around at the piles of uneaten pancakes and eggs and bacon on all the plates and decided to scrape together a brunch from the leftovers. Total big-family move. Father Jonathan is one of six kids and felt as at home with us as we did with him.

After we had a few laughs, he looked at me and said, "So, Jeannie, what is going on with this brain surgery?" There was a moment of uncomfortable silence as I realized that other than the initial toast, we hadn't really been mentioning it, in true lace curtain Irish fashion.

"Well, Father," I started, "I'm going in to Mount Sinai tomorrow, and they are going to embolize the tumor, then on Tuesday I'm going to have the craniotomy." I took a sip of champagne. "And everything is going to be all right." My peaceful smile said it all. "I just need you to look out for this guy." I stuck my thumb out at Jim. Everyone laughed, breaking the tension.

Father Jonathan's huge blue eyes sparked with compassion. "Jeannie, God is guiding you and your family through all of this. I have no doubt that your strong faith and love are going to carry you." Those years ago, when Father Jonathan first came into our lives, I was a mess. I did not have strong faith at all, and my love for Jim was faulty and conditional. Jim and Father were meeting for spiritual counseling, and I was wildly envious and resentful. I was about to give birth to Katie, and I felt abandoned and neglected by my husband. When it was my turn to meet with him alone, I unloaded to him all of my negative feelings for Jim.

His response was totally unexpected: "Jeannie, I spent eight hours yesterday with a woman whose husband and three children all were suddenly killed in an accident." I was shocked. Was I bothering him because he was exhausted from helping someone with a real crisis? Was this meant to minimize my feelings? Bad things happened all the time, but that didn't mean I couldn't vent about my selfish husband! But then something happened in me. I imagined I was the woman who'd lost her whole family. What if the day before she'd been complaining about how selfish her husband and children were and now they were gone forever. I don't know if he knew I would draw this conclusion, but it worked. When I thought I was at rock bottom with my marriage, Father Jonathan had reached down and pulled me back up. However bad I felt it was, it could have been a lot worse. Now, when he was looking at me all these years later, facing a true crisis, I saw admiration. I wondered if he knew he'd had a part in my spiritual growth. If I hadn't made the journey through the hard times before, I probably wouldn't have been able to gather the strength to face this one.

The restaurant was a few blocks away from Dirty Park, and we invited him to walk over with us. He was going to Deacon Paul's house for dinner and it was close by. As we were walking, the blue sky rapidly turned gray and, without warning, opened into a torrential downpour. We all got separated. Each adult grabbed whatever child was closest and ran for cover. It was pandemonium as trucks whizzed by in the pounding rain and I tried to do a headcount, looking for the smallest and most vulnerable in our group. I had Patrick and Timmy under the awning of a bodega, and I spotted Nora and Jim with Michael and Danny a couple of doors down in a similar huddle on the stoop of a paint shop. We were drenched in our Easter finest. We burst out laughing, noiseless under the roar of the rain. Laughter in the face of adversity.

*　　*　　*

That night, as we cuddled in our big bed with the kids, Jim and I told Katie, Michael, and Patrick that Mommy was going to the doctor tomorrow to fix something that was wrong in her brain, and she would probably have to be in the hospital for a little while but would be home soon. "Are you going to a 'talking doctor' to fix your brain?" asked Katie, precocious as ever, concluding that Mommy was clearly going to in-patient psychiatric therapy to resolve her obsessive-compulsive clean-ing disorder. New York kids.

"No, it's a surgeon doctor, like the kind that takes bad ton-sils out, but I have kind of something like a bad tonsil in my brain."

"Do you have to get a shot?" Michael's eyes were as big as saucers. He was terrified of shots. It was pretty much the worst thing he could imagine.

"I might get a shot, but I'm not scared. I don't think it will hurt at all." I didn't want him to worry.

Patrick chimed in: "Then you can get a toy out of the

treasure chest!" Jim put his arms tightly around our youngest and said, "I'll make sure Mommy gets a toy after her shot." The thought of that happy ending seemed to pacify everyone.

After we'd put the kids to bed, and Jim went out to do a set (the best therapy to calm his nerves), I started to experience a bit of panic. Not about the surgery, but about what I was going to eat. I had to leave for the hospital at 6 a.m., and I was to have nothing to eat or drink after midnight. Jim is always game to pick up late-night food for me. He loves me and he loves food, so it's a win-win situation. Over the years when I would be stuck in a chair nursing a newborn baby all night, this tradition became part of our marriage. Jim would come home from his spots bearing one of the unique nighttime delicacies that only New York City has to offer at all hours: shawarma, falafel, Korean hot dogs, and even sometimes he'd happen upon the taco truck on First Street. He'll often call me at 11 p.m. and say, "Do you want me to pick up anything?" I know that means he wants to eat something and knows better than to come in smelling like street meat. I always say "sure"—I just don't ever know what I want. "Just get what you want to get and I'll eat it." That night, I felt like it had to be my choice. I was still kind of full from brunch, but I knew I would not be able to eat for a while, so I had to have something. What do you have for your last meal? Yes, a cheeseburger and fries of course is the correct answer, but I wasn't feeling it. There was a sandwich place across the street that had these amazing salami and parmesan sandwiches on focaccia bread. That's what I wanted. Jim was out doing a spot at a comedy club so I texted him to pick us up a sandwich for my last meal. There was another sandwich place right by the club, so he said he would bring home sandwiches. It wasn't our usual favorite spot, but it was right there.

When he arrived, I unwrapped the sandwiches with the highest hopes for the perfect last meal. I bit into the focaccia bread, expecting the familiar and perfect combination taste of balsamic vinegar, parmesan cheese, and salami. Jim and I took bites at the same time, and though our mouths were full, we exchanged looks as we realized together that these were not the right sandwiches. They were horrible. They were nothing like either of us thought they would be. I felt not-ordering-a-burger regret. Which is a real thing. Even Jim, who has been known to finish an entire meal before remarking, "That was bad!" didn't eat his bad sandwich. How can you mess up a salami sandwich? I opted to just be hungry until after the first procedure. It was too close to be turning into a "nothing after midnight" pumpkin to try for anything else. That's when I started to get a creepy feeling. I knew it was superstitious, like that stupid thought that if you have a bad New Year's Eve, the rest of the year is going to suck.

Something about that bad last meal really shook my confidence. It wasn't about the surgery. In fact, I couldn't wait to get that thing out of my brain. I could feel it back there, taunting me. With all the activity in the last few days, the scans, the Easter baskets, the people to tell, the Vigil, the brunch, I'd forgotten about the evil pear that had caused it all. Now I could feel it. *Get out of my life!* I thought. *No one invited you here. You're ruining everything.* It could probably hear my thoughts up there. I thought it may have throbbed back, menacingly. I held perfectly still. Wouldn't it be ironic if the thing killed me the night before I went in to the hospital? I felt an icky tingling sensation in my limbs. *Oh my God, I'm having a stroke*, I thought. What happened to all that peace I'd felt that day? I thought this new calm Jeannie would be a one-shot thing. I texted John. I knew it was late, but unfortunately for him, he was a neurologist and I had his mobile number.

I believed it.

My mother, my brothers and sisters, my relatives, my friends, my priests, and Jim had all told me that God was going to get me through this, but when John, who was Mr. Science, outspoken in disbelief of all things supernatural, spoke to me about faith, it was somehow the most meaningful and powerful. He knew the odds, he knew the probability, he knew the medical facts, but the night before my surgery when I called him in fear, he told me to have faith. Even if he was just telling me what he thought I needed to hear, that gesture of selflessness and generosity was really the most godlike gift he could give me. Earthy, scientific faith.

Chapter 10

INTO THE WOODS

MONDAY

The next morning, Jim and I left at 6 a.m. for Mount Sinai. The kids were sleeping like babies because, well, they were babies. I thought that getting somewhere at 6 a.m. with no coffee or food would be a lot more difficult, but Jim and I sprang out of bed before the alarm even went off. Turns out adrenaline is way more of a pick-me-up than coffee and a bagel. They should put it in the lattes at Starbucks. Jim and I went into team mode. We don't really need to talk at all or communicate with more than one-word sentences when we have a goal to accomplish: gather up the stuff, get out the door, get to the hospital on time, and get this awful thing over with. We had sitter coverage for the whole day, beginning at 5 a.m. Someone was taking the kids to school. Someone was holding down the fort. Sky was coming in at 9 a.m. to cover the office. At this point we anticipated that we would be gone for at least a week. Still, a week's worth of emails in my in-box is a daunting laundry mountain, so Sky would have his work cut out for him. We had not told anyone but our closest friends and family what was happening. An "out of office reply" would have been difficult to execute in this situation so he would have to handle my email delicately. Jim and I held hands and jumped off the cliff into an Uber. Well, it was a curb, but it felt like a cliff. We made the hour-long journey up to Mount Sinai and the surgery check-in on the second floor.

Up until this moment I was totally consumed with my own situation. I was the only one in the world with a brain tumor that needed emergency surgery. I was the only one whose life hung in the balance and whose family was about to get turned upside down.

Imagine my shock when I rounded the corner after stepping off the second-floor elevator and saw at least a hundred people who were also in the waiting area at 6 a.m. to get surgery at Mount Sinai. I scanned all the tired, worried faces. It was impossible to tell who was the anxious presurgery patient and who was the anxious presurgery patient's support person. I'd been such a narcissist to think I was the only person getting surgery that day. It never even crossed my mind that there would be a waiting area filled with hordes of humanity facing perhaps the biggest challenge of their lives.

After we checked in, I sat with Jim in that big hall, studying the others and imagining their stories. The old woman and her ashen-faced middle-aged son huddled together. Which one was having the procedure? How serious was it? It didn't seem like the type of place where anyone was getting a breast augmentation. Suddenly the idea of elective surgery seemed ridiculous to me. I've always been the person who is totally open to the idea: "When it falls, I'll get it lifted!" Now, as Jim and I were finally called to the check-in cubicle, and they started having us fill out the consent forms, which included a health proxy in the event of death, I started to challenge my own attitude. Why would someone sign up for this if they didn't have to?

After the longest time of filling out the "advanced directive" forms that included many signatures exempting the hospital from all responsibilities of my accidental death, dismemberment, brain injury, long-term emotional suffering, hemorrhoids, acne, bloating, and leprosy, Jim and I had to make the "pull the plug" decision. We had just kind of shown up here after this whirlwind few days and never even discussed any of this. Now in a little cubicle, under the time gun, and in front of a receptionist whose job was to get us processed quickly, we had to make a decision like this. We had thirty-eight seconds to mull it over. There we were, filling out the ultimate form. All previous form-filling had led us to this moment. If I am brain-dead with no signs of recovery, would it be okay if Jim pulls the plug? If I am brain-dead, and the only thing keeping me alive is artificial life support, yes. I think it is unethical to be kept alive by machines. I told Jim yes, he could pull the plug. But I had one caveat before I signed my name: If Jim got remarried to some climbing, comedy fan–girl skank, my vengeful and capricious ghost would haunt him forever.

Stood Up at the Altar

I put my stuff in a plastic bag as Jim accompanied me into pre-op. I was to have two procedures and would be woken up in between. Today, Monday, an embolization procedure was going to be performed to cauterize the blood vessels feeding the tumor to reduce the risk of bleeding during surgery. They would put some wire or something into a vein in my thigh and somehow thread it up to my brain. Tuesday was the dreaded craniotomy. What had happened in my life to bring me to the point where I considered threading a tube through a hole in my femoral artery and up to my brain to glue blood vessels shut a minor procedure? A minor procedure whose possible side effects I'd just signed off on included nerve damage, tissue damage, stroke, and death. Yet it was being treated like a little appetizer before the "crani-entrée."

Jim and I went into a small, somewhat dingy-looking room to get prepped with the anesthesiologist. Compared to Dr. Bederson's office with the lustrous mahogany desk and Friday's MRI experience in a room that could have been the set of a multimillion-dollar sci-fi film, the pre-op area seemed like a big step down. *What, no catering?* I thought, looking around for the tuxedoed waiter holding a silver tray full of medicine cups.

The anesthesiologist, a nice-looking blond woman in her forties, came bursting in with a huge personality, putting me at ease. "Hi, I'm Dr. Patricia Brou; you can call me Patty. I'm going to make this procedure a lot more pleasant for you by giving you some drugs to make you sleep. Sound good?" I could have been in the green room of a comedy club. Just from this brief interaction I knew she was smart, funny, and edgy. Just my type. She explained that in addition to the general anesthesia through an IV tube she would use to put me to sleep, she would control my breathing through a tube. I mentioned my five kids to her, which had become my standard guilt-trip message to all the medical people who held my life in their hands. I learned she lived in Westchester and had school-age kids of her own. I wanted to hang out with her. I realized I might never have the opportunity. Had I not really noticed humans before? Everyone suddenly seemed so kind and interesting. I wanted my kids to have a playdate with this woman's kids while we sat on iron chairs in her Westchester garden with glasses of wine and a cheese tray. Now that I could die or become a vegetable, it might never happen. What a wasted opportunity.

The doctor who was performing the embolization entered my dingy throne room where I was holding court. She introduced herself as Dr. Fifi. Her name seemed out of place for the gravity of the moment. Her name was the star-spangled sweatpants of the tumor embolization. "Dr. Fifi" sounded like a name that my seven-year-old daughter would invent for her Sims video game as the fancy vet that treated only poodles. Unlike her name, though, Dr. Johanna Fifi was very serious. Friendly but to the point concerning what was about to happen. She explained again the procedure of the wire being threaded up my femoral artery and eventually reaching my brain tumor to seal the vessels shut. I mentioned again that I had five kids who needed me. I said good-bye to Jim, and I gave him my computer password and the code to unlock my phone. He would have to learn the teachers' names. Actually, he would have to learn who had which teacher. He would have to learn the after-school schedule and when to call the dry cleaner. Shopping on FreshDirect was easy because they highlighted "your favorite" products on the website. I let him know. He was just nodding over and over, looking at me with watery eyes. Was he having allergies? He should take some Claritin. There was too much to explain. I was about to have surgery of the brain and I was more worried about Jim and the kids. Katie was sucking her thumb while she slept. Michael had to learn to read. Is someone going to pick up Jack's medication? Would Marre start vaping and drop out of school? Would Patrick remember me? It was too late now to think about these things. I had to make it out of there; I had too much to do.

The doctors and nurses escorted me into the OR, where I got up on the table myself. I remember joking around with Dr. Patty while she was preparing the IV sedation. I don't remember precisely what I was talking about but it was probably something like how when the IV sedation kicks in you just stop talking in midsen…

The next thing I knew I woke up in post-op on a mobile bed with five doctors, Jim, and Leslie standing in front of me. It was like the ending of *The Wizard of Oz*, but no one was smiling. The first thing I remember saying is, "What's wrong? You all look like undertakers!"

Dr. Fifi spoke first. "We weren't able to perform the embolization."

"What do you mean?" So I just went under for nothing? What did they do in all that time? I didn't know how long I'd been out, but I knew it was a long time. The team looked disheveled, like they had been caught up in the twister.

"We were going into your brain through the carotid arteries in your neck, but the imaging revealed you have damage that looks like fibromuscular dysplasia."

"Is this caused by the tumor?"

"No, it is something that you were probably born with. We discovered it as we were charting the path of the angiogram." I was speechless. Turns out I have this rare disease of bumpy and weak carotid arteries. The only possible way I could have found this out was if I'd had a perioperative embolization of a brain tumor, or if I'd done a killer yoga headstand and my neck snapped. It would have been literally "killer." *Thank you, brain tumor*, I thought. *You're welcome*, it throbbed back.

"We don't think it is possible to embolize." Leslie was standing there with that "I hate to be the bearer of bad news" look on her face. "But more importantly, this new discovery means that we will not be able to do the brain surgery as planned."

"Wait, you can still remove the tumor, right?" I said in the same tone as a demanding queen hurling disdain at my groveling subjects. Everyone looked hesitant.

"There may not be a safe way to do the surgery," Leslie replied. Anything had to be safer than waltzing around with a pear in my brain that was about to explode the next time I sneezed.

"Can you just fix my arteries? This is a hospital for God's sake!" This was my first of many experiences with feeling annoyed by my caregivers and it surprised me. Moments ago, everyone was perfect and wonderful. Now, I felt like I was the victim of a conspiracy. Being angry with people who are trying to help you is something that contradicts all logic, yet looking back on this scene, it feels strangely familiar to me as a mother, and probably would for anyone who is a caregiver. "But I don't want a bath, Mom! I hate you! You are so mean for making me eat vegetables and wanting me to wear sweaters and go to bed early! You are *evil*."

Leslie was the voice of stern reason: "Let's worry about fixing the arteries later. Right now, we have a new urgent issue to deal with as a result of this complication. Dr. Bederson has to figure out how to position your head during the craniotomy. Since the method we were originally going to use to operate involved twisting your neck to the side, with what we now know about your weak arteries, that position would put your life in danger."

I wasn't thinking clearly. Probably because I had just awoken

from an IV cocktail blackout. A new issue? "Can't you just figure something out?" I was mortified. I had come this far, prepared mentally and spiritually for this moment, and now they
couldn't do the brain surgery. It felt like I was in my bridal
gown at the altar and the groom had bailed.

Dr. Fifi cleared her throat. "There is a possibility there is
one healthy branch that would make it possible. We have to
study it. We have to meet with the whole team and discuss
options." The whole team? How many more were there? The
group that stood around my bed was more than enough for a
basketball game, with Leslie starting at center. Leslie assured
me, "We will figure something out. It will just be more complicated." As if brain surgery was not complicated enough. But
what Dr. Fifi and Leslie gave me was hope, and that's all I had.

They moved me into a room and I fell asleep. I don't remember falling asleep. I was awake, then I wasn't. You expect to
go out with anesthesia, but there was no warning this time.
Maybe a pocket bubble of drugs was circulating around in my
bloodstream and it suddenly popped. I remember nothing; the
only reason I knew I'd fallen asleep was because I woke up. I
was in a room alone and it seemed to be night. There was no
window in the tiny room, but I sensed night. I felt like I had
slept through a party or something. Everyone had gone home.

I found out later that an "alternate solution" had been agreed
upon. I didn't get the embolization, which meant there might
be more bleeding during the surgery, potentially making it take
longer, but the real victory that came out of their strategy meeting was they found a position to put my head in that was not
life-threatening so I could undergo the life-threatening brain
surgery for my life-threatening brain tumor. I didn't understand
it either, but apparently it was a win. I was to have the surgery in

the morning, so while I was out cold, they instructed Jim to go home, as I would probably be asleep for the night. He was told to come back early the next day. Waking up totally alone and having no idea what was going on, I was annoyed that nobody told me anything. I mean, sure, I had been asleep, but at least put up a sign. Where was I? What time was it?

A nurse came in and seemed surprised I was awake. I asked her what time it was. It was almost midnight. I remembered the rule about eating before surgery. I was really beginning to feel the pain of not eating for a whole day, and now that I was quickly approaching the witching hour of "nothing to eat or drink after midnight," I needed to make a move. I asked the nurse what I could have. She said, "Nothing to eat." So I asked her what I could drink. She offered me water or juice, and I settled for cranberry juice. She brought it to me in a can along with a white Styrofoam cup filled with crushed ice and a straw.

I will never forget that cranberry juice as long as I live. It was pure sugar and cranberry flavoring. I kept pouring the juice into the ice and drinking the whole cup in one long, sweet straw sip, over and over. I asked for another can. It was like the best thing I'd ever tasted. I drank so much cranberry juice that I started to feel like I had eaten five cakes. I was determined to get those calories one way or another. Glad I did. It turned out to be the last thing I swallowed for four months.

TUESDAY

The Surgery

I have a very foggy memory of actually going into surgery the next morning. I don't know if I even woke up fully. They just wheeled me in. A gurney is kind of a cool way to get to where you're going. It's so effortless the way they lift you out of one bed onto it, wheel you through corridors and elevators, and then lift you onto the OR bed. It's a good idea for an app: "Uber-Gurney." It might catch on if people don't mind the muscle atrophy.

I'm sure Jim was there, but I don't remember. I have this feeling that Jim was there. Standing by, feeling helpless, but meaning so much to me. I know Leslie was there; I remember her face, but I don't remember what she said. I remember the gurney ride with the ceiling passing overhead. I remember the distorted voices of the doctors, nurses, and orderlies. I remember the blinding lights in the OR and everyone in scrubs. Was Jim in scrubs? I imagined that all my kids were there, in scrubs, just out of my eyesight, but I felt their presence, cheering me on.

One thing I do remember clear as a bell is Dr. Bederson in his surgery gown and hat, smiling at me with perfect teeth. I said: "Can I say a prayer for your hands?" Even with everything I had been through, and everything that was about to happen, I remember feeling a little embarrassed to ask him this. Like he would think I was a Jesus freak or something. Would he say "Yes" because he couldn't say "No" but secretly wish I hadn't asked? When I went under would they all laugh at me? "Ha-ha! Can you believe she wanted to pray over my hands? *Awkward!*" But I did. I needed to.

I took Dr. Bederson's hands in mine and started to talk to God. "Dear God, bless these hands that are about to cut my skull open..." Those hands. They literally vibrated with power. They were like magic hands. He was a magician and Leslie was his beautiful MA (magician's assistant), handing him rabbits and wands. The second I touched them, I knew he was superhuman. His hands felt like he held a million lives in them. Past, present, and future.

I remembered a fun fact I'd learned about Dr. Bederson: in his spare time he was a gifted sculptor. That made perfect sense when I touched his hands. I wonder if Michelangelo and Rodin were also superhumans. Demigods among us mere mortals. I realized that I had nothing to worry about putting my life in these hands. I didn't even need to ask God to bless his hands after all; they felt already blessed.

It occurred to me at that moment that I was surrounded by space-age technology. There were screens and computers all over the OR. They were not magic. They were electronic. Science suddenly seemed less reliable. "I also want to bless all the electronic items in the hospital, that there is no blackout or generator failure!" I blurted. I sensed that all in the room wanted to expedite the anesthesia process so I would shut up.

"Yes." Doctor Bederson smiled. "Pray for the electricity."

And that's all I remember.

FADE TO BLACK

I guess I had brain surgery. I mean, that's what they told me, but I can't be certain because I wasn't exactly conscious. Again, no posted sign. When I first opened my eyes, I was propped up slightly and saw the stark lighting of the hospital and medical people walking back and forth. I couldn't move. Or maybe I could but just didn't try.

It took a couple of seconds for me to realize that I was awake and the surgery was over. Immediately after that, I realized that I realized.

I'm me, I remember thinking. I was me. What a simple

thought. And how horrifying that if I had been brain-damaged, I never would have had that thought.

Turns out it was a different kind of tumor than they thought. It was not a meningioma, but a choroid plexus papilloma. I know, big difference, right? What I later learned was that it was much better that I had the choroid plexus because it was more "flakey" or something, and didn't damage my nerves as much when they spent eleven hours picking it out. Hope you're not eating a croissant while reading this. If you are, sorry. But it really was like a croissant but less buttery.

Apparently, these specific tumors are commonly found in children, whereas meningiomas are more commonly found in middle-aged women. I took it as a compliment: "You have the tumor of a much younger person."

"Why, thank you!"

PART II

The Aftermath

But I was me. I was awake and alive and so grateful. I have flashes of recollections from that day. Doctors asking me questions: "Do you know who you are?" I knew. I knew literally and I knew philosophically. I think, therefore I AM! Of course, I am not a philosopher. I am a mother, a wife, and a comedy writer. All my jobs require agile mental abilities and creative engagement. Losing all or part of my mental faculties would be a total loss of identity and I wouldn't even know it was gone. Instead of having memories, I would *be* a memory, identified only by what I had done with my life so far. But that thought now was just that: a thought. Meaning I still had thoughts. I had a second chance.

"Yes!" I answered in a weak whisper. "I am Jeannie Gaffigan!" Did I know where I was? "Mount Sinai Hospital!" That's right. Did I know why I was there? "I had brain surgery!" What year was it? "It's 2017!" Who was the president

of the United States? (beat) "Uh...It's not Donald Trump, is it?" Maybe I did have brain damage. The room let out a hearty laugh of relief. I remember Jim being there looking like he had just given birth to five babies at once. Leslie beaming. Dr. Bederson smiling down at me. Everyone so happy that the surgery had been a sensational success and then nothing.
BLACKOUT

Total loss of consciousness.

Chapter 11

PEEKABOO! ICU

The next thing I remembered was waking up with something big, uncomfortable, and plastic down my throat. I was in the ICU, and something had gone terribly wrong.

Maybe it was the drugs, but I don't remember feeling fear, just annoyance and bewilderment. I remember fear on Jim's face. I couldn't speak. Something was up my nose. I had tubes coming out of my arm. Maybe they were there before, but now they just hurt. What was happening? Nurses were coming in and out, checking things. Jim talking to a doctor. I know now that at some point during my sleep I had aspirated my saliva and contracted serious bilateral pneumonia. Apparently they told me all this, but at the time, I had no idea I was in the ICU. I was just angry. I wanted to be better. I wanted to get up.

Now as I write this, I know I should have just been grateful that I was alive, but there was something about being stuck there in the ICU without knowing why, and not being able to talk, eat, or breathe on my own, that made me angrier than I had ever felt in my life. I was confronted with the dark part of myself. The part that does not feel grateful. The part that wants to control everything. The furious part.

Even more infuriating than the immobility, the giant breathing tube, the IVs, the nasogastric tube, or the not being able to communicate or understand what the heck was going on, was the hunger. It was painful. I was so hungry. I imagine the tube up my nose with the goopy formula being siphoned from the bag was providing the minimal calories that would keep me alive, and for that, I should have been thankful, but never underestimate the psychological power of eating and swallowing food.

Inside my head I was creative and clear. I knew I had my brain back and was ready to go out and use that new tumor-free gray matter to change myself and the world. My body, however, had different plans. I was so weak I couldn't move. I normally have an excessive amount of energy. I'm not even one to sit on the beach and stare at the water. I'm putting sunscreen on my superpale kids, doling out snacks, and running around finding buried flip-flops. Jim always says, "Would you relax? Sit down and take it easy!" But I explain to him that moving around relaxes me.

At home there were things to do. I had to go to Marre's room and make sure she was not on her phone while she was doing her homework. When Katie made slime, did she put down the plastic cutting boards so that the drips of glue wouldn't take the finish off the floor? I had to tell someone to put a pull-up on Patrick before bed because he still wets occasionally. I have a regimen of washing each room's bedding once a week, and the "safety pull-up" is essential to make sure we can stick to that schedule. Did anyone remember that the Xbox had to be locked up all week so Jack was not tempted to get on it? Whoever was babysitting today would have to remind Michael not to put the Legos in the Star Wars bin or the whole system would be out of whack. I had to plan this week's menu. What did we have in the fridge that might go bad if not used this week? My mind was spinning and I was stuck in the bed. There's no place for OCD in the ICU. As I lay there practically paralyzed, I had to come face-to-face with my demons. I was addicted to control, and I was in withdrawal.

Time is the longest distance between two places.

— Tennessee Williams

There are no doors or windows in the intensive care unit. When you are in the ICU, you have no sense of time. It's like Vegas but without the fun. Instead of the colorful whirring lights and the musical dings of the slot machines, there is the methodical beeping of the medical machinery with flashing numbers and graphs that you are tethered to by IVs and tubes, rather than an obsessive desire to win the jackpot.

In my normal life, and even right now, I am amazed at how quickly time passes. As I write this, I look up at the clock and an hour has gone by and I've barely written a page. I see my children and think, *Where did the years go?* on an almost daily basis. Have I spent enough one-on-one time with this child or that child? I'm one of those pain-in-the-butt people who say, "It's Christmas already? Didn't we have Christmas a couple of months ago? Where does the time go?" Well, now I know where it goes. It goes into the ICU, where it stands still.

I learned to tell time based on twelve-hour nursing shifts, so when a new name was written on the whiteboard, I knew that half a day had passed. The whiteboard on the wall was my main source of news and information. It was like a real-life Facebook post without the Russian bots. When the whiteboard came into focus, I could see my nurse's name, and a little bit into the nurse's personality. If the name was haphazardly scrawled, I knew I had a no-nonsense, couldn't-be-bothered nurse. If there was a neatly written name with a smiley face and a "Have a nice day" message, I knew I was dealing with a lunatic.

To entertain myself during these excruciatingly long hours, and to keep my mind off worrying about Jim and the kids, I would stare up at the tiny dots on the ceiling, which, after a while, I realized were actual blood flecks. I would create scenarios as if I were a blood spatter analyst at a grisly crime scene.

Scenarios:

- Sick of hearing his hospital roommate moaning in agony, an orthopedic patient waited for the room to clear before bludgeoning said roommate with his crutch. The spatter pattern would indicate that the murderer was a left-handed Caucasian man in his early thirties, with a torn right Achilles tendon.
- An unrealistically attractive woman complaining of stomach pains shocked the doctors when a snakelike alien burst out of her stomach, spraying blood on the walls and ceiling. X-Files agents, hell-bent on a cover-up to prevent panic in the civilian population, came in to scrub the scene clean of all evidence, but did not realize they missed a few flecks on the ceiling.

- A comedian's wife who recently had brain surgery experienced a sudden head explosion when she realized that she'd had brain surgery.

* * *

You know how you feel when you have to make a really important call and you get put on hold for an exorbitant amount of time? That's what the ICU was like for me, but without the groovy hold music.

It was unclear what strain of bacteria was behind the double-lung strep pneumonia. Therefore, I was put on a broad-spectrum antibiotic IV, which brought with it a host of other problems and ironically made me feel weak and queasy. The place where my head had been cut open was not painful at all and had been expertly reconstructed and reshaped with some form of synthetic putty or clay, sculpted to perfection by Dr. Bederson. The putty would bond to my skull and not require any plates or screws and hopefully not leave me with a weird bump. The scar went from behind the top of my left ear down my neck. My hair had been shaved off only in that one area. An extra courtesy by Dr. Bederson. I could hide the bald patch under the rest of my long hair. If my hair was in a ponytail, I'm sure I looked totally punk rock, but I couldn't see myself because I was not able to get up to look in a mirror. As an act of kindness and courtesy, no one brought one over to the bed so I could have a look. I could feel what I looked like. My face was slumped on one side with my left eye shut. However, I could open my eye with some effort, meaning that the nerve was not cut. I would regain my face. Eventually. But for now, external beauty was the least of my worries. It was all about survival.

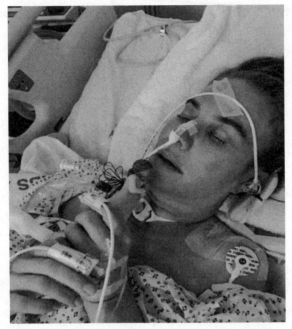

Whose idea was it to take this photo?

My time in the ICU wavered between periods of sharp perception and a total blur. I was getting sicker and sicker with the pneumonia, and there was no sign of it letting up. I remember being in and out of consciousness and waking up to see Jim and other loving, concerned family members at my side. I remember lots of uber-gurney trips down corridors and in and out of elevators, in and out of MRIs, which I now could sometimes sleep through. Though I do recall the first one with my new parasitic friend, the breathing tube, making me feel like I was suffocating. It's not like natural breathing. If you go against it, it feels like you can't get enough breath. In that confined coffin, the added element of the breathing tube made it a whole new horror. I understood why kids were not allowed in the ICU. I would never want them to see this. I was always the one to comfort my kids from their nightmares, not be the cause of them.

On the positive side, I prayed. I prayed like I'd never prayed before. I learned the power of meditative prayer. One time when I was in the tube, I went through an entire Rosary. It takes more than an hour. I know nuns who do it all the time, but as a mother of five with many symptoms of ADHD, I was lucky if I could get all the way through the Apostles' Creed at the top, which is sort of like the overture at the beginning of the Rosary. For you non-Catholics, the Rosary is a series of prayers normally prayed on the string of beads with the cross on the end that Madonna made mainstream in the '80s as a fashion accessory. It's a very holy spiritual tool to help you keep track of different prayers and the number of times you recite them in the meditation. You don't need the actual beads to say the prayers; they just help you keep your place. While having an MRI you can't move or count on your fingers, so I pictured each bead in my mind's eye.

The repetition and the visualization brought me to this deeper, mystical plane of peace. I never really understood meditation until I was near suffocation in an MRI coffin. I preferred to be in the MRI, alone with my peaceful meditation, than out of the MRI in the chaotic ICU. I hope you never have to be in pain like this, or know the terror of suffocation, but if you do, please remember what saved me. I feel like I got out so I could tell you: meditation was my Obi-Wan Kenobi. Okay, I broke the fourth wall again. That was awkward.

Chapter 12

NOTHING BY MOUTH

My brain tumor had been intertwined with my cranial nerves, six of which controlled an aspect of the swallowing function as well as the vocal cords. The nerve damage sustained because of the size of the tumor as well as the state the nerves were in at its removal made it impossible for me to speak or swallow. Anything that went down my throat could end up in my lungs, which was why I had developed the pneumonia. Therefore, the medical instructions for me included "Nothing by mouth." That meant nothing. No water, no toothpaste, *nothing*. Indefinitely. The hope was, with time, we could clear up my serious lung infection and, someday, with rigorous therapy, I could learn to swallow again. Meanwhile, nothing by mouth.

As I mentioned earlier, the way I was fed during this period was through something called nasogastric intubation, which is a medical process involving the insertion of a plastic tube up the nostril, through the nose, past the throat, and down into the stomach. This is not to be confused with the aforementioned tube for endotracheal intubation through my mouth, which ran down my throat into my trachea and was needed for breathing. These tubes were distinguished also from the IV tubes, which would mainline antibiotics and fluids. Basically, there were a lot of plastic tubes compensating for these basic functions that the brain stem was no longer capable of handling on its own. I don't remember getting any of these tubes installed, but suddenly they were there and I was attached to a bunch of machines.

The machine attached to the nasogastric tube was a digital box on an IV stand that held a clear bag of thick yellow-white gunk, which was pumped through the thin tube in my nose. Of course, I needed this gunk to survive, but that bag of gunk was the bane of my existence. It looked awful, and every time I woke up and saw it, I knew I couldn't eat yet.

Days went by. My sensations were "sick" or "empty." Rage and frustration would turn into self-pity and sorrow as I dreamed of a bowl of chicken noodle soup. And I'm not talking about "chicken soup for the soul." I'm talking actual chicken soup. Even a sip of water that I could pretend was chicken soup would do. Did I mention I couldn't have water? It was kind of like being locked in a medieval dungeon, except there, you get water. There was a little sponge on a stick that they used to "brush my teeth" that was lightly treated with either a mint or a coconut flavor, and I looked forward to this every day, just to taste something. I always had a suction tube in my mouth (the kind the dentist uses) to make sure no drop of liquid could find its way down to further exacerbate the lung infection.

To extinguish the negative feelings, I held on to the hope that tomorrow, the doctors would come in and exclaim, "Oh my

God, it's a miracle! Your vagus nerve has completely healed! Let's celebrate with Shake Shack!"

As many of you know, I'm not the person in my family who is normally consumed with thoughts of food, but under the circumstances, I became obsessed. Jim had canceled his tour so he could be in New York between home and the hospital. Instead of being thankful, I would whine and complain that I was starving and miserable and he would look at me helplessly and I would get even more frustrated. My logical mind was being overtaken by my ravenous id. Why couldn't the guy who loved to bring me food every time he'd come home help me this time? I realized I was conditioned to salivate like Pavlov's dog when I saw him, so now seeing him became torturous. But I also didn't want him to leave. I was increasingly jealous of Jim when he left the ICU. I pictured him walking out the door and making a bee-line for the glorious buffet at the cafeteria. I imagined him eating out of spite, muttering, "I'll show her!" between bites of an enormous cheeseburger dripping with condiments. I began to hate people who could eat, which was everyone. I burned inside with resentment. I know I previously claimed victory over my ICU suffering with my nirvana-like Rosary bliss, but come on, even nuns can eat! When it became too much for me to bear, I would remember the Rosary. There I would find peace. Then I would stop meditating, forget again, and seethe with bitterness and loathing. Without the Rosary, I was a hideous monster.

* * *

While the physical hunger was beyond bad, the underlying emotional hunger was unbearable. Remember, no kids were allowed in the ICU, so I felt actual pain longing for the touch of my children. The feelings of craving food and craving my children became so intertwined I was no longer able to distinguish one from the other. I feared that I would be so overwhelmed when I finally saw my kids that I might accidentally eat one of them. Jim would come in and tell me about all the friends and family who were sending dinners over while I was in the hospital. He described the big family meals with tons of food and the funny things the kids would say around the table: "Next time Mommy gets sick can we have this lasagna again?" I was hesitant to relate to Jim how difficult it was for me to hear about food for fear that he would stop sharing these precious moments. Patrick was reading already and could crack the code when Jim would spell something secret:

> **JIM:** The neighbors sent over some c-u-p-c-a-k-e-s. Should we save them?
> **PATRICK:** Cupcakes? Yes! I want cupcakes now!

He told me about how Weezie would always lose her glasses and Katie would find them on her head. My mom was now the one lying in their beds at night reading books and drifting off to sleep midsentence. Michael would pat her cheek so she could finish the bedtime story, though he was perfectly capable of reading himself. It sounded so familiar.

I felt like I was missing my life. I used to complain about waking up under a pile of five kids who individually came into our bed during the night. Now, all I wanted was a pile of five kids. The withdrawal from them was shocking to me. Lately, I'd spent so much of my time as a mother thinking, *If I could just get away from the* kids *for a little while, I could finally get some things done!* Now I was forced to be away from them, and my heart was broken. Maybe my oldest could come?

Jim reminded me that Marre was scheduled to go on an international trip with her school, and he was wondering if under the circumstances she should still go. It did not appear that I was getting out of the hospital anytime soon. I nodded vigorously. She was so looking forward to this major event, and we wanted to keep everything as normal as possible for them. Maybe Jim could talk to the ICU doctors to see if they could grant an exception to the "no kids in the ICU" rule for her to come in before her trip and say good-bye. Just a temporary good-bye. He said he'd see what they could do and then left to take care of all the things I couldn't. I felt empty, so I started talking to God: *Why did you allow this to happen? What does this all mean?*

Lying alone in the hospital, staring at the flecks on the ceiling , I thought about the life I'd been living. I'd already figured out over the past few years that I needed more time with my kids. I'd even made a big career move to make that happen. The main reason we decided not to do season 3 of *The Jim Gaffigan Show* was that it became apparent at a certain point that the television production schedule was going to keep both of us away from our family. Both parents were gone all the time. We knew we could do a great show, but we didn't want to make the choice between the show and raising our own children. We could look back on our lives and say, "We did ten seasons of a fantastic show, but we missed watching our kids grow up," or "We did a couple of seasons of a great show, and we have fantastic kids." The choice was clear. But in the year since this major decision, what had really changed? Perhaps the quantity of time but certainly not the quality. The simple act of moving my production office into our home did not stop me from failing to be truly present for my kids or Jim.

The separation I was experiencing from them now as a result of this medical disaster made me understand that at times I got so caught up in scheduling and running everywhere and trying to be a perfect mother, thinking, *I'm doing this all for the kids*, that I actually became overwhelmed and busy to the point that I wasn't really doing much for the kids at all. I'd been focusing on things I felt needed to be *accomplished* for them while I was missing important opportunities to really connect with them. To get to know their hearts, to enjoy the time we spent together. I guess I just went from being executive producer of a TV show to executive producer of the Gaffigan household, and I wasn't really experiencing the moments. Did Katie really need a printed list of how to clean up and organize her slime or should I just let her teach me how to make slime? I'd been squandering precious time with them. My efforts to make everything run like a tight ship weren't really making me, or probably them, happy. Who the heck really wants to live on such a tight ship? Going around the hamster wheel of schedules and cleaning and homework and grades and appointments was also sacrificing my own ability to have meaningful, soul-fulfilling time with my kids. How I'd been living affected my own personal happiness just as much as it did theirs. And Jim's. Perhaps I'd overcomplicated things so much, now that Jim was thrust into taking over for me *and* dealing with all the medical stuff, I'd made things unmanageable.

Many times over the years I'd planned a magnificent schedule to make sure everything got done, everyone got fed, and everything stayed relatively clean. Jim would come home from a few days away with a bag of trinkets for the kids and announce, "Who wants to go to a movie?" Instead of being overjoyed that their daddy was home and wanting to spontaneously do something fun, I would put a halt to any new plans and say, "Wait! You can't just come in and change everything. Dinner is at six! Where are we going to put that bag of junk? They have baths and homework!" Had I been killing the joy instead of being a source of it? Now that I was away, I wasn't missing the days when all their schedules worked out perfectly and the house was spotless, but rather Katie writing "if you please" in a letter to Santa Claus, Patrick asking for his "uncle-brella" when it was raining, putting a Band-Aid on Michael's boo-boo and having him sincerely tell me I made it feel better. I sensed tears welling in my eyes and running sideways out the corners onto the flat hospital pillow. *God, I'm sorry, please let me survive this. I can change.*

I'm sure God spoke to me in the ICU. This is not "I had the best chocolate cake and God spoke to me" language. Rather, it's "I'm so positive God spoke to me that I'm putting it in my book even though you might think me insane" language. God said, *What are you worried about? Of course you are getting out, silly ye of little faith! Team Gaffigan will be restored. You will be completely healed in body, but you must work to heal your own spirit. Let go of your ego. You are not, nor will you ever be, perfect. Meanwhile, I have some personal commandments, tailored just for you:*

I. Tell Jim and your children you love them every day.
II. Admit when you are wrong.
III. Take time to give each your undivided attention.
IV. Praise their strengths and be patient with their weaknesses as you guide them.

V.   Explore their worlds and let them into your world.

VI. Teach them to serve others.

VII. Remember that people are more valuable than accomplishments.

In this way thou shalt not let thy children grow up to be jerks, nor lead thy husband to be hopping mad at thee. Those weren't the exact words, but you get the idea. Pare down the BS on the to-do list and make room for the meaningful. A "must-do" list. On it. Now I needed another chance. I needed to get out of there. I needed to get up! I had some life-changing to do! But at the time of this epiphany I was really sick, so I put off the commandments for a while. *Sorry, God.*

Chapter 13

JOE

After a week of lying in bed, we had a physical therapist come in to help me sit up, stand, and, eventually with assistance, walk. It was so excruciatingly difficult to do these simple things, but I knew that the harder I tried, the faster I could get the hell out of there (and eat, and see my kids, and avoid confusing the two), so after several failed attempts, assisted by a physical therapist and a walker, I slowly rose and emerged from my cell. I ventured out into the hall of the ICU and saw the picture hanging on the wall (shown on the next page).

Saliva began to pour out of my mouth. I was attached to the IV, but the suction tube was back in the room. Drool was running down the front of my gown. Whose idea was it to hang a giant photo of succulent fruit in the ICU hallway? Adolf Hitler?

* * *

The nurses were busy. It's a chaotic whirlwind in the ICU. You get your vitals taken every hour, including overnight, so

I finally understand "still life."

there's not a lot of sleeping. When you do try to sleep between these night visits, the sounds are surreal. Other patients were always moaning and crying out in agony. I remember thinking, *What is happening to them, and am I next?* The amount of equipment that was dropped at all hours of the night in the ICU was frightening. It always sounded as if the Three Stooges were in the next room, knocking over instruments and heavy objects. My self-entertainment during this time was trying to picture each item that was dropped. (*BANG!*) *Was that an automated external defibrillator?* (*CRASH!*) *A crash cart?*

And there were no doors, no privacy, just people constantly coming in and out, checking machines and vitals. There was not a lot of eye contact, and it seemed as if the machines were getting a closer look than the patient. I started to feel like I was no longer human. There was always a nurse there when I didn't want a nurse, and never a nurse there when I wanted a nurse. I tried not to complain because it was like the TSA: you might have the instinct to be frustrated with the random search, but you can't be too difficult or you will miss your flight.

I was a difficult patient. I didn't try to be, but I just was. As a person who is used to being in control of her own environment, being immobile in a bed was another circle of hell in Dante's Inferno. If I would have been running the place, each patient would have their own concierge. So, God sent me Joe.

Joe was a head nurse in the ICU. From the second he walked into the room, I knew he was the alpha dog. The top guy. The way he walked, the way he spoke to people, the way he handled everything with precision and skill, I knew he was in charge. I decided he was my nurse. I chose him. He didn't know it, but he was my guy. My knight in shining scrubs. Joe was kind, but sarcastic and strong. He didn't put up with any of my unrealistic demands, like noise-canceling headphones, but I could tell he cared. He met me halfway. It was tough love. I always liked guys who played hard to get. I couldn't speak yet, but Joe understood my made-up sign language, and at the time, all I wanted was to be understood. Joe always knew what I was getting at, whether he agreed with me or not.

* * *

Even though there was no infection, and therefore no pain at the site of the surgery, my head was turned to the side, non-incision side down for days on end, so as not to irritate the healing wound. This position caused intense pain and stiffness in my neck. It was the type of pain that brings hot tears to the eyes when you try to move, but you know that moving is the only way to end the stiffness, so you're stuck in a catch-22. The mild painkillers added to my IV did nothing. It was not a good idea for me to take any kind of morphine or sedative because of my difficulty breathing. I was actively involved in not dying. Staying alive was hard work and I needed to be all there.

I wanted a heating pad to put on my neck to alleviate some of the excruciating neck cramping. "We don't have that," I recall Joe saying with enormous attitude and maybe an eye roll, as if I were asking for a glass of champagne and a shiatsu treatment. Yet the next time he entered, Joe put wet towels in the microwave and then wrapped them around my neck. It was heaven.

I learned to complain without words. Even though I couldn't really talk, I employed exaggerated nonverbal communication in the style of Kabuki theater: When I was angry about something, I would open my eyes (or I should say, my *eye*) wide and look at Jim, and he would say, "Look, Jeannie is yelling at me!" and I would be frustrated. We had spent the last fifteen years talking to each other about anything and everything, and this recovery was putting a huge strain on our communication skills. Jim felt helpless about my suffering, and I apparently guilt-tripped him with my tortured glares every step of the way. Joe seemed to understand what I was getting at, so Jim was happy to step aside and abdicate his role as "Jeannie's sole caregiver" to my new ICU husband, Joe. I missed having normal interactions with Jim, but the "Jeannie can't speak" guessing games weren't really working out for us. There was a lot of tension between Jim and me.

Since I couldn't speak, my brother Paul brought me a clipboard where I could write notes with a black Sharpie, my writing instrument of choice. Finally, I could communicate my needs to Jim without hideous facial expressions. With great effort, I would scrawl out a page of detailed instructions and eagerly show it to Jim, or whoever was unlucky enough to be on that shift. I soon discovered that due to my vision, balance, and coordination issues, no one could read my writing. At one point, in frustration, I threw the clipboard across the room. A C-shaped chunk broke off the plastic clipboard. When Paul returned, for a moment he thought I had taken a bite out of it.

"No, she threw it," remarked a frustrated Jim.

"Don't do that anymore, Jeannie," said good old Paul.

I perceived losing my voice as similar to a pianist losing the use of his hands or a marathon runner being confined to a wheel-chair. I wasn't a singer, but I used my voice for everything, not the least of which was yelling at Jim and the kids. I was a direc-tor, and you need to speak to be a director. Also, as a writer, I needed my voice. Jim and I had long conversations about com-edy almost every night. Part of our process of writing was saying the jokes out loud. How was I going to write with Jim anymore? We talked about the kids, discussing all the intimate details of their emotional, social, and academic lives. We talked to each other about our hopes and dreams for the future. We argued and made up. I told long, elaborate stories to our kids when they couldn't sleep at night. Each of them had a character in a story that they knew was them, except the characters lived in a castle a long time ago and far, far away. They were princes and prin-cesses with names like Stone, Adoria, Nala, Michaelangelo, and Bartrick. (I was less creative with the younger ones.) They had magical powers and went on adventures with their flying horses. Who else could tell them these stories? I used to take my voice for granted and now it was gone. I was lost without it. I was told it would come back, just as the ability to swallow would come back, but no one could give me a time, a goal to reach, and I couldn't even throw the clipboard anymore.

Joe was the only one who could understand my silent rav-ings. He was a skilled lip-reader. He always knew what I was getting at. I would look pleadingly at Joe and mouth-beg to take a shower, which of course I couldn't. He reluctantly asked me if I wanted my hair washed, and I tried to nod. Affirmative. He seemed less than thrilled with the response. It was a very busy ICU, but I didn't care about anything other than my own comfort, which was an utterly new feeling for me. The thought of getting my greasy hair with dried blood patches in it *washed* was the bit of cheese this lab rat needed for the motivation to run through the maze of my horrible day.

At one point before this, during one of the days, hours, or agonizingly long minutes in the ICU, Leslie had come by and said, "Let's do something about that hair!" She got a brush and a hair tie from God knows where and went to work on the knots. I remember watching the shining whimsical stone with a sunburst around her neck dangling and dancing while she worked on gathering my matted tresses away from my bandage into a cute side pony. I'd remembered it from our first meeting. Looking at her necklace was the most entertainment I'd had thus far. Seeing something unique and interesting instead of the depressing surroundings that had become my world was the highlight of my day. Because I was so out of it at the time, I was more grateful for that necklace than for the fact that Les-lie, probably in the middle of coordinating and assisting in ten other brain surgeries, would take the initiative to come into the ICU to "do something about that hair!" The important thing about that moment was that it stood as the first time since I'd woke up from surgery that I started to feel something that could be described as gratitude. In my barely conscious state I'd experienced being grateful for the shiny object instead of

Leslie's compassionate sacrifice, but I was so thankful. My black, resentful heart grew a little bit. Flickering with a tiny spark of light.

Like most good things, that feeling was quickly corrupted. After getting that level of attention and service, I now felt entitled to ask Joe to be my personal beautician when he had a break from keeping other people alive. I was more grateful, but still selfish. I wanted my hair washed.

When Joe finally entered my room for this highly anticipated event, he opened a packet of "dry hair wash" and put a cap over my head. There was some kind of itchy powder in the cap that Joe unenthusiastically massaged into my scalp. I don't know if the powder was itchy or my scalp was itchy, but the experience did not live up to my expectations even slightly. I guess I envisioned an exquisite roman bath fit for a queen, or at least *water*. Regardless, I must have let Joe know it was kind of a letdown because I didn't come out as appreciative as I should have after begging him all day for the coif service. Even in my compromised state, I was perceptive enough to figure out that Joe, and probably all the other nurses, thought of me as high-maintenance. Not so much as a smack-my-assistant-with-a-cell-phone diva, but more like a crabby old lady who begged for attention and then just complained when she got it.

Once when he was changing my IV, he extended my arm and looked at me and said, "You got good veins, I'll give you that." That backhanded compliment was the nicest thing he'd ever said to me, and it made my day. He noticed my good veins!

Really? I bet you say that to all the girls! If I had been in seventh grade, I would have doodled that phrase in my math notebook for hours with "Joe" written in bubble letters surrounded by little hearts.

Mount Sinai Department of Critical Care

♡ Joe ♡

Chapter 14

A FAMILY AFFAIR

Jim was torn. He knew that the kids needed him at home more than ever. He knew that I needed him at the hospital. Until this point he had not yet mastered the art of bilocation, something that being a mother of five had forced me to learn long ago. But somehow Jim figured out how to navigate this difficult path. He would come in and sit next to me on a chair and tell me everything was under control. I couldn't do much else besides nod weakly. Jim would describe the plans for the week and who was doing what. He never expressed any frustration to me; he only gave me reports on the action being taken to cover all the bases. If he was feeling overwhelmed, he hid it because I was in such a fragile state.

Occasionally he would ask me if I approved of a decision because that's the way we always figured things out, but during this time I would just indicate my deferral to him. It was not the time for me to micromanage, though it was once one of my favorite pastimes. This was the first time in my life I'd had to let go, and Jim was a champion. He rallied the entire family, my parents and eight siblings, into action. If they were out of town, he flew them in. It was all hands on deck. Jim created a schedule so that somebody was always at the hospital advocating for me and just being there, and there was constantly a family member in my home so my children could hopefully avoid a future spent in therapy, bitching about their abandonment issues. I missed them terribly, but there was nothing I could do. I couldn't go home and they couldn't come to me. Jim's idea was the perfect solution to make sure the kids were all right.

I saw my husband in a totally different light as he took over my job as commanding general of the Gaffigan family. I imagined him as Winston Churchill in the war room, masterminding complex strategies to cover all territories. And he was winning the war. Every time I woke up (which was several times a day since sleep was still an elusive concept), there would be a familiar face. I was also comforted by the thought that the atmosphere in our apartment had transformed into a holiday-like haven, with Grandma and aunts and uncles sleeping on couches and making pancakes in the morning—only this time, unbeknownst to them, the holiday-like atmosphere was to compensate for Mom being near death in the hospital. Just a spoonful of syrup helps the missing mommy go down. And there were other helpers at home. A lot of helpers. To cover the many hats I wear in the Gaffigan household, it became necessary to hire a team of people just to keep everything going. Along with my family staying there, there were three housekeepers, five babysitters, two assistants, and a partridge in a pear tree. It was like *Downton Abbey*, without the fancy clothes and English accents. Anyone who does not appreciate their mom should take down her job description and count the people it takes to fill it.

Jim would painstakingly compile everyone's availability to go up to Mount Sinai and assign times for each sibling to be at the hospital. He referred to this schedule as their "shifts." I was not a big fan of this terminology. Below is an actual example of "The Shift Schedule":

Jeannie Advocate at Mt. Sinai—April 23–28

(O.N. = overnight shift)

MONDAY

Jim did Sun O.N.

7–Noon	Paul
12–5	Pat
5–10:30	Jim
10:30–7am	Liz

TUESDAY

Liz did Mon O.N.

7–Noon	Vin
12–5	Jim
5–10:30	Paul
10:30–7am	Pat

WEDNESDAY

Pat did Tues O.N.

7–Noon	Liz
12–5	Jim

| 5–10:30 | Paul |
| 10:30–7am | Vin |

THURSDAY

Vin did Wed O.N.

7–Noon	Liz
12–5	Pat
5–10:30	Paul
10:30–7am	Jim

FRIDAY

Jim did Thu O.N.

7–Noon	Vin
12–5	Pat
5–10:30	Liz
10:30–7am	Paul

Jim took great care to plan ahead, making sure that the overnight shifts were balanced, noting who had "done" the last "O.N." so no one had to spend two consecutive nights in the ICU, which was really smart, because—trust me—it sucked. I had the overnight shift every night.

My parents and my siblings all flocked to my side. They left their jobs, their own families, their own illnesses, just to come and take care of me. I initially felt guilty and embarrassed about this but they empathetically assured me that everything on their end could wait. All bad feelings about disrupting their lives diminished when Jim would report to me how happy the kids were. They made a huge sacrifice. I remember hearing that one night when Jim was on the overnight "shift" with me, my brother and sister-in-law were sleeping over, in our bed. One of the kids came in in the middle of the night and threw up on them. When I heard about this I felt horrible, but I also laughed. At least there was someone there to throw up on. I also secretly worried about how they cleaned it up because, and I don't mean to brag, I am an expert. I can't believe I was longing to clean up vomit in the wee hours of the night.

The heroism of my family amazed me. Immediately after I landed in the ICU my mother, who is terrified of flying on planes, went straight to the airport and essentially moved in with her grandchildren to be the next best thing to, and probably even better than, their mother. My brother Vincent, who runs a food community center that helps thousands of people get back on their feet, put the reins in the hands of his interns and came straight to New York. My sister Felicia, who works full-time and has two school-age kids, came to the hospital to be with me even though she was sick herself (not contagious). My sister Michelle, who is the director of a child care advocacy organization in Washington, DC, left her own two kids in child care and drove for hours to New York for "weekends with Shelly," where she would visit me in the hospital and sleep at my apartment. The first time Michelle came into my hospital room, I was so happy to see her and I attempted a smile. I must have looked pretty hideous because she burst into tears at the sight of me. She then presented me with a "gift," a huge bag of adult diapers. I mean it was Costco size. The whole scene was hilarious and heartbreaking at the same time. I didn't use the diapers, but it was probably the best gift I'd received in my entire life. What an amazing gesture of sisterly love. Michelle was born when I was in middle school, so when she was a baby, I probably had actually changed *her* diapers. Circle of diapers.

While I was a teenager living in the house with all my brothers and sisters, I took my role as the eldest very seriously. The only way I knew how to express love to them was by being overbearing. I dressed them up, put on shows with them, and told them what to do every chance I had. I'm sure they all resented it, especially since my mother had a very laid-back style of parenting, and I was like Joan Crawford in *Mommie Dearest* but with the maturity of a thirteen-year-old. Much like the sudden role reversal that was occurring in my relationship with Jim, my younger siblings, who probably each had a memory of me cutting their hair, taking them for ice cream, or bossing them around (maybe all at the same time), were now at my side as *my* advocates and caretakers. Being incapacitated, I could observe them in a way I never had before and see what truly amazing people they'd all become. I mean, I knew they were amazing, but I saw qualities in them that were new to me, though I'd known them their entire lives. I also discovered that I'd been a closet "mom-ist." Let me explain.

> Mom-ist: (n) A person who believes that their identity as a parent makes them a superior person to a nonparent.

In ordinary times, the sisters I had the closest bond with were, frankly, the ones who also had kids. In my exclusive mom-bubble, I'd decided there was a secret understanding between mothers that excluded those who weren't. I had many an exasperated phone conversation with my sisters who are moms, baffled by the antics of our non-kid-having siblings. I naively assumed that the experience of having a baby and being a primary caregiver would be a necessary requirement for someone taking care of a sick person in the hospital. Was I wrong. Here is just a sampling of what four of my non-kid-having siblings did for me in the hospital that changed my heart and mind, and enlightened me to shed my backward, mom-ist's ideology.

A Case Study in Anti-Mom-ism: Jeannie's Siblings with No Kids

Patrick is my youngest brother. I remember reading to him when he was a baby and forcing him to be in my plays when he was a cranky preteen. I took care of him the only way a smothering eldest sister can. He recently married an astonishingly beautiful woman who looks like if the sun rose over a perfect Iowa cornfield and became a human, and she has an enormous heart to match. Emilea is smart, funny, and a natural-born caregiver. Patrick definitely must have been looking for a wife with similar qualities to his sisters', particularly the eldest. She takes great care of him and I imagine he is great at, well, letting her. Out of my three brothers, I always saw him as the "tough guy" and never thought he had a nurturing side. That isn't to say he's not sweet and warm and wonderful when he wants to be, but let's just say he once babysat my pet turtle, and the turtle died. Patrick does his own thing and is the type who comes to family events when he wants to, but he isn't governed by any sense of obligation. So when he was there in the hospital, I knew he wanted to be. And he took care of me. Really good care. He wasn't standing around awkwardly asking if anyone wanted a cup of coffee from downstairs. He was like an angel of mercy. I would wake up to find Patrick at the end of my bed, massaging my dry feet with lavender-scented lotion. Yes, my feet. Was this the Holy Thursday callback I'd been waiting for? On his phone, he would play a recording of an Irish priest reciting the Rosary intercut with a beautiful voice singing about peace and love. He was patient with my complaints and took active measures to comfort me. During these times with Patrick, I was transported. Patrick was my shaman of the ICU and he had the peyote. Under Patrick's surly exterior existed a selfless, gentle saint with extraordinary soothing skills—a talent I could learn a lot from as a mother. My illness showed me the gift he has in a way nothing else could have.

*　　*　　*

Paul is my oldest brother. I have always thought of him as self-sufficient, not necessarily a nurturer, although I don't think his dog has any complaints. From childhood, Paul was always deeply immersed in a book, painstakingly drawing wildly imaginative pictures or writing pages and pages of fantastical stories. As an adult, he blossomed in his career by channeling his talent into writing graphic novels and found an outlet for his quiet, biting wit as a cartoonist for the *New Yorker* magazine. I've always admired him, loved him, and been entertained by him, but prior to my sentence of being trapped in my body, I never realized how much I needed Paul. I obviously knew he was an intellectual, but when he came to visit me I saw into the soul of his intellect. Sounds like an oxymoron, but stay with me here. In the hospital, Paul was the caregiver for my mind. He knew instinctively that though I couldn't communicate, my thoughts were racing and needed some TLC. He always came in for his "shift" with the latest podcast to help me pass the excruciating time: the true crime mysteries that would draw us in deeper and deeper and then amount to no answers. The *S-Town* one that sucked me in and then got so incredibly depressing that I tried to smother his iPhone with a pillow. I loved the *Missing Richard Simmons* one so much. I listened to each episode expecting a dramatic explanation for what had happened to him and why he had disappeared, but in the end it turned out that he got tired of being everyone's self-help guru and just wanted to be alone. Richard only desired some privacy, and here I was stalking him in his podcast. Sorry, Richard. But thanks for making my life in the hospital better. You helped me, and you didn't even have to break a sweat to the oldies.

Paul read books and articles out loud to me as he sat in the room in business clothes before he would go to work. He sacrificed his time for me to keep my mind engaged. "Use it or lose it." He was rubbing lotion on my dry brain. His intellectual generosity shone in a way that I'd never seen before. He knew that a mind is a terrible thing to waste away in the ICU.

*   *   *

My sister Maria is a licensed midwife, massage therapist, herbalist, and practitioner of acupuncture. It was her skills as a doula, however, that made her perfect for me in this situation. A doula is a woman trained to assist another woman during childbirth. Having birthed five kids, I could draw many parallels between what I was going through and a traumatic childbirth experience, but without the reward of a happy baby at the end. Maria is an incredible support person, but she also has been known to go rogue in her methodology. When I was nine months plus pregnant with Michael, I was told by my ob/gyn that if I went two weeks over the due date, I would have to go in for an induction. I was terrified of hospitals (ironic,

I know) and beside myself, having tried all the natural ways rumored to bring on labor, so I called Maria and begged her to help. She told me to drink some castor oil. I was skeptical so I WebMD'ed it and basically what I read was, "Don't *ever* drink castor oil!" But Maria told me to ignore the castor oil haters and just drink a little. It was agonizing, but it worked. The effect that horrible castor oil has as it rips through the body is like when you use jumper cables on a dead car battery. Michael shot out like a bullet. I wanted to thank her and kill her at the same time.

After my brain surgery, she was again at my side, but this time in a strict hospital setting with lots of rules against things like drinking castor oil. She had many critiques concerning the ways I was being cared for, such as the highly artificial ingredients in the formula used for my nasogastric feedings, but there was absolutely nothing she could do to change it. She'd stand when the nurses came in to pour a can of formula into my feeding machine.

"Hi, can my sister have a formula without whey by-products in it? I think it's causing a lot of phlegm and exacerbating the pneumonia." The nurse would look at her like she was crazy.

"You'd have to speak to her doctor about that."

"Gladly. Is there maybe a nutritionist I could contact?"

"You'd have to speak to her doctor about that."

As I lay there observing Maria, what I saw in her was smoldering anger at the many contradictions of Western medicine. She appreciated and recognized that special something that all the nurses or anyone who works in an ICU has, and she felt a connection and camaraderie with my hospital caregivers. It was the rules that she couldn't stomach. I considered getting her a T-shirt that read "F the FDA." I saw in her a tortured rebel who longed to throw regulation to the wind and stick needles into all the acupoints of the conventional medical system to purge the big pharma parasites. She was angry *for* me. I felt validated.

* * *

My youngest sister, Lizzy, is the nonconformist of the family. The Divergent. She is the type who would change her favorite color just to disagree with me. Being the youngest of nine children, Lizzy spent her life being parented and advised by all of us ad nauseam. As a result, you just can't tell her what to do. But in the hospital, she turned out to be the most empathetic and understanding of what I was going through.

Whereas some visitors would sit at a seven-foot distance from my bed, Lizzy was never more than seven inches away from me at all times. When she was leaving, she would tell me when she was coming back and ask me if I had any special requests.

"Gin and tonics and chocolate ice cream?" I would whisper.

She'd laugh. "Besides that." Though I couldn't see myself, I was incredibly annoyed by the feeling of tiny prickly hairs between my eyebrows.

"Tweezers?" I acted out plucking.

"You got it!" she said. The next time she came, she brought tweezers and cleaned up my eyebrows, an incredible act of mercy. Think about it, ladies. You're lying there in a bed without a mirror for weeks and you start to look like Eddie Munster. I was elated. Next to my bed, there was a digital meter that showed my oxygen levels. Most people walk around easily with levels of 98 or 99, but due to the pneumonia I was struggling in the 80s—this was a somewhat dangerous level. When Lizzy tweezed me, my oxygen levels would shoot up. Someone should do a study on that: "Pulmonology and the Art of Tweezing."

Sometimes I would get frustrated with the nurses if they went to get something for me and never came back. When I whined, some of my visitors would (rightly) defend the nurses: "They are busy!" But Lizzy would have my back and go find them. If one of my other family members complained about a chair being uncomfortable while I was lying there gasping for breath with purple IV bruises all over my arms, I would shoot Lizzy a look and she would feel my pain. It became funny. If someone was helping me walk and they had their hand on my back in an attempt to steady me but were inadvertently pushing me along, Lizzy would gently intervene. She was the only one I could tell if someone came to visit and they smelled like coffee breath or unshowered, and she wouldn't judge me as an ingrate. She was always holding my hand. I recall seeing her face close to mine when I woke up. Her eyes filled with compassion. "Sick of it," she would say, speaking for me because I couldn't.

Growing up, when my exhausted, overwhelmed mom would get really mad at us for running wild or being disobedient, she would yell, "That's it! Go to your room!" Then, as she was walking away, she would mutter half under her breath, "Sick of it!" This became a catchphrase among us siblings. All we needed to do was say or text "Sick of it!" to each other, and no one asked any questions, we just understood. It was an inside joke. A way to process frustration and also have fun. It was a secret code language that only siblings can understand. With

"Sick of it!" came volumes of history and memories. In those moments in the ICU, Lizzy looking at me with such compassion in her eyes and saying "Sick of it" was my morphine.

But it wasn't always a lovefest in the room. Anyone who has been in a similar situation knows that family members who come to the hospital to help are unique in that they don't have to pretend to act polite. Sure, the first time they see you they're shocked and give you the same fifteen minutes of celebrity that they did on your wedding day or when your first child was born. After that, it doesn't take long for familiar relational interactions to resume. You know how it is when you all reunite for a holiday and everything is great and then mid-meal you regress into seven-year-olds: "Mom, Felicia took the last Coke!" After a few days in the hospital with my siblings, we were back to the same old patterns: Me bossing everyone around, and them not taking it. Me getting irritated by little things, and them being oblivious. But they were *there*, so I really couldn't criticize them without seeming like an ingrate. Except I could complain to Lizzy.

Even though I was usually acting like a cranky, entitled baby, Lizzy was my confidante and understood my reactions to some of the other family members. We laughed about it. I couldn't actually make any noise, but I was laughing. It was therapeutic. Together we created a list of dos and don'ts specific to my family in the hospital. It helped me cope. She wrote it all down. I made her promise that in the event of my untimely demise, she would keep it classified. But I got out, so here it is:

Jeannie's Rules for Jeannie's Family Members Helping in the Hospital

DOs and DON'Ts List

- DON'T talk about delicious food if patient can't eat.
- DO harass nurses when they are hiding.
- DO arrange room and organize personal property since the patient can't move.
- DO declutter room PLEASE! Don't leave your crap all over.
- DO bring lip balm, lotion, mouthwash, or moisturizer.
- DO read stories and play podcasts.
- DON'T say, "It's not so bad."
- DON'T defend the nurses or doctors if your loved one is suffering.
- DON'T call your visits "shifts."
- DO bring a brush and tweezers. Tweezing makes oxygen levels go up.
- DON'T silently check your email for hours.
- DO give lots of touches and hugs.
- DON'T leave open snacks in room when patient can't eat.
- DO brush your own teeth.
- Yes! DO smell good.
- DO bring meditation recordings.
- DO massage feet.
- DON'T massage site of wound.
- When the patient walks, DON'T push them.
- DON'T complain about the chair in the hospital being uncomfortable.

- DON'T complain about not getting enough sleep.
- DON'T complain about anything.
- DO express empathy.
- DO be patient with the patient (it's not about your feelings).
- DO organize cards people have sent.
- DO read cards out loud.
- DO reach out to people who have sent cards on behalf of patient. Thank them. And tell them patient enjoyed hearing them.
- DON'T bring flowers into ICU; give them to the nurses' station.

Jeannie's Rules for Patients (Herself)

- DO love your big family and be kind to them when you are healthy. They will save you when you are sick.
- DON'T make a rules list about your family and publish it in a book.
- DON'T be a mom-ist. Get woke.

Chapter 15

GUESS WHO'S COMING TO THE HOSPITAL

Joking about my family's "shifts" aside, other people come to the hospital just to see you. There's no Emily Post–style etiquette book for how to handle people visiting, but if there were, I imagine it would go something like this:

HOW TO HOST AN (IV) COCKTAIL PARTY

When you welcome people to visit in the ICU, it is imperative for a proper hostess to gently insist that her husband, or her hospital husband, meet the guests at the curtain. A visitor lingering in the doorway for too long could make all present most uncomfortable. A polite greeting would include offering a paper cup of lukewarm tap water and a pump of hand sanitizer from the wall dispenser. Should the guest require two pumps, though it is not standard, graciously allow the second pump in order to dissuade talk of your being stingy with the antibacterials. Before the host escorts your visitor or visitors to your bedside, he should announce each guest by their formal name, for example, "Mr. and Mrs. Eric P. Vitale of the Grand Street Vitale family." After proper introductions are made and the guest has been greeted with a smile, promptly encourage your husband to exit the room charmingly, excusing himself for a much-needed constitutional to "stretch his legs." Husbands are dear creatures, but their tendency toward small talk is not in good form and can quickly render the atmosphere inelegant. Additionally, all successful hostesses will be sure that their gown has been properly closed in the back, to avoid causing a moment's discomfort for their honored guests. Petite, feminine bows are preferable to knots. One wouldn't want their visitor to think, even for an instant, "How is she going to get those knots undone when her gown becomes soaked with drool?" It is uncouth to promote these sort of thoughts when you are hosting. At even the most worthwhile IV cocktail party, it is inevitable that events could go awry and result in a spill, but you must never lose your aplomb. The best thing to do in this situation is to raise one's hand, preferably the one bearing the elegant hospital bracelet (never the one with the unsightly tube inserted), and point toward the entrance as if something exciting is happening outside the room. While your guest looks away, pull a clean blanket or nearby extra gown over the spill, and then pretend to go to sleep and the visitor will eventually leave.

* * *

Visiting hospitals is weird. It used to be a standard thing to visit people at the hospital after they gave birth. You would go see the new mother, congratulate her with a bouquet of cheery flowers, stop by the nursery window and gush about how cute the baby was, twelfth from the left in the Plexiglas bassinet. These days if you have your baby in a hospital, you are usually discharged before anyone can figure out what room you're in. There aren't many "happy" hospital visits left in the world. If you're going to the hospital to see someone, it normally means that it sucks to be them. It's always an awkward situation, but everyone who makes the trip to the hospital is awesome, whether you want to see them or not.

Guests Who Are Told Not to Come but Come Anyway

Tony is an old friend of ours whom we hadn't seen in years. I was in a sketch group with him when I met Jim and we were really close. He moved to Los Angeles many years earlier and we'd kept in touch, but you know, like Christmas card touch. Tony just happened to be in town the day I had surgery, and he contacted Jim out of the blue. Jim told him it was a bad time because I was undergoing brain surgery. Since Jim is a comedian, Tony's reaction was something like, "If you don't want to see me, you can come up with a better excuse than that!" When Jim explained seriously that he was at the hospital and I was undergoing brain surgery, Tony offered to come and sit with him in the hospital cafeteria. Jim politely but adamantly refused. This was a very private time for him, and he preferred to be alone. Jim is not one to discuss very personal matters with others; he prefers to keep things casual. He's not great at processing emotions and usually deals with uncomfortable conversations in one of two ways: by either eating something or taking a nap. About an hour later, the friend showed up. Luckily in the cafeteria. I would've loved to have been a fly on the wall during that meeting.

"So . . . what's been up with you lately? Anything new?"

"Not really. My team didn't make the playoffs, and my wife's upstairs having brain surgery . . ." (bites into a donut).

The irony is that as much as Jim wanted to be alone, it was good for him to talk to someone. Tony is gentle and kind and selfless, and Jim told me later that having him around at that critical time ended up helping so much. Normally I pride myself on being a sounding board and provider of snacks for Jim, so it was nice to have someone do this for me while I was busy having my head cut open. Thanks for ignoring Jim's wishes, Tony.

Guests Who Come Uninvited

During one of the first blurry days in the ICU, I remember opening my eyes and seeing Ms. Alvar, the beloved head of the school my daughters attend. She was standing in front of my bed. It was so odd to see her in this situation instead of behind a podium addressing a packed auditorium of enraptured parents. But yet, I was not surprised. This is the type of woman who is the first person at the scene whenever something goes wrong. It's just in her nature. When a tragedy occurs, it's an awkward time for friends and acquaintances. We don't know if we should call, visit, or what the appropriate behavior is. The people who are closest are allowed in. They're expected. Everyone else is unsure what to do. But Ms. Alvar didn't ask if she made the cut; she just came. I don't even know how she got by the front desk. But she carries herself with such dignity and authority, they probably thought she was the owner of the hospital. Note: Recently she was hospitalized and I tried to do the same thing in return, but her family wouldn't let me in. I guess I didn't make the cut.

Invited Guests

Then there are other friends who ask to come, and you want them there. These are the folks you need on your immediate friends list if anything ever goes wrong in your life. The smart people who look at the big picture in all situations. They come bearing gifts. Not sweet but useless get-well gifts that they purchased five minutes before at the gift shop, but essential supplies like snacks for the round-the-clock family members, lotions for dried skin, and tons of bottled water. You want these people in your group during the zombie apocalypse. Yes, I'm talking about the Fitzpatricks.

Those Who Don't Come

These people can't be called guests; rather, they're nonguests, because they don't come at all. Most folks don't want to visit you in the hospital. And who can blame them? Back in the day they used to just put sick and disabled people on a boat and send them off to sea: "Not my problem anymore!" Truthfully, you don't want a ton of visitors. It's not like you want to run a reception line. It's not a meet and greet after a show. It's exhausting to have visitors anywhere, but particularly in the ICU.

Funny People Help You Heal

Due to the wild and unpredictable schedule, and the fact that Jim needed to be around our apartment with the kids during the nonschool hours, the two of us were somewhat isolated from each other during the longer stretch of my hospital stay. I had taken for granted the fact that I was married to a funny person, and I missed the constant source of humor I was accustomed to. Little moments like when I would be watching one of those bad kids movies with a great soundtrack with the family and Jim would get up in front of the screen and start doing a ridiculous dance. I wished someone would come in and do a ridiculous dance in front of the IV monitor. This new, serious, overwhelmed Jim had not cracked one joke since I'd gone in for surgery. Due to the weight of the situation, it seemed hard for Jim to be funny, which was normally his go-to when things got bad. He'd even come up with a whole comedy routine the time we completely totaled a car. Through the years, Jim's joking in the face of adversity had been comforting and had helped me maintain equilibrium. Now I felt scared and imbalanced, and this time not from high-heeled shoes.

Would Jim ever be the same? The thought that this catastrophe might have stifled the funny man filled me with sorrow. Through the years we'd gotten many letters from people who were going through enormous suffering: a serious diagnosis of an illness or even the passing of a loved one. The letters expressed how they'd seen Jim on television, or gone to a show, and the comedy was so healing for them. They would be filled with such gratitude and often would state some form of *"It was the first time I'd laughed since _____. It meant so much."* I'd be so proud of Jim and thankful that I'd had a part in the writing. We could do what we loved and also bring joy to others. The first time I wrote something for

Jim, I saw the power that comedy had over my life. He used it during an appearance on a late-night talk show. I wasn't at the taping, so I was as nervous about how the joke went over as if I'd performed it myself. Terrified that it might have bombed, before the airing I called Jim: "Well, did you use my joke?"

"I did." Then he was quiet.

"Well, how did it work?"

"It killed." He sounded surprised. I was ecstatic. I never knew I could get such a thrill from writing for someone else. What followed were years of a fantastic comedy partnership. I hoped it wasn't over.

I tried to inject some humor into my hospital life, but my attempts at pantomiming among the medical staff often fell flat. Many times even Joe didn't get me, and I felt comically deprived. When Jim was around for his daily visit (shift), we would be inundated by technical conversations with nurses, prognoses made by doctors, and other general hospital busyness. Jim would of course give me detailed reports on the kids, occasionally bringing me drawings and love notes they'd made, depicting me as a stick figure in a hospital bed, which at this point was a pretty accurate representation. I smiled and cried with Jim over these priceless works of art by our children, who now just seemed like beautiful memories to me. I had no idea how long it had been since I'd seen them in person, because every moment away was like an eternity. The hand-drawn pictures and letters brought me joy, but no laughs. I needed to laugh, and I needed to make people laugh. Laughter was as important as oxygen, so I relished visits from funny people.

My brother Paul has one of those laughs you don't hear much, but it's so good and validating when you do that it becomes a primary goal to make it happen. I would try to find the intelligent yet obscure humor in everything just to hear that laugh. When he would take me for walks down the hall, I would always touch the fruit picture and make smacking sounds with my mouth. It became a thing, and I always got the elusive guffaw. Sometimes I would pretend to struggle more with the walk so he would be distracted and forget about the fruit picture. I would slump over my walker as if to catch my breath and Paul would look at me, concerned: "Jeannie, are you okay?" As soon as he let his guard down I would reach for the fruit picture as if I were stealing an apple. *Smack, smack, smack!* Paul would break up and I would get stronger.

My friend Karen came to visit me as soon as Jim gave the go-ahead. Mount Sinai is pretty much out of the way, and I was always impressed when someone who wasn't on a "shift" randomly came up to see me. It wasn't a place you could just drop by. Karen generously came several times just to hang out with me, and she didn't make a big deal out of it, which totally put me at ease. We could just as easily have been sitting in my kitchen with a glass of red wine, splitting a Domino's thin-crust pizza with ham, pineapples, and jalapeños while the kids ran around and we made each other laugh.

Karen had reached out to Jim right away about wanting to visit me, and it was not just the usual obligatory statement; it was sincere. A sincere desire to come sit with me at the hospital. I don't even know if *I* would want to visit me at the hospital. Karen was a close friend before this ordeal, the type who always asks you about what's going on in your life and really listens to your responses and *cares* what you say. I was so happy that she came. She's a stand-up comedian, and having her perspective on the situation just made everything better. She walked in, took one disappointed look at me, and said, "You're not even bald!" I welcomed Karen's irreverence with open arms. She would joke about my emaciated appearance: "That gown looks great on you. I guess you can wear anything when you are model-skinny." She talked to me about the outside world and brought me out of myself. She brought me a plush, bright blue, anatomically correct stuffed brain with a smiley face on it. Cute, horrible, and funny, just like my current situation in that hospital.

At the point she came to visit me, I was progressing in my daily walks and was strong enough to spit in the garbage cans in the hall rather than drooling all over myself. Even though I had a walker and was really weak, Karen and I would slowly make our way out of the ICU and down the long hallway almost to the end and back. She would roll the IV stand alongside me like my personal assistant as I carefully lifted the walker step-by-step, watching the portable oxygen monitor clipped to my finger. This hallway at Mount Sinai is in a giant open atrium and you can see down all eight floors to the lobby where there is a grand piano, and often there is a concert pianist playing elegant music that fills the whole hospital. One flight down from us there was a gift shop filled with the aforementioned sweet get-well toys, cards, flowers, and balloons.

On the walks, we listened to the piano while achieving my distance goals. Kind of like getting steps in on an Apple Watch, but redefined as my making it twenty feet to the point where I could grab the rail and peer over to get the bird's-eye view of the gift shop. With Karen, it became a fun outing. I created the character of "Karen's grandma," and she played along. My voice was coming back little by little and it sounded awful, like a bullfrog. "I want to look at the gift shop, dearie!" I would croak. We even invented fictitious characters of my other senior friends that I would pretend to wave to between spitting. "Hello, Erma! Gladys, how's the hip replacement? Hi, Otis! Oh, Otis died." We laughed and laughed. Well, I croaked and wheezed, but it was kind of like a laugh.

Chapter 16

THE PEG & THE TRACH

Blowhole

Lucky for me, these days the goal of a hospital stay is "to get you the heck out of the hospital." From what I understand, this is not a financial consideration or a need for beds as much as it is a safety issue. People are not in the hospital for attention, to watch TV in bed while someone waits on them, or for the food variety. People are in hospitals because they are very sick. It is a concentrated population of sick people. The worst germs and bacteria are in the hospital. Unlike a CDC laboratory, these germs and bacteria are not contained; they are floating around in the atmosphere every time a sick person coughs, sneezes, or even breathes. To put it in perspective, a hospital has more germs in it than a public bathroom. Let that sink in.

To make matters even more interesting, when you are sick in the hospital, your immune system is compromised, because you are, well, sick. Therefore, you are more susceptible to being infected by all of this air- and surface-borne ick. For instance, the pneumonia I caught in the hospital was treated very differently than it would have been if, say, I had caught pneumonia at home and then went to the hospital. It was a hospital-borne illness, which is distinguished from a hospital-born baby in that it's very dangerous. I mean, some hospital-born babies are dangerous, but I don't think there are any studies proving that it's due to their being born in the hospital. At least not yet.

Henceforth, it is in everyone's best interests to get you out of these germ-infested hellholes as soon as possible. Since it will take a long time to get you to a place where you can take care of yourself, you have to start thinking about home nursing care. I was thrilled with this idea, because I was at the point where being away from my children was actually making it harder for me to heal due to mental and emotional stress. It looked like my recovery was going to take a lot longer than anyone expected, so if I could have a nurse at home where my children were, it would mean I could recover both physically and emotionally, a win-win situation.

Almost two weeks into my hospital stay, we started looking at things that were keeping me in the ICU that would not be an option for home health care. First, there was the endotracheal intubation helping me breathe. Couldn't do that at home. Dr. Bederson hesitantly suggested that I get a tracheotomy. My only previous experience with this term was on a rerun of *MASH* I saw as a child when Hawkeye had to teach Radar (over a walkie-talkie) how to slit an injured soldier's throat with a razor blade, and then stick the tube from a pen cartridge in there so he could breathe again. I was assured that they performed this procedure a bit differently at Mount Sinai.

Apparently, this option of the tracheotomy would allow me

to go home sooner, because it would replace the intubation that I periodically needed. The thought of getting rid of the huge plastic tube shoved down my throat brought me closer to a feeling of joy than I had experienced since this whole ordeal began. It wasn't actual joy, but it was very close.

Of course I wanted the tracheotomy! I felt like a puppy that was about to get off the leash for the first time.

"Yes! I'll take the trach!" What had been holding us back from doing this before?

"There will be a scar on your neck," said Dr. Bederson.

I didn't care. I mean, I *really* didn't care. It suddenly struck me how amazing it was that for all of the seriousness of the medical procedures, Dr. Bederson was always thinking ten steps in the future: He was hell-bent on saving my facial nerve so I could keep my face. He shaved only the minimal portion of my hair needed to enter my skull for the craniotomy. Now he was worried about a scar on my neck.

I had been so consumed with just getting through each moment, I was completely unconcerned with the future, even though my surviving this had everything to do with my future. Dr. Bederson was so confident in my *living* through this and recovering completely that he was considering how I would feel about my appearance in the future, because there actually *would be a future* when I was well! That's the kind of confidence you want in a doctor. But meanwhile, a scar on my neck was nothing compared to getting out of there. "Let's do it!" I mouthed enthusiastically and gave a weak thumbs-up.

What I didn't know about a tracheotomy, or having a hole in your neck in general, was that things normally contained in your mouth when you coughed had new freedom to escape. Jim called it my "blowhole." Enough said.

It's Your Favorite Foreign Movie

The next thing to do away with was the nasogastric food tube. A more home-care-friendly option was something called a percutaneous endoscopic gastrostomy or, for short, the PEG. It's when a hole is cut in the abdominal wall and a tube is inserted so that you can get the food goo, water, and medicine pumped directly into your stomach. When I was given a choice to stay on the nasogastric tube or switch to the simpler PEG, I was overjoyed. It's the little things. Sure, the complication risks included:

- pain at the PEG site
- leakage of stomach contents around the tube site
- dislodgment or malfunction of the tube
- infection of the PEG site
- bleeding and perforation (an unwanted hole in the bowel wall)

…and other charming side effects. But compared to the tube-up-the-nose-attached-to-a-machine-in-the-hospital option, it sounded like a piece of cake. Did I mention that I could not have cake? The point is this: When given the choice between staying in the hospital unmolested further or being able to go home if I underwent more surgical procedures, it was a little bit like meeting a crossroads demon. Would you sell your soul to save your child? Would you get holes cut into your body to get off the hospital machines? I had to make sacrifices in order to get home, and I was willing to make those sacrifices. Maybe if I had been a Victoria's Secret bikini model, I would have hesitated for a moment, but for me, if it meant getting home, bring on the knife.

Lizzy was there when I was uber-gurneyed into the OR for the PEG procedure. We sat in the waiting room outside the OR for a long time. *The Chew* was playing on the high-mounted TV. Does every medical waiting room show *The Chew*? In my current state, the show seemed like a form of medieval torture. Liz kept looking for a way to turn off the TV as she saw that I was mesmerized and tormented. There did not appear to be a button on it. "Sick of it," said Lizzy.

I cheered her on: "Throw a medical gown over the screen!" I remembered it was her birthday. I kept mouthing to her, "This is the best birthday ever!" She agreed. Some new characters in scrubs appeared to wheel me into the procedure room. Lizzy waited outside the door for me to emerge reborn in all my new PEG-inserted glory.

*　*　*

After the procedure, Lizzy was next to me, holding my hand. I blinked my eyes open, face-to-face with a blurry doctor I'd never seen before. "How are you feeling?" he asked.

"Hungry," I replied. I couldn't wait to put my new PEG to work, ingesting large amounts of highly processed foodstuffs directly into my stomach without passing "GO." The doctor started coming into focus. "Thank you, Dr...." I had to look at his name tag, there were so many doctors. "...Hamburger?" Either I was hallucinating from hunger, or his name tag actually read "Dr. Hamburger." I looked around for Nurse Mustard and Orderly Milk Shake.

"Umm, is your name Dr. Hamburger?" I whispered trepidatiously.

"Unfortunately, yes," he replied sadly, as if this question

dominated his career. I imagined his name trumping all other achievements he'd made:

> **Dr. Hamburger:** I've discovered the cure for indigestion!
> **Other doctors:** Oh, great, now patients can eat *hamburgers*! lol!

Lizzy was grinning from ear to ear. Happy birthday.

"Wait, you are a gastroenterologist and your name is Dr. Hamburger?"

"No, I'm an anesthesiologist." He seemed defeated. It would have been much cooler if he were Dr. Hamburger, the stomach doctor.

Chapter 17

THE ICU "LITE"

Before actually going home, I would need to stay in a transitional room at Mount Sinai. I started to hear rumors about the luxury oasis known as Eleven West. *Eleven West*, I was told, was the place where Cleopatra would have been recovering had she had a craniotomy at Mount Sinai Hospital. During Jim's visits, I was spending most of my precious time with him pleading to find a way to get me out of the ICU. He was painfully aware of my suffering and he wanted to bring me some relief. Since he couldn't whisk me away to a beachfront resort on the shores of Thailand, he started talking about Eleven West. If you were lucky enough to find yourself a patient recovering in Eleven West at Mount Sinai Hospital, according to the brochure, you would be treated to *"private suites, a gourmet kitchen, daily afternoon tea, and soaring views of Central Park."*

I could see it in my mind. In fact, it was all I could picture. Jim was determined to get me a room there. Nothing was too good for his ninety-pound-half-head-shaved-tube-fed-multiperforated queen.

When the time drew near for me to leave the ICU to go into this transitional phase of my recovery, I was beyond disappointed to learn that I didn't qualify for Eleven West. I required a level of care that denied me access to this white-collar prison section of the hospital. However, I was assured that I would have a similar resort-like experience in Eight West, which was near the neurosurgery ICU and therefore adjacent to all the specialty care still required in my multitube existence.

Eight West was a tiny private room with a small window (did I mention there were no windows in the ICU?). It did indeed have a view of Central Park, if you walked over to it and looked straight down. But it was a room. An actual room! Not a multiple-patient area divided by curtains with people moaning in pain and crash carts crashing all night. Also, there were flowers allowed (did I mention there were no flowers allowed in the ICU?), and the flowers came pouring in. A note about flowers in the hospital: If you happen to be lucky enough to be someone's primary caregiver in the hospital, part of your duties should include moving flowers to where the patient can see them, and also throwing them away when they die. There's nothing worse than waking up in a room surrounded by dead flowers (see Rick Grimes waking up in the first episode of *The Walking Dead*).

Also important is to let the patient know who sent the flowers, and to record the names of those people, because inevitably when the patient finally gets out of the hospital, any of those who sent flowers might ask, "Did you get my flowers in the hospital?" only to be met with a blank stare that says, "I don't remember," and they will respond back with a look of disappointment. At this point, you're probably saying to yourself, *What an ingrate!*

She's complaining about people sending her flowers and not having a nice Central Park view?! but truth be told, I would have been overjoyed at leaving the ICU and landing in Eight West had it not been for the concept of the elusive Eleven West beckoning to me like a beautiful siren to a sailor lost at sea.

The thing I was most grateful for about moving to Eight West was that, theoretically, my children could visit me. This started a serious debate. Jim was hesitant about this happening. He was afraid of traumatizing the kids. At this point they had put a speaking valve in the trach hole in my neck so I could wheeze-talk.

> **JEANNIE (wheeze-talking):** Jim! Thank God I am out of the ICU! When can you bring all the kids to see me?
>
> **JIM:** Jeannie, I don't know if that's the best idea right now. They are really happy with Gramma Weezie.
>
> **JEANNIE:** But I miss them and I want to see them as soon as possible, please!

The force of her voice blows the plastic valve across the room, where it hits the wall and click-clacks to the floor.

> **JIM:** I don't know, Jeannie, you don't really . . . I'm not sure if they should see you right now.

In other words, I looked like death warmed over. There was a playground within eyeshot of my window with the straight-down view of Central Park. Jim compromised, saying he could bring the kids there and they could look up at me in the window, close enough to see it was me, but far enough not to see that I was breathing through a hole in my neck. "Look, everyone, there's Mommy! Doesn't she look great from that window eight flights up across the street?" I would wave at them and they would wave at me, and no one would be traumatized—except me, of course, but I was already traumatized.

If you look straight down, there's a playground.

Upon giving this plan some thought, I expressed to Jim that I felt, with every molecule of my being, that it would help my healing immensely if I could *touch* our children. I didn't want to be selfish. I didn't want to traumatize anyone, but I really needed it. I felt that if Jim carefully explained the situation, warned them, at least the two older kids would comprehend that how I looked now was only temporary. Marre was still out of the country on her epic class trip. I barely remembered her brief visit to the ICU that Jim had finagled. She'd come in for like five minutes while I was barely conscious. I'd opened my eyes and saw her sitting on the edge of my bed with a weak, scared smile on her face, and then I must have fallen asleep. That left Jack, who was eleven. He was old enough to understand how I looked and why. Jim decided that Jack made the cut, and he would bring him to Eight West to see me after school the next day. The long train ride up would be great father-and-son alone time and give Jim a chance to prepare Jack. I advised him to describe me as a hideous monster, so gruesome that by the time Jack walked in, I would look like a supermodel.

If I were to try to describe how long it took for the next day to arrive, it would take up three chapters. So I'll spare you the excruciating anticipation of this visit, but as I was waiting, I envisioned spending time with each of my kids. Kissing Patrick's palm when I dropped him at nursery school. Shampooing Michael's curly hair in the tub and forming a Christmas tree on top with the suds. Making up formulaic Scooby-Doo stories with Katie where she was central to the mystery and inevitably the one who pulled the mask off the scary witch, revealing that it was just the greedy hotel clerk. Lying on Marre's bed, holding her in my arms and rubbing her back while she cried hot tears of preteen angst. Jack, my little monkey, my Dennis the Menace. Chasing him around the house to get him to brush his teeth. I would always start out mad, but by the time I caught him we would both collapse in gales of laughter. Jack is a handful, but despite his naughty capers, I'm captivated by his odd humor and offbeat way of thinking. I remembered the time in church when I observed Jack gazing up at an elaborate stained-glass window, an angelic, peaceful look on his face. I wondered what profound, spiritual thoughts were going through his head. He turned to me and with the innocence of a cherub asked, "Mom, do zombies poop?" When would he get here? I was dying inside.

Jim finally brought Jack in and the part of me that had felt dead sprang back to life. He was wearing a blue polo and blue pants that were way too similar in color. It was a monochromatic abomination. Obviously, his mom hadn't dressed him in weeks. Normally this would have bothered me, but now I thought he was perfect. A huge, wide-eyed, concerned smile spread across his face as he dropped his backpack and came right over and gave me a hug. He smelled like dirt and Fanta. It was the best thing I've ever smelled. Without thinking, I licked his cheek. It tasted like dirt and Fanta. He didn't seem to care at all.

Chapter 18

GOING HOME

Nearly three weeks after surgery, which included ten days in the ICU, and five days in Eight West, my time at Mount Sinai was hopefully coming to an end, so we had to develop a concrete plan for my home care. Karen was connected with a team of Irish nurses that provided this service and she was looking into it. Meanwhile, Jim had to learn to perform basic Jeannie care. One of these tasks was cleaning and changing my tracheotomy, which, as I mentioned, was sometimes a treacherous endeavor—more for the changer than the changee—because if I coughed or even exhaled too hard, let's just say you would be safe only under a large umbrella. But Jim learned to do it, God bless him. He was calm and methodical. Not making jokes (at first), but focused and strong.

Jim is surprisingly good in medical situations. He keeps his head under difficult circumstances. When I was nine months pregnant with Marre, there was a plumber at our apartment fixing a leaky sink. Noticing the size of my "due any minute" belly, he asked me if my husband planned to be at the birth. "Of course! Why?"

"Don't let him see it," he warned me. "I had to leave the room when my wife gave birth. He'll never look at you the same again."

Jim, on the other hand, insisted on being part of all my deliveries. Sure, he got better at it with each one. With Marre, my first baby, I waited too long to go to the hospital and I was in too much pain to walk anymore. Rather than risk my having the baby on the stairs or in an ambulance, Jim called two home-birth midwives to come over and save the day. He was on standby to help. "What do I do?" Jim asked. "Boil water?"

"Warm up some towels!" said one midwife. We didn't have a clothes dryer, so Jim turned the oven to warm and put towels in it. She also asked for plastic shower curtains. Jim came up with some plastic paint covers we had stashed somewhere. Suddenly we had a plan and I found a burst of strength to carry me through the pain. An IV bag of antibiotics (just in case) hung from an oval shower rod that was suspended above my tiny clawfoot tub where I sat in a bath of steaming water. I felt like I was fading in and out of consciousness: sharply aware of what was going on and then when the contraction pain would start going to another place where I was surrounded by blue and white light, until the peak would subside and I would return to the reality of the bathtub. The midwife suggested we take this show out to the living room where a bed of plastic and towels had been placed and she could set up her equipment in an area larger than the four-by-five-foot bathroom. The two midwives half carried me out of the bathroom into my birthing nest, where I heard my mother praying loudly behind the closed bedroom door and, from the living room, the distinct sound of duct tape ripping. We rounded the corner to find Jim, dripping in sweat, taping yards of plastic sheeting over the wall where our new forty-two-inch flat-screen TV was mounted.

"What do you think is going to happen in here?"

"My friend told me not to wear my good shoes," Jim said. "And they told me to put plastic over anything that could get damaged." Through all the pain I was going through, the sight of Jim taping plastic to the wall to protect his TV remains one of my fondest memories of the entire experience. That and seeing the live human being who entered the room three hours and two Sunday morning services later (I could hear the bells chiming through the epic pushing phase). There I was, holding a deliciously healthy (nine pounds) baby girl. She had a thick shock of black hair on her head (we are both blond), and her chubby face was squinched up as she cried out, taking her first breaths. She looked like the Buddha wearing a Beatles wig. Jim looked like he was the one who had just given birth. After that first experience, he became something of an expert.

Therefore, Jim was no stranger to gore. At this point he had assisted with five unmedicated home births, so learning to pull a long rod out of my throat, unscrew the cap, rinse it out, and sanitize it before sliding it back in and tying it back to the bib thing was as second nature to him as putting a microphone back in the stand.

As we prepared for my discharge from the hospital, a new nurse was walking Jim through this procedure, but he was explaining it too slowly and neglected to fasten the ties right away. Suddenly, a sneeze came over me and the metal trach ejected from my throat like a silver bullet and shot across the room, missing Jim's gigantic head by an inch. Initially, this struck me as very funny, until a trauma team came in and there was a lot of hubbub about getting the trach back in my throat. I guess it was dangerous not to have one, even for a moment.

The day before I was supposed to leave, Jim and I were like giddy six-year-olds on the night before Christmas. The mundane medical interactions that I had become so used to were infused with happiness and excitement: "Yes, I would love nothing more than to have my vital signs taken, thank you!" We stared at the door of the room, holding hands, like we were waiting for Santa to come down the chimney. Enter a team of serious-looking doctors. Due to the incident with the tracheotomy, there had been an important debate behind closed medical doors about whether or not it was safe for me to leave the hospital as previously scheduled. "No! I'm fine, I'll be fine, I need to go home!" I begged. I turned to Jim, who seemed crushed. There may be no presents under the tree this year.

"We will let you know tomorrow," replied Dr. Robert Rothrock, one of my doctors, who looked like he should be on a soap opera and had a name to match. Normally, Jim and I would have laughed about the perfect Dr. Rothrock, but not today.

Anyone who has spent any time in a hospital knows that waiting for doctors to come in and give you updates is agonizing. Your day revolves around it. If you address a question to any hospital staff, the answer is likely to be, "Your doctor will come in and let you know." The worst is when you wait all day to find out what is going on, you doze off, your caregiver runs down for a coffee, and then you miss the doctor. It's like staying up all night and then sleeping through the sunrise, or going to India and finding out the Dalai Lama just left. The doctors hold the key to the mystery of life in these rounds of enlightenment while you lie in wait, floundering in bewilder-ment and ignorance.

The next morning, the doctors came in and explained that they had decided to allow me to leave, but only under the non-negotiable condition that I be accompanied home by a regis-tered nurse who we would have had to hire from the outside. We didn't have one. The Irish nurse squad was unavailable. Jim reached out to one of our neighbors, a working actor who also happened to be a registered nurse, but on that fateful day, he was not around. We were at a loss.

Later, one of my sisters was taking me for my daily grandma walk to gaze down at the gift shop at a balloon or something to slightly raise my sinking spirit, when through my blurry, one good eye, I saw a nun in a full habit walking toward me. Had I died? "Excuse me," said the nun. "Do you know where Eight West is?"

"Sister Mary?" I asked. Sister Mary, of the Sisters of Life order, was an old friend who had previously helped Jim and me through one of the more traumatic times in our life. We had known her for about ten years, and although she was now reassigned to Washington, DC, we had remained close friends through handwritten letters and monthly call days. She had become my spiritual adviser—my "nun on call."

On April 7, 2008, when Jim and I were twenty-two weeks pregnant with our third child, I was rushed to the hospital because of cramping and bleeding. We were stunned because a couple of weeks earlier, we'd gotten the anatomical scan that assured us our baby girl was in perfect health and already almost two pounds. In the hospital, it was discovered that somehow the umbilical cord had gotten infected, and my body was going into premature labor to try to eject the infection. The baby, whom we had lovingly referred to as "Bean" since we first saw her at eight weeks, was in mortal jeopardy. I was put on a course of antibiotics and told by the neonatologist that although some babies are born at twenty-two weeks and survive, this baby did not have mature lungs or eyes yet and was on the "cusp of viability." I had to stay pregnant and hope that the infection would clear. Since I was in the hospital, we weren't really worried because I was surrounded by doctors and experts. Jim and I were confident that this was just a little bump in the road. Suddenly there was an extremely painful cramping sensation. Doctors rushed in and checked the baby via sonogram. I was in full-blown labor. The neonatologist sat with Jim and me and explained that the baby was coming and there was no stopping her. She would be born alive but would be unable to survive on her own. Her little lungs were just not ready. They could put her on a breathing machine to prolong the inevitable, but that would cause her a severe amount of unnecessary discomfort. Jim and I were shocked. We clung to each other, crying. What would we tell Marre and Jack? They were so excited for their new sister and were already making her cards and drawings welcoming her into the family. I was beyond devastated.

Jim took my face in his hands and looked deep into my eyes: "Jeannie, I am so, so sorry. What can I do? What can I do?" The familiar labor pains had started.

"Jim, I have already had two unmedicated births," I said through my tears. "I can't go through another painful labor knowing this baby is going to die. Please, go get an anesthesiologist and tell them I need every painkiller known to humankind. I do not want to feel anything." The emotional agony was crippling. It was too much for me to bear as it was; I couldn't go through anything physical. Jim ran out of the room to oblige me.

On the way to the anesthesia station he literally ran into a nun in an old-fashioned, full habit. This was the first encounter with Sister Mary. She was at the hospital with another nun supporting one of the pregnant women from their shelter. They were just leaving. Jim blurted out to her: "Sister! My wife is about to lose her baby! We are Catholic and it would mean so much if you helped us through this!" The nuns explained to Jim that they had been at the hospital for twelve hours and ensured him there were other people there that could support us. Jim pleaded, and Sister Mary relented. She told her colleague to leave without her, that she would stay. She entered my room like a ray of sunshine cutting through a deep fog. I looked at this nun with the white veil as if she were an angel that could save me from this horrific misery. "Sister! My baby is going to die! Please save her!" Sister Mary sat down on the bed next to Jim and took both my hands.

"Jeannie, I don't know why God is calling your baby home, but you have to let her go." I didn't want to. I wanted this baby so badly. Jim had his head in his hands. His shoulders were trembling. "Jeannie and Jim, it's your goal as parents to get your children into heaven. This one is already going." This statement could have made me furious, but instead Jim and I were filled with an inexplicable peace. When trying to recount this feeling later, it was described to me as "grace." Sister Mary brought out a small bottle from her bag. "This is blessed holy water from Lourdes, France. I am going to say a prayer over your baby. What's her name?" Her name had been "Bean" up until this point, but that didn't seem very holy. Though I found out later that there is actually a "Saint Bean." Catholics think of everything.

"Her name is Maria. Maria Lourdes," I just decided.

"Maria Lourdes' short life is going to have so much meaning for you. She is your child, and you and Jim will always love her and cherish her as your dear daughter. She will always be with you." Sister Mary's ethereal words were cool water poured on our parched souls. A short time later, beautiful Maria Lourdes was born. She was regal and elegant. A perfect tiny baby. Jim and I spent the next several hours talking to her, singing to her, and cuddling her. After a while, she went to sleep, never to wake again. I held her warm body close. I looked over at Jim sleeping in the corner chair. I felt more love for him than ever before. To his left, the air appeared sort of misty, and then some colors began to take shape. Blue and white. The room smelled of roses. I blinked my eyes and I saw what appeared to me to be a shape like the Blessed Mother holding a seven-month-old baby girl in her arms. The baby looked at me with big round blue eyes and smiled. I shook my head. The vision was gone. These drugs were really strong. Then I remembered that the anesthesiologist had never made it into the room.

We never found out conclusively what had caused the spontaneous infection, but the expert medical staff advised us that it would be dangerous to have any more children. My body might not be able to handle pregnancy anymore. In the whirlwind year that followed, while we grieved the loss of Maria Lourdes, we became pregnant with Katie, who was born full-term and flawless the following May. On Mother's Day. Around Christmas that year, Jim entered my room holding Katie, who looked at me with big round blue eyes and smiled. I recognized her as the baby I'd seen in my vision in the hospital. That was the miracle I was afraid to tell you before, but I thought you might be ready now.

Kidnapping a Nun

So Sister Mary was there at one of the most significant moments of our lives, and now, with her improbable appearance in the hallway, she was with us at another. Materializing seemingly out of nowhere on the eighth floor of Mount Sinai.

I vaguely remembered she was going to be in New York to visit her nephew around this time. I believe she had communicated with Jim about stopping by the hospital to pay a visit. But the moment she arrived could not have been more timely. I was down in the spiritual dumps. She helped me back to my room. I asked for her prayers and told her about how this was the one day that my neighbor happened to be unavailable, so I couldn't leave the hospital.

"But you know, *I'm* a registered nurse," said Sister Mary. Jim and I were aghast. Suddenly it made total sense that she was a nurse—all those years ago we had met her in a hospital. She was there all day taking care of pregnant women. We called the doctors and told them my registered nurse was here to escort me home. We also mentioned to Sister Mary that she'd probably have to call her nephew and postpone her personal plans because we would likely require her services for the entire day. After all, she was a "nun on call," and we needed her. We kidnapped a nun.

* * *

Eight weeks after our fateful, frantic car ride up the FDR to Mount Sinai, Jim and I prepared to leave. I slipped on the fashionable Chloé cat-eyed sunglasses my cousin gave me and, with my husband and my nun at my sides, I rolled down the hallway of Eight West for the last time. Good-bye, random crashing noises in the middle of the night. Good-bye, incessant beeping machines. And, especially, good-bye, specter of death hovering over me. I'd had an entire pear removed from my brain, and I was ready to face whatever came next. Bring it.

When I was pushed through the exit doors into the bright sunlight and took my first breath of fresh outdoor air, I felt like a butterfly emerging from a cocoon.

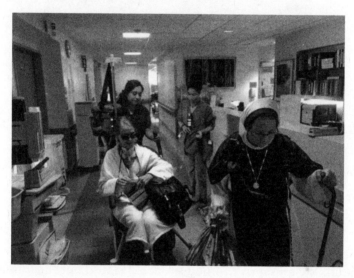

Jim hoisted the oxygen tank and related tubes into the back of the SUV that he had arranged to take us, and Sister Mary, home. Traffic was horrible, but still, it seemed less tumultuous than the ICU. The horns honking and sirens blaring were music to my ears. I was heading home! My kids were waiting! I sat in the backseat growing impatient as the journey from 103rd Street and Fifth Avenue to the Lower East Side, which should have been forty minutes down the FDR at that time on a Saturday, took about two hours. How different this was from the ride up the FDR when I had no idea what was about to

Drugstore Cowgirl

happen. We all sat in stunned silence. I stared out the window. There was the Pepsi-Cola sign that I'd thought I might never see again. Memories were mine. Memories are everything.

The driver took the Twenty-Third Street exit instead of Houston and I found myself annoyed. *Now we are going to hit more traffic*, I thought. The feeling of irritation was quickly replaced by exaltation as I realized that I was having normal traffic impatience. Normalcy! I was feeling what normal people who were not in a hospital felt! During this long drive through the city to the "no place like home" at the end of the Yellow Brick Road, I noticed there was a Mister Softee ice cream truck on every single corner. I was incredulous at the thought that in all my many years of living in New York City, I had never once gotten myself a Mister Softee cone. I had bought them for my kids so many times, but I had been that mom who never got herself one. I vowed on that day that once my "nothing by mouth" restriction was over, I would make it my life's goal to never pass a Mister Softee without getting myself something.

Jim and Sister Mary ushered me in through the back door, which was the shortest distance to my bed, and they helped me lie down. I was exhausted by the journey, though I'd been sitting the entire time. Being home felt surreal. Our bedroom had been meticulously cleaned by someone unknown and I was impressed by the made bed and spotless surroundings. I inhaled deeply and smelled no hospital aroma, except me. I was still wearing the gown. The kids were not home from their outing yet, which was a huge disappointment, but I was also somewhat relieved because the first thing I wanted to do before they saw me was take a shower and change into some normal-looking and normal-smelling pajamas. Jim had already gotten a shower chair that I would need to sit in, and that chair remains there to this day as a monument to my freedom. Since I couldn't walk on my own, Jim and Sister Mary got into the shower as well to set me in position so I could hose myself down in privacy. Before you think this book just took a dramatic turn in genre, there were still several places on my body that were wrapped in bandages and could not get wet. So, this "shower" was with the handheld hose only, I was partially clothed, Jim was fully clothed, and Sister Mary was in her full nun's habit.

Though I should have been enraptured by the first sensation I'd had of actual water hitting my body in weeks, my mind was otherwise occupied with constructing the joke "a brain surgery patient, a comedian, and a nun walk into a shower..." The rest of the afternoon was spent with me watching Sister Mary and Jim struggle to put together all the in-home care machines: the IV feeding machine, the oxygen, the suction thing, and all the plastic tubes. There were so many tubes that my room looked like a mad scientist's lab. "Miles and miles of tubes," as Sister Mary put it. Those two would have blown George Burns and Gracie Allen off the "best comedy duos" list in a heartbeat. Jim was following Sister Mary around the room as she connected tubes. The tubes were so long she was concerned the oxygen would be too weak by the time it reached my mask. She wanted to cut them. Jim, at the ready, quickly fetched her a scissors, and they went around together through the forest of tubes.

"Okay, this one goes *here* and that one goes *there*...Now, where is the little connector thing? Oh, there it is!" Sister Mary stopped to pick up the plastic piece. Jim bumped into her.

"Whoops. Sorry, Sister!" They seemed to be tangled up in the tubing. I think Jim stepped on her habit. Even though I was short of breath, I chuckled and felt the rush of joy bring color to my cheeks. I was moments away from seeing the kids. I was home!

Playing Doctor

When the kids got back, they were instructed to take a decontamination shower before they could come in to see me. They had been prepped by a nurse about what condition to expect to see Mom in, and how they could not touch certain parts of my body. I asked Jim for details about what they had been told. He said that the nurse sat them down and gave them important information and responsibilities.

"Your mom has a little hole in her neck that she needs to help her breathe, so you might see that and think it is scary, but it is actually really helping her get better. She also can't eat or drink like you or I can, so she has a special tube going into her stomach where she can take food, water, and medicine. She's only going to have these things for a little while, but during the time she does, you have to be really careful around her. She's going to want to get hugs and kisses, but you must be gentle around these areas."

Michael raised his hand. "Can we sleep in the bed with her?" The nurse said that wouldn't be the best idea for now, because when people are sleeping they can't be as careful and they could accidentally pull the tube out. "If the tube gets pulled out, will all the air go out of her like a balloon?"

This is the post on Instagram that announced to the world that I had come home.

Being (sort of) careful around Mom.

I heard the familiar noises of the kids and my heart pounded in anticipation. When they entered the room, I was reborn. They stood awkwardly for a beat in front of my bed, allowing a moment for us to take one another in. They were a feast to my eyes. My seven-year-old, Katie, was like Florence Nightingale. She was concerned about my temperature, my comfort, and if it was time for my medicine. My four- and five-year-olds, Patrick and Michael, were carrying toy doctor's kits, and they carefully used their plastic instruments to analyze my condition.

They brought in gigantic, shiny, individual balloons that spelled out "WE LOVE U!" and put them in front of my bed.

There were stacks and stacks of cards from friends, and more drawings and love that expressed joy, gratitude, relief, and well-wishes.

I was back. Not as the boss, not as the organizer, not as the house-runner, but I didn't care. I was surrounded by love and family and I felt I had finally turned a corner.

I was under a pile of kids.

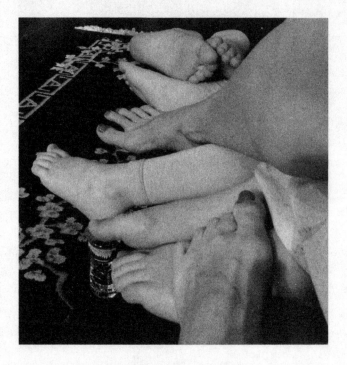

And that's when the real work started.

PART III

An Uphill Battle

All fears I had of Jim losing his mojo of funny dissipated after we got home. He went from stern commander to court jester almost instantaneously. He treated every day like a victory celebration at the end of a brutal war. Having Jim as my primary caregiver at home was probably the main reason I made such impressive progress in my recovery. Though the nursing role was totally novel to him, the role of comedian was already his thing, and laughter truly was the best medicine for me. Jim found a way to make everything funny, and, since everything was really horrible, this was the key to my survival. During this time, it was pretty clear that God had designed our marriage specifically for this moment.

* * *

My younger kids used to wake me up in the middle of the night because they were scared to go use the potty alone, so

215

I would take them. Now, because of the physical weakness caused by the pneumonia and the muscle atrophy caused by lying in bed, I couldn't even get to the bathroom by myself, and it was depressing and frustrating. The kids would come in and be so sweet: "Mommy, when you get better I am taking you to Disneyland!" And heartbreaking: "Mommy, when you get better, can we get a dog?" I would nod weakly, but inside I felt powerless and ineffective as a mother. I remember lying in bed at night, wide awake, and hearing noises. Was it an intruder? Was one of the kids wandering around the house in the dark, an accident waiting to happen? I could no longer protect them. I felt like I was in one of those nightmares when you have to defend yourself against something awful but you can't move. I remember saying, "Jim, I feel worthless. It's like this will never end!" Jim wouldn't let me dwell in this dark place for long. He knew how to read the room. He invented this character of "the horse," who would put me on his back and carry me to the bathroom. Jim would appear at my bedside and say, "Your carriage is waiting, m'lady," lift me out of bed, and make clicking noises like a horse trot. My noble steed transporting me to the bathroom made something that was unimaginably difficult into a sweet, romantic, and hilarious comedy sketch. Now that I was home and Jim took more time off from work to take care of me, I no longer had to rely on funny people visiting me at the hospital to lift my spirits. My constant companion was my comedy concierge. It made me realize how much I'd missed this time with him when I was in the hospital and explained and alleviated the tension we had been experiencing for the past three weeks.

One of the funniest things he did was wash my hair. Hair washing in and of itself is a very unfunny task, but a ticket to watch Jim Gaffigan, hairstylist extraordinaire, do it, is one you want to buy. I leaned back in a chair next to the bathtub, and Jim used the sprayer hose. My husband has, shall we say, drastically less hair than I do, and it probably takes him about thirty seconds to shampoo, rinse, and condition himself, so this was entirely new territory for him to complete the same actions with my hair. It was at least a two-hour process, including a thorough blow-dry so I could get back in bed. To pass the time, Jim became a gossipy salon owner lady with a thick southern accent. He went on and on with this character, chattering away: "Now, honey, my third husband was as cute as a button but dumb as a rock. He would always say, 'Mabel, don't you cut the back of my hair or it ain't never gonna grow back!' He was not the sharpest tool in the shed, but he loved my cookin' and ooh-wee, he was a looker! Now, girl, you've got a fine-lookin' husband yourself; all he needs is a good mullet…" He kept me in

hysterics the entire time. And he did a decent job on the hair too! I forgot all about my hair affair with my hospital husband. It was a meaningless fling and rather disappointing. After Jim was done with the blow-dry, I confided in him, "You are way better than Joe."

Chapter 19

JIM AND BRUCE

Jim was thriving in his new role as primary caregiver, but he was being spread really thin between being "daddy day care" and Jeannie's home entertainment system as well as surrogate nurse, so God sent us Bruce. You know that really awesome, friendly neighbor in your building that you see in the hall and you think to yourself, *Boy, if I had time, I would love to hang out with this guy.* That's Bruce. And I got my wish, just not in a way I would have ever expected. Sometime while I was in the hospital and Jim wasn't able to book the highly in-demand Irish nurse squad that Karen had recommended, he approached our neighbor, Bruce. We knew that Bruce was a busy actor in New York City. We had only recently learned about the nurse part when I was diagnosed with the brain tumor.

Technically, what I needed was a live-in nurse, but since my home was already bursting at the gills, the fact that Bruce lived in the building and agreed to be on-call as my nurse twenty-four

The Unlikely Nurses.

hours a day was another miracle that is beyond explanation. Don't get me wrong, Jim was still on duty, but Bruce was the cavalry. He would come over five or six times during the day or night to take my vitals, change my food bag, clean my tracheotomy, and administer my variety of medications. He quickly became a member of the family. He also continued to train Jim in the complexities of Jeannie care as I watched in amusement. A favorite moment was Bruce teaching Jim physiotherapy to clear my lungs as they took turns pounding on each other's backs. Jim and Bruce were like act II of my personal vaudeville show. Now I had two funny people taking care of me! It was terrific for Jim to have not only the medical support, but also a peer and friend to share the hard work as well as the laughter.

Chapter 20

THE FOOD CHAPTER

When someone dies, has a baby, or has serious surgery, food appears in abundance. When people don't know how else to help a family in need or crisis, they send food. This explosion of generosity results in a massive accumulation of meals, desserts, and gourmet baskets. This is a wonderful communal gesture and helps alleviate the stress of cooking and shopping. As I mentioned before, I'm the oldest of nine children, so my mother was constantly having babies. Rather than associating each of my mother's trips to the hospital with the thrill of anticipating a new sibling, my fondest memory of those times was the arrival of the new and fun things that the neighbors would send over for dinner. "Mom's having a baby, maybe we'll get that hamburger casserole again from the Thiels!" I knew my kids were coping the same way. Food makes everything better.

During the height of my illness, the baskets of cookies, lasagnas from the school Loaves and Fishes committee, and a variety of delicious-looking meals from friends started pouring in, much to the delight of my husband and children, but not so much for me. The sights and smells of this free-flowing feast of delicacies were the final nails in my nothing-by-mouth coffin. They would try to hide the food from me when I'd struggle through my daily lap around the house, but there was too much of it. Towers of treats were piled high in every corner. It got to the point where, during meals, we had to hermetically seal my room off from the smells. Jim would close all the doors leading to the bedroom and stuff towels under the door. He would burn scented candles while I inhaled aromatic oils to take my mind off the deprivation. I tried to pray, but this was admittedly torturous. Jesus fasted for forty days and forty nights, but now I had him beat.

Food had always been a major theme in my household and in my life. Jim's relationship with food is very primitive. In other words, he sees it, he eats it, regardless of its nutritional value. This was the guy who had mindlessly eaten chips and stinky guacamole in my face while I was in labor. I have always been the voice of reason, saying, "Suppress the urges of the id! Be conscious of what you put in your body! If there is free pizza, you do not have to eat it! You are not hungry. Be mindful of *why* you are eating and *what* you are eating." It's also the job of the parent of a young child (or a dog) to monitor food intake, so kids (or dogs) don't make bad choices. Food and eating should be reflective of how you honor and respect your body, and the bodies of those you are feeding. I have always thought of it as my responsibility to reinforce this message for my family, which has earned me the prized nickname "the Food Nag."

Once I became deprived, my whole perspective changed (remember my Mister Softee observation on the ride home from the hospital). I had lost more than twenty pounds so far and was making plans, as soon as I was able, to gain it all back and then some. I told myself, *When I can eat, I am going to eat anything and everything.* That I had deprived myself of food that I wanted in the past seemed so ridiculous and an obvious attempt to exercise my now glaringly evident control issues.

Whenever someone visited, I'd only want to talk about what meal we would enjoy together once I got my swallow back. With Karen, we would have the Hawaiian pizza with hot sauce that we perfected during years of playdates, followed by an entire cake from an incredible Italian bakery we both know. With my friend Niels, who was the DP on *The Jim Gaffigan Show*, I would have that merguez sausage sandwich with egg and avocado from Café Gitane that we'd once shared during a beautiful afternoon of filming; and so on. I remember one day after a particularly disheartening home visit with a swallow therapist, I needed some cheering up. I texted Niels: "Soon: Merguez Sandwich!" and he replied, "Sorry, honey, I'm not eating bread now. Drains my energy." The arbitrary decision to "give up bread" because it is supposedly bad for you used to seem to me to be not only logical, but smart. Now it was the stupidest thing I'd ever heard. Like cutting down on air to make your lungs more active. I wondered if you offered a starving man a loaf of bread, would he ask, "Is that gluten-free?"

The other things I missed about food were shopping for it, prepping it, cooking it, and serving it. Food preparation and serving are acts of love that nourish the body, soul, and spirit. Being bedridden, I couldn't do any of those things.

Meals have always been a time of togetherness in our home. When Jim is back from touring, it's our tradition to celebrate with a big family dinner. Oftentimes we will have guests over.

There is seating for twelve around our big wooden table, and on Sunday nights, every chair is filled.

Jim and I decided early on in our lives as parents that if we were going to have this nontraditional lifestyle with five kids in an apartment in Manhattan, we would hold on to some traditions of our childhood that gave us a solid foundation as adults. In fact, the table we sit at is the same table where Jim and his six siblings ate Sunday night dinners in the 1970s. This tradition has evolved somewhat. For example, Jim and his brothers are probably still traumatized from the itchy coats and ties they were required to wear, so we've made ours more casual affairs. But we still start our meals with the traditional Catholic grace, and the kids take turns being the leader. Before you think we are the Flanders family from *The Simpsons*, know that grace normally results in bickering among the kids: "Mom, Michael did the sign of the cross *wrong*!" At least we try. After the prayer, we attempt to engage them in some kind of statement of thankfulness, and then while we are sharing the meal, we do our aforementioned "best and worst" of the day or some other conversation starter that encourages them not to just shovel food in and ignore one another. If there is a guest there, we try to prompt the kids to let them have food first, and we also warn the visitor not to be shy, because if they blink, our kids will have eaten everything! Mealtime at the Gaffigans' is a really raucous party every night where as soon as the plates are clean, there could be an impromptu game of charades, Marre playing the piano, Jim being silly ("How does it feel to have the best-looking dad in the world?"), the kids being smart-alecky (Jack: "I don't know, Dad; do you know someone who does?").

Now that I was at home recovering, they still carried on the same way at mealtimes, but I felt separate and disconnected.

If you caged a bird whose mission was to feed worms to her babies, she might die. I get it. The hunger I was feeling was also a soul hunger. I would try to put on a brave face and sit with them, just to be nourished by the togetherness and laughter, but I was too weak, too dizzy. My family would be embarrassed and awkward, apologizing for eating in front of me. I was once a force in this house, and now I was treated like a fragile piece of china that might break if you breathed on it too hard. So someone would carefully help me back to bed where I would lie and listen to the laughter and conversations that I was no longer a part of.

* * *

When you think about recovering from surgery, you can't help but envision long, boring days at home with enormous freedom where you'll finally be able to do your scrapbooking and other rainy-day tasks you've been putting off throughout your life. There were so many times in the past where I was caught up in a whirlwind of to-do lists, schedules, and deadlines that I would think to myself, *I need a bed day! I need a bed week! I just need to stay in bed and catch up on all the books and writing that I long to do. I could finally organize all my photos! Maybe I even could do some crafting, if only I could just stay in bed all day.* Now that wish had come true, and I was more miserable than ever. I had so many ideas swirling around in my head, but I did not have the health or energy to even sit up and write. What good is a laptop when you don't have a lap? But I did have my phone so I could send texts to people about food, or text Jim in the other room and say, "Hi, could someone send a kid in here?" The novelty of having Mom home had worn off and everyone was going about their lives, popping in only now and then to check on me. I started to miss the constant train of interrupting nurses in the ICU. Well, not really, but you catch my drift. The smartest thing about the smartphone is the Notes app. I couldn't really write down my feelings in a significant way, but I could make notes.

This is a poem I wrote after a week of lying in bed, smelling food I couldn't eat, and hearing everyone in the next room that seemed a world away.

i am a Ghost

```
life rushes by and i stay the same
i see people laughing and living but i
    cannot participate.
they know i am there but they are too
    scared to really look at me.
when i get mad i throw dishes.
i groan in the night.
cup of coffee is dream of a past life.
    it's like i can smell heaven from
    purgatory;
i know i will eventually get there
but it's just out of reach.
```

Now that I existed as a wandering soul looking in at life from the outside instead of being in the middle of it all, something began to happen to me. God was giving me the opportunity to sit back in silence and develop a new awareness of what was really going on. To observe my life without living it. Even being stuck in bed, in other circumstances I would have been busying myself with *something*. Okay, maybe not crafting, but something. If I could eat, I would be stuffing myself until I couldn't feel my feelings. If I could take sleeping pills or pain-killers, I would have welcomed the escape and binge-slept. All I could do now was see and hear.

Jim was fully engaging in fatherhood in a whole new way. I saw Jim spontaneously teaching Jack how to tie his necktie before a bar mitzvah. He saw me staring and said to Jack with a sideways look at me, "Your mother doesn't do a good job on the knot." I started to notice that the kids were approaching Jim in a new way. Whereas before there was a little bit of a "What did you bring me?" approach to Jim when he walked in the door, I saw things like Katie showing Jim her sketch pad and asking him if he liked a new character she was drawing. "Katie, I think you should design a tour poster for me!"

She blushed with pride. "Really, Daddy? Are you joking?"

"No, I think that rabbit with big eyes is amazing and I think he could sell a lot of tickets!" I joked that he should review the child labor laws.

It wasn't just a change in Jim I noticed. Marre had blossomed into a young woman. She was thirteen now and was getting herself around the city. I used to be paranoid about her walking half a block to school when I dropped her off at the corner, and now she was taking Katie to the art supply store on her own. She came into the bedroom and shared with me that on their way back from buying glue and glitter, Katie had stopped and given her unopened juice box and goldfish crackers to a homeless person on the street who was asking for change. "I let her do it, Mom, because we only had pennies and I thought it would be rude to put pennies in the cup. Is that okay?" It was more than okay. My kids were coming into their own as people, and they didn't need me breathing down their necks to survive. They were doing great.

Chapter 21

THE DOG DAYS OF SUMMER

"So, you have five kids, a touring husband, are recovering from brain surgery, and you decided to get two puppies?" is a question you might ask an insane person. Or a Gaffigan. True, the Gaffigans like a challenge, but while some of these seemingly overly ambitious, self-sabotaging exploits—such as a decision to put a date on the calendar to film a special without any new material, or to bring five kids along on a comedy tour of Asia, or the absurd undertaking of writing a book shortly after a medical crisis—are taken on purposely, some craziness happens by accident. And so it was with the two puppies.

My kids, particularly Katie, have always asked us for a dog, but there was never, ever a good time to get one. Because of the brush with my own mortality, I realized that a "good time" would likely not ever happen. Why not get one now before the dog got sucked into the "mini-kitchen effect." Let me explain.

When Katie was in nursery school, her favorite playtime

activity was the mini kitchen. She would walk into the class-room, put her coat in her cubby, and bee-line straight for the toy kitchen. She would don the apron and busy herself with organizing the pots and pans to create delicacies out of wood and plastic food. There were many organized activities in nurs-ery school, including art, music, alphabet, and counting games, but when it was free play time, Katie would always go back to the little kitchen. When I would pick her up she would ask, "Mommy, can I *please* get my own little kitchen?"

"Of course you can!" I already knew from my Amazon Prime addiction that I could get an affordable little play kitchen delivered to our door in three days or less. The problem was, where to put it? At the time we had seven people, one of whom was a new baby, living in a two-bedroom apartment. We barely had room for our actual kitchen, let alone a play one. We had been "in the process of moving" for a couple of years already. After finding an apartment we wanted, we would start packing up our stuff in boxes, and then not actually move because the deal fell through for one reason or another. The boxes became part of our furniture. They were sat on, used as side tables, and accumulated other things on top of them. At least we had more seating for dinner guests. I could start a shabby chic trend. Sometimes I'd throw a tablecloth over a pile of boxes and stick a scented candle on top so it looked more purposeful. It was like in the Winnie-the-Pooh story where he got stuck exiting Rabbit's house so Rabbit put a frame around his butt. The walls were closing in on us, and I could not find room for the promised Katie kitchen, though she would not give up the dream, as we understood from her constant reminders. We eventually found a space to move into, but it would require a huge time-consuming renovation to combine two apartments.

But at the end of the long tunnel there would finally be an area for the kids to play in!

When we walked around our future home while it was under construction, Jim said proudly, "Look! Here is where we could put Katie's kitchen!" After a full two-year process of building, and promising Katie she would finally get her wish (as she continued to ask for the play kitchen on almost a daily basis), we were emancipated into an apartment that could accommodate all of us, with no boxes as furniture, and a playroom for the kids complete with a little kitchen, which we proudly unveiled for Katie. Unfortunately, by this time, she had outgrown the kitchen and had transferred her love of mixing plastic food into science experiments and making slime. The kitchen got plenty of use by Michael, and eventually Patrick, but I had tremendous guilt about my unfulfilled promise to Katie. One of the best (and worst, depending on your mood) things about kids is their resilience. Their dreams and desires are constantly evolving, so not getting the kitchen in a timely fashion did not kill her spirit. The latest Katie ask-obsession was her ceaseless begging for a dog, which I also had been putting off for years. While I was lying in the hospital, my thoughts often went to Katie and the dog. I thought, *If I die, there will never be a dog, and another promise will have been put off and remain forever unfulfilled.*

Now that I had survived and was home I resolved, "We are getting that dog Katie asked for!" But how could we do it now—when I was too weak to even take care of myself, or my own children for that matter, and I wanted Jim to be able to get back to work? I felt the old determination fire driving me. I needed to take action, but I also knew I couldn't do it alone.

As providence would have it, my brother Patrick and his

wife, Emilea, had recently relocated to our neighborhood from up in Harlem so that they could be closer to help my family while I recovered. Yes, I know, we should nominate them for sainthood. While they were over one day, everyone ended up sitting on my bed, which, at my request, was becoming the new living room/hangout place. Pat and Em were talking about how much they loved their new place, the whole area, and how great it was to be neighbors. The discussion turned to dogs. They'd just taken the kids to nearby Washington Square Park, which blossoms in the warm weather with young people, families, musicians, and tons of dogs playing around the giant fountain. "I wish we could get a puppy!" said Emilea. Patrick agreed, but since they each occasionally traveled for work, it didn't seem realistic. Jim and I concurred, noting that before I got sick, the Gaffigan travel schedule was a main factor preventing us from getting a pet. I had a crazy idea: "What if we share a dog?" It was like the "you got your peanut butter in our chocolate" moment. Jim, Patrick, Emilea, and I simultaneously realized that if we shared a pet, the out-of-town issue would rarely be a factor. We could co-adopt a puppy from a shelter. Jim was incredulous. He always had this joke whenever someone asked us if we had a dog: "No, Jeannie hates animals." When I suggested the dog-share, he said, "Are you sure? You are still really weak!"

"We can get a small dog! Patrick and Emilea will help. They are a block away, and the kids will have to do their part!" Our two apartments would be one big house, one big family. This was a huge decision and something that was not like me at all (more messes!), but it seemed right. It was something active, something that would present new challenges but also be a new chapter in life! Katie just about lost her mind when she heard the news. "*Really*, Mom? *Really?*" Her reaction was one part bliss, two parts skepticism as she smiled at me in disbelief, as if my brain was going to heal a little and I'd suddenly exclaim, "Wait, no! What was I thinking?" The truth was, I was serious. It was the first big decision that I'd had a part in since coming home and it gave me a feeling of engagement and taking charge that I badly needed.

I lay in bed with my very smart phone, trolling different dog shelters' Instagrams. They were all adorable, but in the "profiles" they gave projections of how large the dog would grow. I skipped over the ones that would get big enough to pull me off my feet into oncoming traffic, since I had no idea when or if I would ever get my strength back. I fell instantly in love with a little mutt puppy named Sharon. She was white with brown spots and had her head tilted to the side, making direct eye contact with the camera. I told the kids, "Look, we are going to adopt this one!" They weren't picky. Who could be after seeing a photo of a cute puppy on Instagram? Though, full disclosure, my brother Patrick wasn't a huge Sharon fan (she was super girly). Our next step to making this whole thing real was meeting the dog. We contacted the shelter and they let us know that Sharon had been adopted already, but they had many other needy puppies. I wondered if Sharon was even real. Maybe she was the model they used to hook people like me. By this time, the kids were totally amped that we were getting a dog ASAP, and by "the kids" I include Emilea, Patrick, and Jim, and Sharon's adoption was not a deterrent. The kind people at the shelter invited us to arrange a meeting with the foster parents (the people who temporarily kept the dogs during the adoption period) of another puppy who was available and in need of a permanent home.

All nine of us made our way to the neighborhood animal shelter we'd been stalking and drooling over on Instagram, me with my oxygen tank and tracheotomy, Katie skipping ahead impatiently, to meet a little black puppy named Esther that my brother Patrick was head over heels for after looking at that litter's Instagram posts. The kids were all talking at once about how much fun it would be to have a dog as part of our clan. Emilea and Patrick were thrilled about the joint custody arrangement, and hopeful that it would bring them closer to my kids long after they needed to be there to help me get out of bed and get around with my tank and walker.

We waited at the shelter for a while, but the foster parents were a no-show. We were all about to disappointedly drag ourselves out of there when someone who'd adopted two sister puppies came back to return one of them because it turned out two puppies were too much for her (she was an actual sane person). When she took the tiny dog out of the carrier, I saw the white puppy with brown spots. She tilted her head to the side and looked at me with sad eyes like she was posing for an Instagram photo with the caption "Please, adopt me!" I croaked, "Wait…is that *Sharon*?!" It was Sharon! I viewed it as a sign: We were meant to adopt her! It was in the stars!

We started the paperwork. The kids were overjoyed and Emilea, Patrick, who had now fallen victim to Sharon's wiles, and Jim were beaming over her. Just then, a family walked in with another puppy, Esther, who was tiny and black. The foster family had gotten stuck on the train, but they were elated to find us still there. They had a little boy about Katie's age, who said, "I'm so happy that my dog is being adopted by a family with kids!" Katie looked up at me with her big blue eyes: "Mom, they could be *sisters*!" I looked over at my brother

Patrick, who was busy getting his face licked by Esther. Instant bond. "Okay," I said. "We'll take them both." Jim and I caught eyes and shared a smiling look that said, "Are we crazy?" and "Yes, but together we can do absolutely anything," at the same time. And that's the story about how, in the middle of this family earthquake, we ended up with two rescue puppies that we promptly renamed.

Peggy and Larry the Girl

Chapter 22

FEEDING FRENZY

My recovery seemed to be at a standstill. I wasn't getting worse, but I wasn't making progress either. I was so congested and my lungs weren't clearing. Over time, it occurred to us that it might be the canned formula, just as Maria had theorized in the hospital. When Bruce would "fill my feed bag," as I put it, occasionally there would be drops of back spray that would land on the wooden floor next to my bed unnoticed. The next day the droplets would be as hard as cement and someone would have to scrape them off with a plastic knife, taking the poly on the floor off with it. This was what was going into my stomach. I was surviving on this processed liquid cement while I was trying to recover from the most traumatic health crisis in my life, and I would never have put something like this in my body at the height of my fitness. When I got better I resolved to treat myself to junk food more often (carpe pizza!), but for now, I had to heal! After a post on Instagram that showed my

Time for your pouch of goodness!

feeding setup, people who had tube-fed children started reaching out on social media with recommendations for alternative formulas that were organic and natural.

With Jim's help and advocacy, I started to use a variety of natural tube formulas for my PEG. Rather than using a machine that pumped in the processed goo, the new formulas were mixed and PEG-ed through a syringe.

* * *

Food, fun, and family were always interconnected in my life, so this new existence with the food PEG tube was seemingly the opposite. Just to keep me alive, nutrition was pumped into my body in an awkward, humiliating way and was not enjoyable at all. All the other elements that made food part of life were

237

gone. So Jim creatively made the process the best experience it could be for me. The double meaning of the term "pegged" was not lost on my comedian husband. I am not sure what it means and I never looked it up because I am sure it's gross and dirty, but I can guess. The one thing I am sure about is that its principal meaning is not mixing up a bag of puréed food formula, sucking it up into a plastic syringe, and injecting it into a rubber tube running into the stomach.

Jim was the primary "pegger." I remember the first time Jim brought me into the kitchen for this; he was all set up with the mixing cup, the food pouch, and the big plastic syringe displayed on the counter. "What is all this?" I asked.

"Are you ready for your pegging?" Jim asked seductively.

"Not really..."

"Uncap your food hose and get ready for Chef Jim to mix you up some...(looks at a pouch) chickpeas, carrots, and spinach! Yum, yum, yum! Somebody, film this!"

In true Jim form, he turned this escapade into a cooking show–style sketch that he posted on YouTube called "Feeding Frenzy":

When it was time for a "feeding," the iPhone camera would be rolling. Jim would shake the formula around like Tom Cruise in *Cocktail*, describe what type of ingredients were in the formula, and then explain in step-by-step details to the "audience" how to expertly PEG his wife. He even lit a candle in one episode to make the process more romantic. Every time we had a visitor and it was time to PEG, he would create another installment of this show with guest peggers, like Trish. "Would you like to 'PEG' my wife?" He would then proceed to criticize the way the guest was doing everything. Even though one could think that this was a silly, infantile way to deal with a delicate, somewhat gross activity, we received an outpouring of support from tons of nurses, speech pathologists, and patients, thanking us for "normalizing" this not-so-uncommon medical procedure. Peggers of the world, unite! No not *that* kind. Get your mind out of the gutter.

The romantic dinner.

Again, Jim found his stride in caregiving, not only helping me to get through this awful time by being hilarious, but also helping the food tube community that until this point I had no idea existed. Sharon's new name was not a random choice; she was named after my food PEG. Thank God for comedian caregivers!

"Peggy"

Chapter 23

DIRTY DANCING

I'd always taken for granted how physically active I was in everyday life. I probably have some kind of hyperactive disorder and should be popping Ritalin like Tic Tacs. When I was nine years old, I could race to the top branch of the highest tree in the neighborhood the fastest and beat all the big kids, and I was always covered with scratches and bruises that these days would raise some eyebrows among social workers. Jim would mock me for getting up during writing sessions and acting out all the characters: "You are the only person I know who makes writing an aerobic exercise!" I got in there deep with the mothering and housecleaning too. When the other moms were going to the gym and asked me if I wanted to join them for a workout, I'd say, "I bench-press babies!" Or, "I'm going to go hit the vacuum machine and work on my quads." The old neighborhood joke was calling me "the bag lady" because I was always schlepping way too many heavy things around. A neighbor describes a regular, imaginary encounter with me as, "I saw Jeannie hurrying down the street with ten bags of bricks. I said, 'Jeannie, what are you doing?' She said (breathless), 'I'm building a brick wall for Jim, but I need more bricks!'...and then she ran off!"

Being a waiflike shadow of my former self with no muscle tone was like being trapped in a crate. Even though I was exhausted all the time, I knew I had to get up and work on getting my strength back. I was grateful for my life, but now that I had proper nutrition, "pegged" though it was, I needed to get back the quality.

Part of my rehab was that a physical therapist would come over a few times a week for an hour at a time. He was a really sweet Filipino man in his fifties, but it was awkward to be sleeping and have my husband come into the bedroom with a strange man and announce, "Jeannie, wake up, it's time for physical therapy!" Since I could barely move, we would do a short series of exercises while lying flat in bed, then sitting up, and then a few standing. These ridiculously easy, incredibly boring exercises totally wore me out, even though it appeared as though I was having a vivid dream about synchronized swimming. I was totally annoyed by these mundane activities I struggled to do. I'd never been bored and challenged at the same time. I found myself loathing the three-times-per-week visits, but I hid my annoyance and put on a smile for the therapist so as not to appear impolite (see the Amy Vanderbilt handbook for PT manners).

My brother Patrick thought the whole thing was hilarious, so he filmed some of this and then put together a video montage paired with "Super Freak" and songs from *Dirty Dancing*. Although I was absolutely mortified that anybody would see

me this way, doing lame exercises in my striped prisoner pajamas, there was something hysterical about it, so I let go of my
humiliation and agreed to post it on my Instagram. The feed-
back I got was so inspiring, it was like I had a team of cheer-
leaders rooting for me to get through my ten stupid leg lifts. I
felt like the Beyoncé of physical therapy patients.

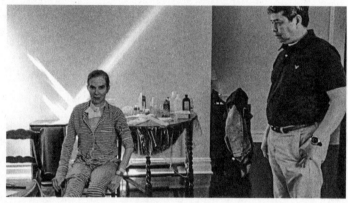

Crazy in leg lifts.

One of the things I dreamed about during my recovery at
home was riding a bike. I'm not much of an everyday rider,
but there was something about looking out the window at the
beautiful weather while being so immobile that made me crave
riding one, something so easy yet so out of reach. The first
time I walked outside, I felt a step closer, like the end of the
long road was finally in sight. The sun was shining brightly in
a clear blue sky with a cool, gentle wind blowing. I made it all
the way to the end of my block with my physical therapist. We
slowly strolled down the street like we were on a date in the
1900s. I held my head up proudly as my gentleman companion
ushered me with an appropriately placed hand on the small of
my back. I savored the breeze hitting my face and smiled at

passersby. The funny thing was, no one on the streets of New York gave me a second look, even though I was wearing pajamas and using a granny walker. Gotta love this city.

After this first walk outside, my temperature shot up to 103°. Paul was visiting that night and noticed how hot I was getting and that my oxygen levels were dipping dangerously low. He alerted Jim, despite my protests that I was fine. Jim called Bruce, who insisted we go right to the emergency room at Mount Sinai. "No! I can't go back there! What if they don't let me leave?!" I started to cry. I was the prisoner who got released and now they were bringing me up on new charges. "Please don't make me go!" I was traumatized. Jim and Paul consoled me: "Jeannie, if you don't go to the ER it could get really bad, and then you'll have to go back to the ICU!" That was enough to convince me. I knew there were patients in the ICU who never made it out. I'd been so lucky. I might have to spend one night in the county jail to avoid months of solitary confinement. Jim called Dr. Glen Chun, the pulmonologist who had managed my pneumonia in the hospital. He said he would meet us in the emergency room so we wouldn't have to wait around for hours like mere hospital amateurs. He would be like the bouncer who escorts us to the roped-off table at the back of the club. My lungs were "VIL" members: Very Important Lungs.

When we got to the ER they were waiting for me as I entered with my entourage of Jim, Bruce, and Paul. I was given a CT scan of the lungs by a radiology technician whom I jokingly referred to as "the paparazzi." Looking at the scan, Dr. Chun determined that the pneumonia wasn't completely resolved and my lungs were still filled with gunk. They gave me an IV of antibiotics, a prescription, and as a result of my pleading and tears, let me go back home, with strict instructions for Bruce and Jim: "She needs to take it easier." Which meant no more walks outside for a while. I didn't really know how anything could be easier than walking half a block, but I complied.

I felt unproductive lying in bed, but my schedule was packed. It was aggravating for me to be so busy without "getting anything done." I was on a strict medication regimen, my other aforementioned accoutrements needed constant service, and there was a revolving door of home therapists.

Occupational Hazard

An occupational therapist is supposed to help you relearn day-to-day things as you go back to your life at home. I barely remember these sessions. She came by only twice because I think I scared her away. I couldn't really handle buttons yet, so we focused mostly on this exciting job. Buttoning and unbuttoning multiple times under supervision was awkward. "Take off your clothes and then put them on again." I felt like I was auditioning for an ingenue role in Hollywood before the #MeToo movement. Once it was apparent that I was perfectly capable of doing the basics of getting clothes on and off, I asked what I had to do next for OT. "You should do something that is meaningful to you," she said. "Something you would do in everyday life."

"Okay, can I clean out my basement storage?" I couldn't wait to get to that project. The therapist looked mortified. "You have to do something very simple at first. Like, why don't you try to cook breakfast for your children?" It was so me that I wanted to jump into a huge project when doing something directly for my kids was obviously the right choice.

Do other people do things like this? Feel like they have to

take on the most ambitious project in order to prove...what, exactly? Don't get me wrong, the storage needed cleaning. Before I got sick, it was on my "projects to do" list. Over the winter, the skateboards, bikes, and scooters sat unused under the beach stuff and coolers. I'd planned to organize the closet for easy access when the weather got warmer. But even now, as I was recovering from brain surgery, it hadn't even occurred to me to delegate this. Not because there was no one to do it, but because, as usual, I had convinced myself that I was the only one who knew whose skateboard was which and who outgrew what; therefore, I was the only one who could do it right. This was what I did to "nurture" my family. But I guessed I would try the breakfast thing, as simple as it seemed.

When I make scrambled eggs, I don't scramble them. I push the edges into the middle of the pan and fold them on top of each other. I also don't beat them one solid color, and I never use a blender or add milk. I actually think they are better if they are not mixed that well, with big pockets of yolk and a few white bits. As I was making breakfast that next morning, I was getting really into my egg cooking. I let go of my hunger in the name of something bigger. It was as if I were someone grooming their ex for a date with another person for the purpose of a greater good.

Katie noticed my intensity. "Mommy, I love the way you make scrambled eggs; you can pick up a whole piece with the fork and you don't make them little crumbles like everyone else does." I was beaming with pride. "Katie, would you like me to teach you how to make them that way?" She was so excited to pull a chair up next to the stove and learn my OCD egg method. Once she had mastered my perfect folded egg, she said, "Mom, now can you teach me how to make a sunny-side

The perfect egg.

up?" I paused. In a past life, I would have retorted with something like, "What do you think this is, Denny's? I'm busy! I have to get to cleaning out the basement storage!" But that morning, I took a deep breath and said, "Of course I will!" After all, I was the only one who could do it right.

Chapter 24

DO IT IN STYLE

All day after I made breakfast I felt fantastic. I didn't push myself too hard, but I stayed engaged with life. I was getting back on a normal schedule where day felt like day and night felt like night, and I ceased to envision myself as a lonely spirit wandering the darkened halls and rattling my chains all night. That evening I could sit with the family at dinner and not feel any awkwardness or resistance to being around food. My taking on the eggs with Katie must have broken the spell. I spent quality time with all of my kids that night, outside of my own bedroom. I brushed Marre's hair while she told me about a movie she'd just seen with a friend and I wasn't sarcastic about her hyper-PC opinions. Jack showed me a funny video he'd edited in iMovie that was a compilation of famous film scenes intercut with a guy talking about chocolate cake, and for once I kind of got his humor. Katie taught me how to make "fluffy slime" with shaving cream and I didn't complain about the mess. Patrick, Michael, and I sat in the playroom tent telling scary stories, and not once did I correct them for being too gory about alien zombies eating brains. I already knew they weren't serial killers, so what was wrong with a little macabre creativity? I'm sure Tim Burton's mom got over the worry at some point.

That evening I actually "went to bed" since I hadn't been in it all day, as I had in the past few weeks when "going to bed" was redundant. Jim had my pillows propped up around me so that both my head and feet were elevated in sort of a U shape. My legs were up so the blood would not pool in my ankles, and my head was also raised so I could breathe while I slept. This may not seem like a very comfortable position, but I was happy in my little U nest. I was actually exhausted. Not the bad exhaustion that I'd been feeling for weeks, but a good, "I had a long, productive day" exhausted. I felt human. I told Jim I was ready for him to go back on the road. Jim loves performing, and I was sure he missed it. I knew he was wanted back, according to the endless comments on Twitter. The funnyman was resurrected and I needed to share him. "Are you trying to get rid of me?" he asked.

"You caught me," I answered. "There are a lot of gentlemen callers who are dying to change my trach pad." I assured him that his going back to work would be the best thing. Pat and Emilea were five minutes away if I needed to go back to the hospital. Family members were still popping in on a regular basis. Lizzy's boyfriend (now husband) Rudy had even stepped up to take little Patrick to a birthday party when no one else could (Rudy: "The pizza was pretty good"). Jim said he would call his manager and give the green light, but he'd feel more comfortable if he started with venues close by on the East Coast in the event he'd have to return quickly. We laughed about how it was just like the ninth month of all my pregnancies when we were afraid he'd be onstage doing the "Hot Pockets" routine and I'd be having a hot pocket moment alone. We both agreed: It was time for him to go back to reality.

I turned off our lamp and Jim turned on the news, which before all this had been our routine at the end of the day. I found myself suddenly interested in current events. It struck me that during all that time from discovery of my tumor through recovery thus far, I was very mentally removed from what was happening in the world, and there was a lot going on.

Years from now, this particular period in 2017 would probably be viewed as one of the most politically volatile times in modern American history. There was a new president. Half of the country hated him like poison and the other half felt he could do no wrong, despite alarming evidence to the contrary. I'd hear bits and pieces of news here and there, but I was too sick to really comprehend anything. It seemed like every week there was another huge protest or march going on. As if the turmoil in Washington wasn't enough, there were also horrific sexual harassment scandals in the entertainment, religious, and business worlds, and mass shootings on what seemed a regular basis. The country was bitterly divided and civil discourse was a thing of the past. Whereas before, I would have been quick to pick a side and decide who was good or bad, going through the personal trauma that threatened my very life and the lives of my family, I'd become out of touch, disconnected from the political vitriol. It didn't suck me in anymore. Of course it's important to care about gun violence, racial inequality, gender inequality, or persecution of any kind. It's not that politics don't matter—obviously the policies of our politicians affect people's lives in grand and small ways, but what I'm talking about is the spectacle of politics. The thing that robs us of all capacity to see nuance and to find the humanity in others beyond the political label. Back in the ICU all the people who came to help me could have been from diverse political viewpoints, but they weren't fighting with one another. They were working together around a common cause: love for me.

But since I was feeling better that night, I quickly forgot about this epiphany and got sucked right back into caring about what was happening on cable news. It was something incredibly salacious like Trump covering up a payment to a porn star and I was captivated, hook, line, and sinker. This gossip was like the chocolate-syrup-covered dessert I was craving. I recognized this icky part of myself in the moment, but I didn't turn off the TV. I reached for the remote to change the channel and saw a silver dollar–sized spot on my right hand with large pink bubbles on the skin between my thumb and my wrist. "Holy crap! What happened to my hand?" It looked like a severe allergic reaction—maybe hives or bites from a giant extraterrestrial mosquito, or even a brain-eating zombie. I showed it to Jim, who examined me with concern.

"It looks like burn blisters," said Dr. Jim. "Did you burn your hand?" It did not take us long to realize that on my right side, I'd lost all sensations of pain and temperature. When I was cooking breakfast for the kids, I must have rested my hand on the hot frying pan and because of this numbness, I did not immediately react in pain and pull it away. I must have just let it rest there and sizzle. Here I was feeling so capable, yet I wasn't even aware of this major injury to my own body. The oddest thing about this discovery was that I could move my hand really well. I mean, I couldn't tie shoelaces yet, but I could open and close my fist and isolate each finger.

Jim called Leslie, who was afraid I might have a blood clot. She called me in for an MRI. So much for cable news and chill. Up to Mount Sinai again we went. Turns out I had no blood clot and the numbness was just another cool residual side effect from having a pear in my brain that would "probably resolve itself eventually." I got back in bed and resumed feeling sorry for myself. Jim started second-guessing his decision to go back to work. "It wasn't a blood clot, Jim. Don't worry about me. I'm just a mutant. Maybe I'll join *The Avengers*."

Life Is Beautiful

I really needed a pick-me-up. I had been in pajamas for two weeks, and though I had constant medical care, I needed to do something for myself. I mean, everything I was doing was for myself, but I viewed all the therapy work really as the need to get back to me, the caregiver. I wanted to do something purely for my own vanity. Get a manicure or buy a scarf to cover my hideous blowhole. Something for my appearance that would make me feel less like a revolting monster. Of course, health is the most important, but taking care of appearances gets a bad rap.

My first adventure back into the world of beauty was getting my hair done. The half-shaved look had gone from punk rock to scraggly. My fantastically stylish cousin, Tina, set me up with her beauty guru, giving him fair warning that I was part invalid, so he wasn't shocked when I rolled up to his high-end studio with my multitube couture. The thought of doing this sort of extravagant thing for myself made me happy. Finally, I had something to look forward to! The night before that first haircut, when Jim got into bed I was excitedly chattering about how I was going to Chelsea for some beautification. He was like, "You look fine to me." He so didn't get it.

I asked for "the horse" to take me to the bathroom to brush my teeth. As he helped me up, I noticed that my right leg was completely numb. I was used to the dullness because of the bedrest and general atrophy, and the lack of feeling on my right side, but suddenly my leg was tingling. Jim was concerned, but I was hoping it was a sign of the feeling coming back. He sent a "just in case" text to Leslie asking if we should be worried. We didn't hear back right away, so I figured it was nothing.

In the morning, my mom, who was still living with us, took me to the fancy Chelsea hair salon with my tracheotomy and oxygen tank to do something about hair that looked like David Lee Roth on one side and Eleven from season 2 of *Stranger Things* on the other. I did not feel quite ready for real clothes, so Jim bought me a beautiful pair of green satin pajamas with white piping that Weezie said looked like something a 1940s Hollywood icon would lounge around in: "You are *so* Kate Hepburn!" Apparently my mom felt like she was a close personal friend with Katharine Hepburn.

We arrived at the salon in the elegant brownstone. Mom came around to my side and helped me out of the cab. I had a white silk scarf loosely tied around my neck to cover the tracheotomy. I felt like there should be flashbulbs popping. I pretended my portable tank was a fashionable handbag as I limp-waltzed into the salon with my head held high. Tommy cut and styled my hair like Edward Scissorhands taking on a topiary while he gossiped with Weezie. I listened, smiling, while I tried to ignore another customer, just a few chairs to my left, eating cut fruit out of a plastic cup—a cruel reminder that no matter how glamorous I felt, it would take time before I could have a normal life. *Ignore the fruit, ignore the fruit...*, I told myself.

Tommy spun me around to admire his work in the beautiful framed mirror. Weezie had put red lipstick on me, saying, "My grandmother Mimi would never leave her apartment in Tudor City without lipstick!" I felt marvelous. I forgot about the cut fruit. I got such a lift from this little bit of self-pampering. I thought about all those mornings before I got sick that I would pull on leggings and throw my hair up in a ponytail, caring less and less about my appearance over the years as I stressed about

Princess for an afternoon

what the kids were going to wear. I wanted to bottle this feeling and open it up when I was feeling glum to remind myself that it's okay to have these little indulgences. I needed them!

My phone rang. I had just texted Jim a photo of "the new me" and I figured it was him, wanting to see me immediately so he could plant a kiss on my ruby-red lips. It was Leslie. She had just gotten the text about the tingling in my leg and was very concerned. "But I feel fine now!"

Leslie was adamant. "It could be a blood clot. I want you to come in right away for another CT scan." Just as I was getting the last touches on my fab new coif.

"We have to go in," said my mom, concerned.

"Maybe I'll run into Joe." There's nothing better than running into your ex-nurse when you're looking fabulous.

After the five-hour ordeal of going to the hospital, finding out I couldn't go in the tube with my metal trach, having an otolaryngologist come swap it out for a plastic one, and the familiar hour-long ride through the noise tube, my beachy wave blowout was transformed into more of a hurricane-mangled matted-dreadlock look. The best-laid plans of mice and women who have their hair done at fancy salons. On a more positive note, again it turned out I didn't have a blood clot. Just another false-alarm urgent trip to the hospital.

The bizarre juxtaposition of beauty day and medical drama united me and my mom in female power like Wonder Woman and Supergirl. Beautiful, powerful mutants. She with her nine kids and me with my five kids plus brain tumor surgery, which has to equal like at least four more kids, right? We agreed on the way downtown, life is hard, but women are so *strong*! When we arrived back at home later that night, we were a dynamic duo who could survive anything, and look good doing it! Jim greeted us at the door. "Wow, your hair looks amazing!" He was serious. Note to self: to impress husband, get hair done, then walk through a tornado.

Setbacks Keep You Moving Forward

After the elation I had felt when being discharged from the hospital, going back so often was a major disappointment and it started to really weigh on my spirit. At this point, I was making so many trips up to Mount Sinai, I started to refer to it as "my summer home." Throughout our careers, Jim and I had become used to setbacks and remaining strong in the face of disappointment. The entire time we'd been together, the "chance of a lifetime" was presented several times a year and then abruptly yanked away. Regardless of the momentary devastation, over the years we'd come to recognize that cumulatively we had it really, really good. We'd gained invaluable wisdom, worked even harder, and become seasoned by our professional frustrations, understanding that every failure was a necessary part of a long game. But this self-assured hubris as it applied to our careers did nothing to inform us in this new roller-coaster ride we were on. The definition of a "setback" changed profoundly when it came to life and death. Not getting a script deal or a lead role in a pilot as opposed to finding out you have to go back to the hospital is like the difference between climbing a flight of stairs and climbing Mount Kilimanjaro. The constant mini victories followed by devastating disappointments of the health crises stripped us of all our mature wisdom and turned us into wide-eyed amateurs who thought they were going to be discovered by sitting at the soda counter at Schwab's, only to find themselves dressed as pizza mascots handing out flyers for a lunch special.

We needed to pull ourselves together. We wanted everything to go back to business as usual far faster than humanly possible. This was to be a new exercise in patience, something that maybe we had learned in the entertainment business but now had to relearn in just living life. Based on my tumor-related experiences so far, I had come to understand that time would be the only salve on the burning frustration of not being able to quickly get better and put this all behind me. I wanted to get back to being a hands-on mother before all my kids grew up and flew the coop. There'd been so much high-stakes drama in this brain tumor saga already, and it didn't seem like it was going to end anytime soon. It was a series of mini steps forward and giant steps back: Making peace with the brain surgery and then discovering the fibromuscular dysplasia. Getting through the surgery successfully and then suffering the enormous setback of pneumonia. Finally being discharged from the hospital and then having the trach accident.

I had to get a grip on the fact that this heart-wrenching ride I was on was making me stronger and teaching me not to give up. I wanted to jump right on a bike, but I learned that I had to take it slower. Even though I'd lived my whole life as if racing in a 50-yard dash, now I had to take the attitude of a long-distance runner: pace yourself at the beginning in order to run the second half faster than the first, and finish strong. Having to relearn the same lessons that you thought you'd already mastered in life is humbling. Even more humbling is being honest with your kids that you are dealing with disappointment and that it's a necessary part of life. You can't hide from pain.

Things aren't always going to go your way. Nothing is going to get handed to you, and if it does, it's not going to have much value.

I remember little Patrick coming into my room and saying, "Mom, are you going to be able to eat soon?" I answered, "No, Patrick. I really want to eat, but it's probably going to take a lot of work and a really long time." I thought it was so sweet of him to bring that up out of the blue, but I wondered what had prompted it. I asked him the reason for his question. "Because, Mommy, when you don't have a PEG and a trach anymore, I want to take you for a picnic. But don't worry, I won't go without you. I'll wait for you to get better. Keep working hard and all your dreams will come true."

And they did.

Chapter 25

THE ANNIVERSARY

Marriage is like recovering from a serious illness. It's a lot of work, and it's painful, but it's better than dying. Sometimes. Just when you think you get over a hurdle, you get comfortable and then *WHAM*, you get hit with a setback.

I think Jim was more excited than I was the day I was allowed to have my first swallow of food. Jim and I went together to Mount Sinai for the big moment. We'd built it up so much in our minds that we'd anticipated we could start off with a steak dinner, and then just eat our way across New York. We would be the couple that ate New York.

My long-awaited reunion with food was very anticlimactic. I was required to pass an x-ray test where I had to swallow tiny bits of white barium paste with my strict yet sensational speech and swallow therapist, Leanne Goldberg, closely monitoring a screen to see if it went down the right pipe. Jim had a field day watching me swallow the barium paste: "You know, with some salt and pepper that doesn't look like it would be that bad. I would spread that on a bagel!" I passed the test; the barium went down without aspiration. I graduated from the "nothing by mouth" sentence, but instead of the glorious feast I'd been dreaming of for months, I was allowed three spoonfuls of applesauce per day.

On the way home, Jim was so elated that I'd passed, he stopped and bought two giant grocery bags full of assorted flavors of applesauce. "You are going to par-tay!" I forced a smile. "C'mon, Jim, it's not like it was the bar exam!" He went on, "Nothing is too good for my lady! Today, cinnamon applesauce; tomorrow, Smith & Wollensky's (his favorite steak house)!"

I just wanted water, but water was a no-no. I had to stick to "nectar-thick" liquids such as applesauce, because anything thinner would just go down the wrong way and I would choke, or else it would immediately run out of my nose. Gravity helped the more substantial liquid down my throat, so I had to add this starchy, powdered thickener to water and coffee. If you want to know what that tasted like, I'll put it this way: I actually missed nothing by mouth. Not really, but almost. It was easier to PEG than eat. But Jim was ready to celebrate for me and with me.

July 26 was our fourteenth wedding anniversary. The number 14 doesn't really mean anything as far as anniversaries go, but it was a huge year for us because unlucky 13 could have been our last. Furthering the grand celebration was the fact that my tracheotomy had been removed and I was left with a neck scar that looked like a stitched-up belly button. Luckily it was an "innie."

A chef friend, who had been wonderful about sending food

to my family during the nothing-by-mouth days, invited us to his fancy restaurant to celebrate this milestone in our marriage. He knew about my dietary restrictions and had custom-designed a five-course menu consisting of all liquid delicacies. Jim, in communion with his ailing wife, decided that he, too, would just have the liquid menu.

After dinner Jim produced a beautifully wrapped jewelry box and presented it to me: a gorgeous necklace that was intended to cover my garish trach scar. With a romantic gesture, he fastened it around my neck. I excused myself to the ladies' room to admire it in the mirror. When I saw my reflection I was horrified. The front of the necklace formed a little V, which sat directly under the scar on my neck, as if it were a glittering silver pedestal showing it off. What was I going to do? I had to wear it; it was a gift from Jim. He had picked it out with the best intentions in mind, but it just accentuated my pink neck-button deformity. Staring in the mirror, repelled at the sight of myself, I resolved to wear it only for him. He was back to work on the weekends now, so he would never know that I hated it.

I returned to the table, and through a big toothy smile I exclaimed, "Thank you so much. I love it!" Jim looked sad. Either I'm a terrible actress or else when you're married for fourteen years, your husband knows when you're full of it. I backpedaled: "Maybe we can get it adjusted a little higher."

"Of course we can. You look beautiful in it. I hardly notice the scar." Maybe he was a bad actor too. Time to change the subject. The dinner conversation quickly turned to all the things we had recently been through as a couple, and how we were rock stars in our fantastic marriage. We had overcome so many obstacles over the years—and how we'd grown from all the hardships! The struggles we'd been through, from baby Bean to Father Jonathan counseling us through our marital discord, had shaped and prepared us for this latest catastrophe and for the many more that were sure to come. I apologized about my reaction to the necklace.

"I'm sorry, Jim. Am I still in the doghouse?" I put my fingertips together over my head, forming a little roof, and peered my head out like a sad dog. This was an inside bit we'd been doing since the first year we were dating. If one of us was in trouble with the other, we could disarm the situation by putting ourselves "in the doghouse" and making a sad dog face. It always cracked us up and broke the tension. Stupid, I know, but it's our thing. Jim responded by putting himself in "the doghouse," and we both started laughing and clinked champagne glasses. As soon as we let our guard down, the mood changed dramatically. Jim asked me if I remembered something very specific he did when we were at the hospital. I replied, "I barely remember you at the hospital." Now before you also misunderstand this, what I meant was that the hospital was very foggy and confusing for me, and I remember only spurts of time. I *should* have said, "I barely remember the details of being at the hospital." But I accidentally added the "you" part. What he heard was, "I don't remember *you being* at the hospital at all," as if he hadn't come.

Jim was hurt and enraged: "I was at the hospital all the time, Jeannie! What do you mean you don't remember me being at the hospital?" Instead of clarifying what I meant, I was wildly defensive. "You're mad at me for not remembering everything that happened in the hospital after I had *brain surgery*?!" So there we were, in the fancy restaurant, seething with fury and resentment toward each other, with champagne I couldn't handle drinking yet dripping from my nose directly onto the unwanted silver trach pedestal.

Jim had canceled sold-out shows to stay with me. He became the master of ceremonies for the Gaffigan household, and now he thought I didn't remember any of it. But I did. I was just too stubborn to admit I was wrong. God wasn't kidding with those commandments!

Seeing the look on his face at that moment, I believe Jim finally understood how I felt sometimes as a mother. To give and give to the one you love until you feel you have nothing left, and it seems they don't even notice you are there. Or even more so, what it's like to be God. He's probably pretty bummed being a benevolent giver who just gets ignored and blasphemed in return. I know I'm guilty of that. I understood how Jim felt, but he was wrong. I did notice, and I remembered. I'll never forget what he did. And I'm sure, someday, the kids will look back and appreciate me.

*　*　*

At the beginning of our relationship we'd figured out that we fit together based on who we were already. That's how we knew it would work. Sure, we'd tweaked and adjusted a bit, but our identity as a couple was based on how the two puzzle pieces we'd individually brought lined up, and as we added kids and other elements, we continued to view each other through the same lens as we always had.

The tumor reset had switched our roles like *Freaky Friday* and as we emerged from the depths of the crisis, our ability to adjust and redefine who we were as a couple was presenting us with a big mess o' growing pains, as illustrated by our failed romantic dinner. Jim felt underappreciated, as I had so many times in the past. I felt like I couldn't say the right thing, as Jim had pretty much *every* time in the past.

Over the year that followed this anniversary and through many long, honest conversations about the challenges we faced as we evolved into our new relationship, I came to realize that as painful as this experience was, our marriage benefited. Jim understood what it was like to be Jeannie. Jeannie understood what it was like to be Jim. This deeper level of empathy reshaped who we were as individuals and fit together in a new and better way.

Once a day we each make a point of communicating love and appreciation for each other. It may be something as simple as "Thanks for buying that cheese I like," or even texting a heart emoji. This was something that we'd overlooked as a necessary part of a strong coupleship over the past fourteen years. The anniversary wasn't a disaster after all, because in our failure we'd gotten the greatest gift either of us had ever received from each other: the daily gesture of a simple "Thank you." Okay, was that too corny? Am I in the doghouse now?

Chapter 26

WHEN JIMMY MET JEANNIE

Looking back on my young adulthood, I never thought my life would get so intertwined with someone else's. We weren't always an enmeshed couple with five kids trying to navigate through the same life with two different minds. It's difficult to imagine that a chance meeting could change everything so dramatically, but I guess that's how it always happens.

When I first met Jim, we both lived on Mott Street north of Chinatown, south of Houston Street in Manhattan. The area is now one of the city's most sought-after stylish neighborhoods (yes I'm obsessed with NoLIta), but back then, pregentrification, it was sort of no-man's-land. It wasn't Little Italy and it wasn't SoHo. I loved it. It was distressed in the way a shining stainless-steel sink becomes etched and scratched over time and develops a beautiful patina that tells the story of its years of use. The once charming prewar tenement buildings had fallen into disrepair, layers of paint peeling off elaborately patterned tin ceilings. Old marble tiles warped, cracked and filthy.

There were some people remaining from the Italian neighborhood that Martin Scorsese had grown up in, but it was mostly inhabited by immigrant Chinese and Dominican families. The playground on the corner had cement tables where old guys would sit all day playing dominoes. There was a bodega on the block that I don't think sold anything, at least not legally. It had a wooden fruit stand, partially visible from the street, and I think the fruit had dust on it. There was a suspicious storefront where some wannabe goodfellas met up and "played cards" while two or three lookouts sat on the sidewalk smoking cigars in folding lawn chairs with a friendly word for all who passed. There were open windows with dripping air conditioners precariously placed on the sills high above the sidewalk, elevating the exhilarating feeling of impending danger. Loud salsa music was always blasting from somewhere. A Chinese great-grandma foraged for cans in the curbside recycle bags.

Central to the neighborhood was a Catholic church with a brick wall around it: St. Patrick's Old Cathedral. This church defined the block because within its walls was an old cemetery filled with grass and trees, a rare sight for a nonpark area in New York City. It gave the whole area a unique charm and made it unlike any other neighborhood. It became my church. Jim's building was on Mott between Houston and Prince, and mine was between Prince and Spring. I had *seen* Jim for a few years as we passed each other on the street. When you pass the same person so often, eventually you should acknowledge they exist with a nod or a smile, or it's just weird. Years later, Jim and I would recount passings-by and the number of times we had "met" before we actually met.

There was that one time in the late '90s when my sister Maria, a junior at a Milwaukee high school at the time, was staying at my apartment while she toured colleges in the New York area. Jim, whom I then thought of as that blond guy who lived on my block (he stood out like a pale thumb), was jogging by with headphones on. I smiled at him and said "Hi," to show my sister that even in New York City people are friendly with their neighbors. Jim reacted as if he were at the beginning of some "I never thought it would happen to me" story, stopped jogging, and said, "Hello, ladies!" We stood there awkwardly for a beat because I guess we didn't expect him to stop. I must have babbled something about heading over to the NYU campus. He looked at us skeptically and said, "How old are you?" My sister quickly replied, "Sixteen!" and Jim said, "Bye!" and sprinted away.

A few years later I was directing a play with seventh and eighth graders in the St. Patrick's Youth Center. It was tech week, and the next morning the kids were having their dress rehearsal. The backdrop and scenery had taken a beating from the day's run-through and needed to be patched up. At about 10:30 p.m., I ran over to the Korean market on Prince Street to buy some duct tape. A Korean market sells everything under the sun. Amazon probably got its inspiration to move on from being only a bookseller after walking into a New York City Korean market. When I got to the duct tape section (yes, there was a duct tape section next to the gourmet crackers), I realized I had forgotten to grab a shopping basket and I needed about five rolls of tape. In my usual manic state, I slipped the multiple rolls over my wrist and up my arm like bracelets, checked out at the counter, and bolted out the door.

Jim, having finished a spot at one of the comedy clubs, was entering the Korean for a late-night snack. As I was exiting, I literally collided with Jim like we were in some bad romantic comedy. As we bumbled through our apologies, I smiled and said, "How are you?" He replied, "Sorry, do I know you from somewhere?"

I was wildly offended: "Are you kidding me? We live on the same block! We have passed on the street hundreds of times! We smile at each other! We nod! Are you really that arrogant that you would ask me if you *know* me?" I caught my breath. I'd had a rough day staging fifty rambunctious middle schoolers in *Romeo and Juliet.*

Jim looked at me. A wild-eyed, dirty, crazy woman with duct-tape bracelets up to the shoulder. "You know, we're probably going to get married," he said.

Two years later, we did.

* * *

That prophetic pickup line kicked off the beginning of my story of surviving a brain tumor. At the time, I was shocked by Jim's unabashed confidence, yet intrigued. After I accused him of being arrogant, he said probably the most arrogant, obnoxious, entitled thing I have ever had directed at me that wasn't catcalled from a passing car window. Married? I wouldn't even go on a date with this guy. Not my style to be pushed around. Married? I was busy. Not interested in a relationship. My experiences with relationships up until that point were excruciatingly painful time drains. Then again, I was starting a not-for-profit theater company for local urban preteens, and I needed the support of the neighborhood, so I gave him my email address. I didn't want to seem too available with a phone number. That night when I got home after midnight, I sat down in front of my gigantic computer and logged in to AOL, as we did in 2000. As soon as I began to check my email, a little instant messenger popped up. It was Jim.

jimgaffigan: Hi. Did you miss me?

Jlnoth: Wow you are really confident.

jimgaffigan: What are you doing?

Jlnoth: Logging into AOL.

jimgaffigan: Wanna go see a movie?

Jlnoth: When?

jimgaffigan: Now.

Jlnoth: It's 12:16am!

jimgaffigan: There's a 12:35 movie playing at the Angelika. Let's go.

Jlnoth: What? No! i don't even know you.

jimgaffigan: What do you want to know?

Jlnoth: Um... where you get your arrogance?

jimgaffigan: What are you doing tomorrow?

Jlnoth: Laundry.

jimgaffigan: Cool. I have laundry too. Let's do laundry together.

Jlnoth: i'm not doing laundry with you. You're not my boyfriend!

jimgaffigan: Not yet. Do you want to have dinner with me?

Jlnoth: What is your problem?

jimgaffigan: Ok, how about lunch?

Jlnoth: Ok, fine.
jimgaffigan: Great. Lunch tomorrow. I'll meet you at Spring Street Natural at 12pm
Jlnoth: Tomorrow?
jimgaffigan: lol
Jlnoth: What's lol?
jimgaffigan: laugh out loud.
Jlnoth: oh.

For some reason that I could not explain at the time, I met him for lunch the next day at Spring Street Natural. I brought brochures for my "Shakespeare on the Playground" initiative. We started talking. He was a stand-up comedian. Only. I was a teacher, an actor, a director, a caterer, and I had just started a not-for-profit theater company. In other words, he was successful; I wasn't. Ironic that the more jobs you had, the less prestige. I offered to let him pay for lunch. I ordered some fancy thing with brown rice, avocado, and a poached egg on top. This was the nicest restaurant I had ever been to in New York. In fact, it was the first time I'd ever gone out to lunch in New York.

"Do you come here for lunch a lot?" I asked.

"No, I've never been here before."

"Why did you pick it?"

"I've always wanted to come here since it opened. The neighborhood is really changing."

We talked about all the changes we were witnessing. It was interesting to hear the perspective of another midwestern transplant who had such a similar experience of ending up in this neighborhood and then realizing they were the hillbilly that settled on top of an undiscovered oil well.

He talked about how he was going out of town for a while to do gigs at various *improvs* around the country.

"I don't really follow stand-up comedy," I admitted.

"Do you have a favorite comedian?"

"I guess the Monty Python guys."

"Oh, you're a nerd!" he replied.

"Wow, you're really good at talking to girls!"

Navigating through a conversation that ranged in tone from jocular to downright hostile and would have made Beatrice and Benedict seem chummy, we discovered that we both grew up on Lake Michigan (him Indiana; me Wisconsin). I knew we were both from the Midwest, an area that a New Yorker would describe as anywhere between Pennsylvania and Utah, but the coincidence that we grew up on the same lake was wild. And both from unusually large Catholic families. He was the youngest of six, I the eldest of nine. "Nine? That's just weird," he said. Our cultural sameness was further highlighted when the food came. He took a forkful of mine without asking, so I took a forkful of his. He asked me about the play I was directing. I handed him a brochure across the table. "I really think you should get involved. The kids in this neighborhood have nothing to do."

"Did you just agree to go out to lunch with me because you wanted me to volunteer in your theater company?" He seemed irritated.

"Did you just ask me to lunch so you could bed me?" I retorted.

"Touché," said Jim, and he took another bite off my plate.

Just then, my flip phone rang. The guys I had buying an amp for the show were at the Guitar Center in Queens. Yes, there was only one Guitar Center at the time. And it was in Queens. They were at the register and didn't have enough money for the purchase. "Excuse me," I said to Jim. Then into the phone, "Let me talk to the cashier. (beat) Hi, can I just give you a credit card over the phone?"

"No. We don't do that," came the voice on the other end, obviously suspicious that I was trying to steal the amp. "We need to see the card and ID."

"Okay," I said. "Let me talk to the guys. (beat) Hey. Okay. Stay there. I'm coming." I snapped my phone shut and said to Jim, "Thanks for lunch. I've got to go." I grabbed my bag, and the brochure (they were expensive to make, and I'd decided that Jim was not brochure-worthy).

"Okay," said Jim. "I'll walk you to the train."

He paid the check and walked briskly beside me as I made another phone call to the guys.

"Hey. What train do I take to get to where you are in Queens? No. I don't want you to get a smaller amp..." While I was talking I paused and leaned against the brick wall of a building as I fumbled for the MetroCard in my bag. Jim put both hands against the wall on either side of me. Not touching me, but kind of trapping me, like the "London Bridge Is Falling Down" game. I ended the call, ready to knee him in the family jewels. "What are you doing?" I asked incredulously.

"A strong woman needs a strong man," he said and gave me a firm kiss right on the lips. Then he walked away. "Bye."

I stared after him. He was a strong man.

In the time between the collision of the duct tape diva and the arrogant pale guy in the Korean market and the day we walked down the aisle of St. Patrick's Old Cathedral, the dying-on-the-vine neighborhood began to transform into the height of New York chic. It was like our own Disney movie. As our love blossomed, so did Mott Street. When we walked down the block hand in hand, it was like stardust shot out in front of us and an old abandoned storefront transformed into a romantic French bistro. It was a nonstop adventure as new boutiques and restaurants sprang up everywhere, as if just for us. We both worked long, hard days late into the night, but in the city that never sleeps, two night owls meeting for midnight indie movies and small plates and red wine, at new places that people from all over the city were crowding our neighborhood sidewalks to get into, was magical and thrilling.

We started working together right off the bat. It was sort of an accident. Yes, I did force Jim to volunteer for "Shakespeare on the Playground." The neighborhood kids were part of this renaissance we were all experiencing, and they had to come along for the enchanted ride. There was a young man in my hip-hop production of *Midsummer Night's Dream* who was naturally funny but shy and self-conscious. His role was Robin Starveling, the tailor, and it was a funny part. Every time Billy would say his lines, he would turn bright red and hide behind his script. Jim worked with him one-on-one, and Billy gained tremendous confidence. I couldn't tell who benefited more, Jim or Billy. Jim's willingness to take time out of his schedule and help this kid showed me that under the tough, irreverent, funny-guy exterior was a compassionate saint. It was buried deep, but I saw it with Billy.

I also started dragging Jim to Mass. His apartment building was directly across the street from St. Patrick's Old Cathedral, but he had never once entered the church. "Are you afraid you're going to burn, like foil wrapped bacon in a microwave?" I asked incredulously. Jim had grown up Catholic but was more of a cultural Catholic; in other words, he rooted for Notre Dame. But when he saw it was important to me, he was game.

One day, Jim sprang it on me that he had written a TV pilot and it had been picked up by David Letterman's production company, Worldwide Pants. I was like, "Wow, that is so amazing! Can I be in it?"

Jim seemed annoyed by my naïveté.

"I'm trying to make sure they keep *me* in it." He explained that it was for CBS and it featured all well-known actors, except him, the unknown.

"But it's *your* show!"

Jim was a little frantic. "I have to do a bunch of scenes with Christine Baranski, and she's a *real* actress."

If there was anything that years of theatrical training had taught me, it was how to break down a scene. Jim had the comic timing and the natural charm already. He had helped me by helping Billy, and now it was time for me to help him. "I'll work on it with you!" Great. We made plans for later that night to work on the scenes. Jim gave me the key to his apartment so I could let myself in after my catering job in case he was not back from his set at the comedy club. It was my first time in his apartment. When I flipped on the lights after keying in, I was pretty sure I had just stepped into the apartment of a serial killer. Jim lived in a cramped, filthy, railroad-style one-bedroom with eleven-foot ceilings and a bathtub in the kitchen, the room I had just entered.

I looked around. Books and dirty dishes were piled high on the counters. There were three rooms visible from the center kitchen where I'd come in that led into one another (like railroad cars), and each was sponge-painted a contrasting hideous color. The paint was cracked and chipped and peeling off the tall steam pipes that heated the room with a hiss. There was a robin's egg blue living room area to my right toward the front of the building. The windows with moss-colored curtains partially masked the best view in Manhattan, which was St. Patrick's grassy courtyard surrounded by the redbrick walls. In that room was a desk with stacks of papers and CDs, the walls lined with shelves of hundreds of books. Standing in the yellow kitchen with the bathtub, I heard an imagined whisper: *Run for your life!* To my left was a room that looked like a cramped closet with a lofted bed, painted in a too-dark forest green and an open door to a tiny gross-looking bathroom with only a toilet and sponge-painted orange walls. The commode was six inches off the floor and there was a three-foot stack of magazines and mail in front of it. It was a pull-chain toilet circa the 1920s, and most likely had not been cleaned since then, the tank high above, and no sink.

I didn't know what to think. Jim seemed so normal, and now I was standing in the den of a madman. As my heart stopped pounding and I started to think more rationally, I walked around as if on another planet. The environment told the story of a workaholic artist. This guy was reading, studying, eating, sleeping—and showering in the kitchen—rinse, repeat. Yes, it was a mess, but it was an aspirational mess. However, now I was working with him, and I couldn't work in a mess. I pushed up my sleeves and started cleaning. For me, as the oldest of nine kids, cleaning is second nature. I was not intimidated by any mess; I'd seen them all. In fact, I was more uncomfortable being *around* a mess than cleaning a mess. Cleaning gave me the sense of some sort of control over my environment.

I don't know if Jim was delayed, or if I worked really fast, but when he showed up for our scenework session, his apartment was totally clean.

"You cleaned my apartment?!" He didn't seem embarrassed

or freaked out. He seemed overjoyed. It was at this moment that I believed I'd created my own monster. I also suspect that I may have been tapped as potential wife material.

"I didn't do it for you; I did it for me. Next time, we are working at my apartment."

This began a series of work sessions where Jim and I really clicked into team mode. I lived with my sister Felicia, who soon got used to Jim coming over every night for our scene study. We nicknamed her "the Judge" because we often would call her in to settle our arguments (fights), which she did fairly, giving equal time to both sides. Our apartment down the block was a five-flight walk-up, which Jim didn't mind, because at that point he was actually trying to stay in shape. He was "eating healthy," so I always had a salad with Annie's Shiitake Vinaigrette and veggie burgers ready to go along with our work. Jim made himself right at home. Not thirty seconds after he walked in, he would take off his pants, drop them on the floor, and spend the rest of the evening milling around in his boxers.

My sister just got used to it. She was slightly irritated the time when a brand-new, ultra-buttoned-up boyfriend came to pick her up for a date and Jim answered the door in his T-shirt and boxers. The guy was stunned. It was also Felicia's last date with him, and we always joked that Jim ruined the relationship with his "butler in boxers act."

But the work was where we really found each other. If the changing neighborhood had helped our romance bloom, the work revealed that we would be able to be compatible long after the magic of the late-night dates gave way to the practicality of the real world and there was no more time for red wine.

Welcome to New York was a baptism by fire into the world of network television, but Jim and I were a tight team. We went through the ups and downs of the show getting canceled, multiple pilot seasons of brutal auditions, stand-up shows that I was now producing, home-made CDs (compact discs, for those of you born after 1997), trips around the country and the world, and lots of work. Jim was a true romantic, and he booked gigs in exotic places like a cruise ship whose route was around Alaska's Inside Passage. Jim performing on a cruise ship was the antithesis of his personality, being someone who would finish a gig, put a baseball cap on, and scurry out of the club so he didn't have to interact with anyone. On a cruise ship you are trapped with the same audience who saw you the night before for a week: "My wife thought you were kinda funny. I didn't get it. Pass the eggs." Jim hated performing on the cruise ship, but he did it so he could take me on these amazing adventures.

Off and on for two years, Jim asked me to marry him. I couldn't say yes. I felt like marriage would be the end of my life. I was having too much fun being the girlfriend. Every time I felt like Jim was gearing up to ask me to marry him, I would say something like, "I hope you are not taking me to Rome just so you can ask me to marry you." Every time this happened, I would watch the disappointment wash over him, like I just blew a surprise party he had been planning.

"Listen, when you're ready, give me a two-month warning so I can plan something."

"It's a deal."

Jim had been cast in a sitcom at one point and had to relocate to LA. He'd asked me to come with him, but I'd already let go of so much of my life to be part of his team, and I couldn't move to follow him. I had a lot going on in New York.

"Move out here!" he would say when I would complain that the long-distance relationship was too much for me to deal with.

"I'm not following some guy across the country unless we're married."

"Then marry me."

That's not how I wanted it to happen. "I'll give you a two-month warning when I'm ready."

"Is this the two-month warning?"

"No."

I went to a therapist to talk about why I couldn't make a commitment to Jim. I already "had" a therapist, as most New Yorkers do, even starving artists like me. My favorite aunt had been diagnosed with cancer a few years before, and her health was deteriorating quickly. When she was very sick a bunch of family members had gone down to Florida to help out. One of my jobs was to drive her from her home on Marco Island to the hospital in Naples for radiation treatments to keep her cancer at bay. She refused chemotherapy. A doctor herself, she had seen the havoc chemo wreaks on the body, and she wanted to enjoy the little time she had left. The radiation therapy was to keep her brain tumor from taking over. As we drove along that long highway, I was overwhelmed with emotion. How could she be so resigned about facing death?

After her funeral, I returned to New York. My life was different. I was terrified of getting cancer. I felt like I had cancer. I would make appointments at the clinic every week and see the doctor with lists of imagined symptoms that I was sure were cancer. About the fifth time I saw the same doctor and was questioning the results of my normal blood test, she said to me, "I think you need a different kind of doctor." So that's how I came to "have" a therapist.

I didn't see that therapist very often anymore since I had worked through the anxiety caused by the trauma of losing my beloved aunt so quickly, but this whole "Why can't I marry Jim?" question brought me back to her. That, and my sister told me that at a recent Halloween party when Jim was in town, he confided in her that he thought I might be crazy because everything I did indicated that I wanted to marry him, but every time he broached the subject, I would run away.

My sister was concerned. "Jim is the most normal boyfriend you have ever had. He is an *adult*. You are going to blow it, Jeannie. You have to do something!" I *was* crazy. I knew it. And I was about to blow it. So I went back to my therapist.

"What are you afraid of, Jeannie?" she asked.

"Jim's career is taking off. I feel like if I marry him, all I will do with my life is continue to help his career, and give up my own life. He's going to steamroll me."

She looked at me through her thick-lensed glasses. "Close your eyes. Picture yourself in five years. In ten. Is Jim there?" I closed my eyes. Jim was there. He was always there. If I lived in a mud pit, life would be fun with Jim. As our session ended, she handed me an illustrated cartoon of a woman sitting on a bench. She was covered in cobwebs and had the face of a skeleton. The caption below said, "*Waiting for the perfect man.*"

*　　*　　*

I walked home to my apartment in the brisk December air. I found myself talking to God. "God, why didn't you tell me that I was supposed to marry Jim?" and God said, "Why did you ask a therapist instead of me?" Well, that's probably what He said. I called Jim. In a week, he was flying to Milwaukee where I would meet him to spend Christmas with my family.

"Jim, I'm giving you the two-month warning."

"Finally," he said. "What made you change your mind?"

"A skeleton," I said.

"I knew you were crazy."

My family had the tradition of the "Secret Santa" out of necessity. There were just too many people to buy for, so someone had the job of assigning gifts for one other person. Of course, we all bought gifts for Danielle. No one had kids yet, and she was like an adult kid, so surprised and gleeful with every present she unwrapped. We all should experience life with such joy. After about an hour of exchanges and laughs, we were sitting surrounded by piles of ripped paper and bows. I was doing my usual act of cleaning up and looking for wrapping that was "still good." I asked, "Is there anything else, did everyone give their gift?"

"There's one more," Jim said. I turned to face him and he got down on one knee while opening a box that had his mother's engagement ring in it. "Jeannie, will you marry me?" For the first time I could remember, my eight siblings, their significant others, and my parents and cousins were completely stunned into silence.

"Oh my God!" I said with tears in my eyes. "I thought you said two months!"

My sister-in-law chimed in, "Well, what are you going to say?!"

"Yes!"

And that's how Jim steamrolled my life. And I let him. The oldest of nine children, the ultimate caregiver, marries the youngest of six, the ultimate care-getter. A match made in codependent heaven.

PART IV

Life Goes On

Chapter 27

ROME WASN'T BUILT IN A DAY

If cleaning Jim's apartment that day created a monster, I spent the next fifteen years cultivating the monster and maybe inadvertently spawning five additional mini monsters. I took it upon myself to handle everything: the logistics with the kids and household as well as juggling all the productions for our company. And I didn't stop there. If there was not a project to be done, I created one. My executing the never-ending to-do list was not because Jim was dumping all the work on me, or my kids were lazy, or that no one else could do it. It actually gave me a false sense of fulfillment to be needed. Maybe that was the subconscious reason I cleaned Jim's apartment in the first place. When everyone had to take over for me, I saw that doing everything for people might not help them at all and could actually hurt them. Was I acting on impulses to take care of people just to feed my own ego?

Watching Jim and my family and friends take care of the

important things (the well-being and safety of my children, my health and recovery), while the unimportant things fell apart (the house was messy and disorganized, there was way too much food in the fridge, and it was—gasp—*unlabeled*), showed me that my priorities had been a bit out of whack. My being too weak and incapable of running my house like a well-oiled machine showed me that the machine may not have needed that much oil to work. Many times when my kids asked me to lie down with them and tell them one of our great stories, I would say, "Later, I'm busy right now. I have to finish cleaning the kitchen and make the menu for tomorrow." By the time I showed up in their bedroom, they were already sound asleep. I was taking so much time to make sure my garden looked perfect that I was missing my chance to smell the flowers. This was what God was trying to tell me in the ICU. That, and how I made myself so busy I almost missed a diagnosis that saved my life and was almost killed by a giant pear. That would have really sucked.

Many times I am asked, "How has this experience changed you?" I wish I could say that when I got some of my strength back I was a changed woman. I recall being asked this question during a radio show interview shortly after I knew I was out of the woods. My answer at the time was, "Above all, I learned, *don't sweat the small stuff and always take time to smell the flowers!*" Several months later the same radio host, Jen Fulwiler (also a crazy busy mom but with *six* kids), was doing a recap of the year's stories, and I was invited back via call-in to be on the 2017 wrap-up show. It was in the middle of the holiday rush, and though I was participating in life fully, I was still feeling like a shadow of my former self. I was absolutely buried in to-do madness. On the air, Jen asked me how I was doing and I admitted, "I'm sweating the small stuff and forgetting to smell the flowers."

As Weezie always says, "Rome wasn't built in a day," and I realize that I will have to learn and relearn my new perspective on life for a long, long time. I felt my recovery from brain surgery dragged on endlessly, but recovery from needing to be busy all the time was going to last a lifetime. My ability to let go was going to require assistance from a higher power.

Chapter 28

THE NEW NORMAL

I often hear the question "When did you get back to normal?"

I respond, "I'll never be back to normal." You don't just move on from something like this; it becomes part of you. You change and grow. You may change into a bitter person and grow in self-pity, or you may use the memory of your suffering as an opportunity to transform your life into something more beautiful and meaningful than you could have ever imagined. I'm going to go glass half full here. If not, what was it for?

Long ago in our marriage, Jim and I decided that we would always travel as a family when the kids were on their school breaks. Granted, it's much harder traveling with children—especially at times when every other school is on break—but because Jim has a job that geographically removes him for long periods of time, it's just not right for us when he returns from a tour to announce, "Mom and Dad are taking off for the weekend! See you losers later!" It is essential for our family's survival that we stay together whenever possible.

At the end of August, a year and change out from my surgery, we took a family trip. Jim was performing at the Alaska State Fair and wanted to do something really unique as a family. My recovery was going faster than any of us had expected, so I told Jim I was totally up for something like this. I think we were both surprised when we arrived and realized that maybe we had jumped in too deep. We'd traveled a lot over the past year, but this time we went rugged. Not quite camping, but a cabin in the Alaskan wilderness miles from civilization and phone service, where the activities would include hiking on harsh terrain, deep-sea fishing, and physically challenging activities even for those in good health. I didn't plan the trip, and I was a bit shocked that Jim would take us somewhere so remote. I naively anticipated that I would be "glamping," experiencing the beauty of Alaska out of an enormous picture window, while lying in a big comfy bed enjoying room service. Closer to my postsurgery speed.

When I saw the cabin, I asked Jim if he knew it was going to be so remote. He was surprised as well. The website he had studied made it look like more of the Disney version of Alaska, but it was the real deal. I told him, "Don't worry. If I feel like I can't handle something, I will just stay back in the cabin and read." Turns out I wasn't the one to worry about.

The first morning we woke up for our guided hike, Jim was doubled over in pain. In the fifteen years we have been married, Jim has never really been sick, so I knew he wasn't just trying to get out of hiking. I told him to stay in bed and that I would handle the kids on the excursion. I was a little nervous about having all five of them on an isolated mountain surrounded by majestic beauty and treacherous cliffs. We did have an expert guide with us, but no daddy disciplinarian. It was scary but somewhat empowering to be in this incredible place as the sole parent in charge. It had been awhile since I'd been in my former position, and I felt like the retired sports star trying to make a comeback. When we returned, I felt great that no one had fallen down a hole or been dragged away by a wild animal. Jim was still in bed, so I thought he'd be recovered and ready to take over while I took a much-needed rest.

"How are you feeling?"

"Like I'm going to die."

"What?"

"I can't walk. I have a sharp pain in my stomach. Is there a doctor here?" The reason I had been concerned when I saw that the place was so remote was that clearly there were no doctors for miles. But I had been concerned for myself.

"Jim, there are no doctors here! What should I do?"

"I don't know!" Jim was curled up in a ball. I ran out of the cabin and hiked up to the main lodge, but there was no one there. I ran to the back of the lodge and knocked on the door of the room where the guides were. I told them about the situation and two of them went to the cabin with their first-aid packs and walkie-talkies. I went to gather the kids, who at this point had dispersed into the surrounding woods and may have been seconds away from being a five-course meal for a bear.

After I rounded up the children and got them into playing fetch with the campground dogs, one of the guides emerged from our cabin. "Has Jim ever had problems with his appendix?" A stomachache after eating three burgers, yes. Appendix? Never. "I think we should get him to a hospital in Anchorage."

"Okay, how?"

"We'll call a helicopter," said the guide matter-of-factly.

"Sure," I replied, as if this were just another day at the office. No roads, no phone service, middle of nowhere, five kids, and me. Jim was in pain. He was having a medical crisis. It was *his* turn. I couldn't be weak. The roles had reversed again. Couple survival instincts kicked in. "Good cop/hysterical cop" was now "sick cop/well cop."

As I watched Jim take off in the helicopter and disappear over the mountains, the adrenaline was pumping through my veins. I closed my eyes and said to God, "You got this, right?" I was overcome by that familiar sense of peace. We had been through so much; this was just another step on the path. There was only one way I could describe the feeling I was having: "Back to normal." The new normal.

P.S. Jim survived the appendectomy and returned to his family in the Alaskan wilderness, who greeted him with open arms and gentle hugs. Then we all almost got eaten by a bear. But I'll let him tell that story.

Chapter 29

THE NECTAR OF LIFE

I'm grateful for the tumor. Grateful I had a chance to almost die so that I could be more appreciative of life. Every time I take a sip of water, it feels different. It feels amazing. Swallowing water. Something I've done my whole life, and then couldn't do anymore and didn't know if I could ever do again. Once I could, the feeling didn't change—*I* changed.

It's a strange concept to express gratitude for something that really messed everything up for a while, but had it not been for this catastrophe, I never would have had the opportunity to see what my marriage could survive. I wouldn't have experienced the same kind of painful separation from my children, which was necessary for me to realize exactly how I could love them without being a drill sergeant.

I wouldn't have imagined that my mother, father, and siblings could literally drop everything to rush to my side, and be there for *my* family. Maybe I would've expected one or two of them, but literally everyone came. I built deeper friendships. The friends who were really the true friends were highlighted in a sea of acquaintances.

I never would have experienced the ecstasy of a Mister Softee cone on a hot summer day. The first time I added on to my kids' order of the push-ups, rocket pops, and SpongeBob-shaped ice cream bars, saying, "And I'll take a vanilla cone for myself," I sat on the cement with them watching a group of street musicians perform in front of the fountain at Washington Square Park. The sweet, icy, creamlike substance, which was probably as antinutritious as the formula that I loathed in the hospital, felt like manna from heaven as it easily glided down my throat, causing me to forget my struggle with swallowing.

My kids were more excited than I'd seen them opening up a first birthday present at the sight of me communing with them in this new way. "The Food Nag" had transformed into Princess Softina!

Without my suffering, it would have been impossible to achieve this higher level of joy. Things I took for granted my entire life have new and profound meaning. Someday, I may just swallow water and not feel how good it is. I hope not. My prayer every day is to not forget how good it is to swallow water. My wish for everyone is to be grateful for swallowing water.

I am so thankful for this new perspective. This new directive to take advantage of a God-given second chance. This chapter is not the end, but rather the beginning of a new life.

If the pear (the actual fruit, not the tumor) is indeed a metaphor for life, my old life was a rock-hard pear that cut really well with nice sharp angles, but the flavor was lacking. Now it's a misshapen overripe pear that just mushes under the knife, but the juice is the sweetest thing you'll ever taste.

Life goes on and children grow up fast. Some of you might be in "baby land" and be like, "This is too tough! When am I getting my life back?" There *are* periods that seem to take forever, but then you blink your eyes and they are borrowing your shoes. One of the many gifts that I received from my blessing of a brain tumor was the recognition of the passage of time. You know those people when you were a kid who every time they saw you were like, "You have grown so much since I saw you last!" Well, now that's me to my own kids, every day. Another gift this sickness gave me was the opportunity to look at my life from the outside and realize that my concept of caregiving for my kids was actually preventing me from fully experiencing them. When I was recovering at home, I saw that my having been the alpha controller of the whole operation was actually stealing the power from my family and preventing them from blossoming into masters of their own lives. I'd been overwatering the garden.

Removing the mama bear from the caregiver role had helped everyone around me, and especially Jim, to discover their innermost power and figure out how to make their own damn porridge. Or the story of the person spontaneously finding the strength to lift a car off of someone who is trapped. They always had it in them, but they needed a crisis to let it out.

I'm filled with gratitude that over the past two years, I've been given new eyes to see the goodness, the generosity, and the compassion in my community. There was something about observing people—the nurses, the doctors, the therapists, the friends, the husband—offer so much of themselves to help another human being that was totally inspirational and life-changing.

It has become an absolute necessity for me to look around at my life and find little ways that I can cultivate in myself the kind of generosity that was shown to me. And in turn inspire it in my children. The hand that rocks the cradle changes the world. Unless it's that one cradle where the bow breaks; that's a disturbing nursery rhyme.

* * *

You don't need to have your own kids or be a parent to understand this. In fact, it's probably easier if you don't have kids.

293

Heck, *everything* is easier if you don't have kids. Especially writing a book. I would have been done with this chapter about six weeks ago if I didn't have kids. But kids can be wonderful canvases. We can model our behavior as if we are shaping someone else because we *are* shaping someone else. We are shaping our world, and we alone have a very short time on this planet, so let's use it wisely. Maybe get a group of friends and families together and help out at a soup kitchen. It's incredibly bonding and meaningful. Sometimes it's hard to figure out who benefits more: those being served, or those serving. Or find someone in need and reach out to them in kindness. It doesn't have to be a major production. A small gesture can have a huge effect.

In the past year, with some gentle guidance and suggestions, my kids have all found their own little ways to make a difference in their communities. Katie started a "Box of Sox" drive at her school to help a neighborhood shelter. Marre, in high school now, initiated a "Women Helping Women" collection of products for the homeless. Jack, full of compassion for the disabled, is forming friendships across barriers, and all the boys are engaged in Zero Waste and motivated to save the planet! And their friends are encouraged and inspired because goodness spreads.

"The children are the future" may be a tired old cliché and also a line in a top ten song from 1986, but it's true. If we can give them simple examples of tolerance, kindness, and gratitude and provide ample opportunities for them to express those attributes, we can give them greatness. And that is better than money, toys, and all the Mister Softees in the universe.

In conclusion, I'll leave you with a little to-do list:

To Do:

1. Spend more quality time with your children

2. spread goodness

3. Execute numbers 1 and 2 without getting a brain tumor.

Epilogue

My morning now goes something like this:

6:00 a.m.   Wake up to iPhone alarm, roll over, smell a kid's head, hit Snooze.

6:30 a.m.   Drink coffee and stare at kids jumping on furniture.

6:40 a.m.   Hold myself back from micromanaging the kids making their own breakfast.

7:00 a.m.   Get picked up by Sixto car pool. My kids are the whole car pool.

7:02 a.m.   Marre and Katie teach me to understand Snapchat.

7:30 a.m.   Drop off Marre at her high school on Eighty-Fourth Street. Remind her to take her "Women Helping Women" bag, and say "I love you."

7:37 a.m.   Drop off Katie at her middle school on East Eighty-Second Street. Remind her to take her Box of Sox drive bag, and say "I love you."

7:40 a.m.	Cross Central Park on Seventy-Ninth Street, down the West Side Highway to Chelsea, read a book with Michael and Patrick about zombies eating brains.
7:55 a.m.	Get dropped off with the three boys, take Jack, Michael, and Patrick into school early to help sort the Lost & Found for the Zero Waste Initiative.
8:10 a.m.	Hug Jack good-bye (in front of all his middle school friends), then do "Kissing Hands" with Michael and Patrick.
8:11 a.m.	Yell "I love you" to the boys, loudly and embarrassingly.
8:30 a.m.	Text Jim the emoji with the two heart eyes.

The sprint has begun to get anything at all accomplished in the next seven hours before the kids get home and life can begin again.

Acknowledgments

I would like to dedicate this book to my brain tumor. I understand this may confuse, well, everyone, but I do feel the need express my sincere gratitude to that pear-shaped mass that occupied the most precarious spot in my head and almost killed me. After all, my brain tumor is why you are reading this and why I got to be exposed to so many incredible humans.

So here goes. Thank you, Brain Tumor. That seems formal. Do I even have to include the word "brain"? It's the only tumor I've ever had. It's not as if half of you are thinking, "Which tumor?" Anyway, thank you, Brain Tumor. Without you, I never would have seen a side of humanity I thought only existed in the sappiest of Hallmark television movies. If you weren't growing at the base of my brain stem, I never would have met the genius **Dr. Joshua Bederson, MD**, who saved my life, and **Leslie Schlachter, PA-C**, who coordinated **the entire Department of Neurosurgery at Mount Sinai**. I would never have been exposed to the motley crew of hospital characters like **Dr. Robert Rothrock, MD**, who has a soap opera name but is too good-looking for a soap opera and no one would believe he's really a doctor anyway so he wouldn't get cast. Speaking of great names, Brain Tumor (Can I call you BT for short?), you brought me the brilliant **Dr. Johanna T. Fifi, MD**, who together with the fabulous anesthesiologist **Dr. Patricia S. Brous, MD**, performed the *almost* embolization that revealed I also had fibromuscular dysplasia (FMD), which led me to meet the great **Dr. Jeffrey Olin, DO,** who happens to be the principal investigator and director of care and research of this very rare disease. Thank you, Brain Tumor, for landing me in an ICU where I fell head over heels (and flat on my back) for **Joseph "Joe the Nurse" Waugh, RN**. Thank you also for compromising my breathing and swallowing so that I could develop a life-threatening pneumonia and wake up to find **Dr. Eric P. Neibart, MD** (infectious disease specialist), standing over me in his bow tie telling me to "get up, get better, and get back to quality of life." You also gave me the pleasure of working with **Dr. Glen B. Chun, MD** (pulmonology), who will always have a place in my heart and deep in my lungs. Thank you also for exposing me to the stellar team of **Dr. Mark Courey, MD,** and **Leanne Goldberg, MS, CCC-SLP** (otolaryngology), who were there from me croaking through a tracheotomy to singing scales up to a high *C(?)* after a palatal adhesion surgery. (Great job on fixing my innie neck button scar, Dr. Courey.)

Because of you, Brain Tumor. Can I call you Tumor de Cabeza? I know that means "tumor of the head" in Spanish, but what a cool nickname, right? Either way, thanks for getting me to the point where I actually looked forward to having a PEG feeding tube inserted in my stomach like, well, a tube being inserted in your stomach. After not eating for two weeks, having an anesthesiologist for that procedure named **Dr. Joshua Hamburger, MD**, was a hysterical touch.

Without you, my dear Tumor, I would never have received the amazing care of all the **physical, occupational, speech and swallow therapists** and **Visiting Nurse Service of New York**,

ACKNOWLEDGMENTS

and I never would have adopted into my family the incredible **Bruce Macvitte (RN, IMDB)**, whose talents and skills as a nurse are outnumbered only by his appearances on *Law & Order*. Thanks for bringing **Lida Ahmady, Lac**, and **Daniel Camburn, Lac**, over to my house to give me acupuncture and nutritional and wellness therapy. Thanks for making **Sara Hester** come over twice a week to give me Pilates-based physical therapy that made me even stronger than I was before.

Thank you, Tumie (I can call you Tumie? That's cute, right?), for showing me that we picked the right schools for my children because their communities took care of me and my kids while I was recovering from you, especially **Concepcion Alvar, Donna Corvi, Cathy Callender**, and all the faculty, staff and parent body at Marymount, and of course **Nancy Schulman, Rachel Gordian, Jena Krueger, Kim Turner, Roberto Baldeschi-Balleani, Alexandra Gerba, Libby Hixon, Eric Ogden, Avery Barnes**, and all the faculty, staff, and parent body at Avenues. Thanks for the home helpers that made the staff at Palace of Versailles in 1789 seem small (**Kathrina Anunciacion, Eve Novak, Abby Diette, Kira Koffskey-Smith, Val, Anita, Melanie**, and **Victoria**).

And Tumes, Can I call you Tumes? Who am I kidding? You can't answer. Well, I hope you can't. That would be really scary. Anyway, thanks for giving me such street cred with the holy people in my life such as **Deacon Paul Vitale**, his amazing wife **Helen Vitale, Monsignor Donald Sakano, Father Jonathan Morris**, the one and only **Sister Mary Doolittle**, and **His Eminence Timothy Cardinal Dolan**, who actually called me from Lourdes, France, and gargled holy water for me when my throat was paralyzed (it worked, by the way, Cardinal; now I can't shut up).

Tum-Tum, you showed me that my friends and family are saints on earth. **Dr. John Broderick, MD**, who gave me a plan; **Shana Broderick** my BFF; **Karen Bergreen**, who is funny and wonderful; **Tricia Heine**, who made me feel strong *and* beautiful; **Danielle Blumstein**, who is my work wife and taught me about proper manners and to always keep my aplomb; **Sky McGilligan**, who is not a girl; **Tony Hale**, who sat with Jim during the scariest time in his life; **Gina Larucci, Dr. Laury Cuddihy**, and **Samantha Sheeler**, for the best non-food gift packages; **Susan Isaacs**, for the best customized hospital workbook; **Sarina Ogden**, for taking care of Katie; **Ali Lesch**, for hanging out with Weezie in the ELC; and all the people who sent food and made Jim even fatter. Thanks for allowing me to grow closer to my extended family, **Marita Haggerty, Beth Haggerty Steers**, the entire **Haggerty Family** (including **Anne** in heaven), and **Tina Langley Walsh**. Thanks for finally revealing to me why being one of nine siblings makes perfect sense and how lucky I am to have **Dom (Papa Dom) Noth, Louise (Mama Weezie) Noth, Felicia Noth, Paul Noth, Vincent Noth, Jessica Noth, Danielle Noth, Patrick Noth** and **Emilea Wilson Noth, Maria Noth, Michelle Noth, Elizabeth Noth, Rudy Behrens** (who #tookaNoth), and also **Nora** and **Trey Fitzpatick** (who looks like a Noth) in my life.

Also thank you, Brain Tumor, for bringing me to this book through **Simon Green**, my agent, who told me to write a memoir instead of *How to Organize a Laundry Room*; **Nancy Rose, Isaac Dunham**, and **Liza Montesano**, for having me sign a legal document I didn't read; my great level-headed manager **Alex Murray**; **Rob Greenwald**, the publicist who made people care; **Tina Constable** and **Tammy Blake**, who believed in me; **Eric Vitale**, who stopped me from total hysteria as I wrote it; and all of the people at Grand Central Publishing: **Suzanne O'Neill** my editor, who I called and emailed three hundred times a day; **Linda Duggins**, who helped get eyes on it; **Albert Tang**, who let me have creative freedom with design; and **Carolyn Kurek**, the production editor who was clearly sent from the Holy Spirit.

And most of all, I'd like to thank you, Big T, for showing me that I made the right choice in marrying my best friend, **Jim Gaffigan**, who I partnered with in our most successful productions so far: **Marre, Jack, Katie, Michael, and Patrick.**

About the Author

Jeannie Gaffigan is a director, producer, and comedy writer. She cowrote seven comedy specials with her husband, Jim Gaffigan, the last four of which received Grammy nominations. Jeannie was the head writer and executive producer of the critically acclaimed *The Jim Gaffigan Show*, which was loosely based on her and Jim's life. She collaborated with Jim on the two *New York Times* bestsellers *Dad Is Fat* and *Food: A Love Story*. Jeannie, with the help of her two eldest children and some other crazy moms, created The Imagine Society, Inc., a not-for-profit organization that connects youth-led service groups. Most impressively, she grew a tumor on her brain stem roughly the size of pear.

Jeannie presently lives in New York City with her five children, which feels more like six children if you include her husband, Jim.